MW00643917

THE FORTUNES OF POETRY IN AN AGE OF UNMAKING

JAMES MATTHEW WILSON

Wiseblood Books

Oregon

Published by Wiseblood Books
www.wisebloodbooks.com

Cover: Dominic Heisdorf

Printed in the United States of America

Set in Arabic Typesetting

Library of Congress Cataloging-in- Publication Data

Wilson, James Matthew, 1975-

The Fortunes of Poetry in an Age of Unmaking/ James
Matthew Wilson;

1. Wilson, James Matthew, 1975-
2. Literary Criticism / Poetry

ISBN-10: 0692556931
ISBN-13: 978-0692556931

For Cecilia Rae Wilson
Who brings a lovely balance to our line

From Harmony, from Heavenly Harmony
This Universal Frame began.
When Nature underneath a heap
Of jarring Atoms lay,
And cou'd not heave her Head,
The tuneful Voice was heard from high,
Arise ye more than dead.

TABLE OF CONTENTS

Appendix

PREFACE

These chapters were begun as something like a cry: a cry of dismay at what was being made of literature in our time; a cry of exasperation that the worst tendencies in both the contemporary art and scholarship of poetry were consistently heralded as advances rather than symptoms of degeneration; a cry of incomprehension, as unreason was heralded as intellectual sophistication, charlatanry as rigor.

A cry of alarm, too. In the first chapter, we hear references to a few scholarly panels at the annual meeting of the Modern Language Association, and though I am nowhere present in those portions of the text, a younger version of myself was in attendance in those rooms. Possessed already of two advanced degrees and soon to be awarded a doctorate in literature, I had for a time joined the multitudes wandering through the hallways of that convention, but was not at all sure what they had to do with me and the literature I studied, or us to do with them. Everywhere I turned, it seemed there was a lovelessness, a contempt for life, and a vision of the world so suspicious, impoverished, and barren as to be unrecognizable. I was about to marry; I did not know it, but before the next year was out I would be a father. Was there a place in the academic world for someone who wanted to feed his family by talking about the truth, goodness, and beauty of literature? Was the demolition of literature the ransom one paid to be allowed to profess it?

I feared the answers were, respectively, no and yes, and in the oldest of these pages I can hear that fear just beneath the surface of the indignation, satire, and sententiousness. The man who first thought to write them was thumbing through literary journals—each one worse than the last—while waiting for his wife at the obstetrician's office, mulling that "no" and muttering that "yes." The one who carried the argument forward in the months ahead girded himself for combat as a young professor at a large state university whose conception of knowledge was strictly technocratic. And then, he found a home within that small remnant of the academy that prized the life of learning as something good in itself, literature as a way of knowing, and beauty as a reality. He did that and had more children. The argument was left, outlined but incomplete, as he turned his hand to other things.

In the years since the first chapters of this book were published under the title, *Our Steps amid a Ruined Colonnade*, it has remained on my mind. Should I have forgotten it, the occasional letter from an admirer of its argument asking after its completion would remind me. I knew how it needed to end, but was not ready to give it an ending. And then, last winter, my publisher at Wiseblood Books, Joshua Hren, asked if he could publish the completed *Colonnade*. I had by then traveled a sufficient distance through the halls of academe, and a sufficient distance from dismay to hope, from alienation to contentment, that it seemed time for this book to show itself whole.

If it begins with a cry against good things being ruined, it ends, I hope, with the authority built of definition. Truth defined is truth discovered; and truth can be discovered only because it is always there, it abides, waiting for those who come to know it because they have first loved it. I hope the readers of this book will find something in it worth the knowing, because it seeks to defend something that they love, the art of poetry and all that it does to enrich human experience, to form it and orient it to the permanent things. I hope also its first chapters will have a certain incisiveness and novelty to them, as they chip at some of the individual idols of our age; by the end, however, I hope the value of this book will be judged not on any originality of detail but in its clear dependence on and fresh expression of a few of those permanent things. The last chapter and the appendix should bring us to rest in what has long been known; the test of the worth of what I write there is whether it is in accord with what is old. My debts there to other thinkers therefore are many, but I do my best to acknowledge them both here and at the back of this book.

At the outset, I want only to offer thanks to a few individuals. This book was made possible by the encouragement first offered by Garrick Davis and Ernest Hilbert, in their offices as founder and editor of *Contemporary Poetry Review*, where most of these chapters first appeared serially, between July 2007 and July 2008. It benefited from the comments and criticism offered by colleagues and fellow poets, and, not least, the enthusiasm for the project of Joshua Hren. But before and alongside all this was the ongoing company of my wife, Hilary, whom I first saw cry not in dismay but joy over a good poem, and who reminds me why literature is a thing worth fighting for, but only because it is one of many good things.

—Villanova, Pennsylvania
July 2015

PART I
TIME REVERSES

1/ THE RUINED COLONNADE

While arguing amid the colonnades,
Tired in the noon-day by the badly taught,
Or resting, dubious, in the laurel shades
I have impinged upon a firmer thought
                                        —Yvor Winters

Poet-critics occupy a privileged place in literary
culture, even in an age such as ours when few persons
claim to read poetry. From Ben Jonson and Samuel
Johnson to T.S. Eliot, Louise Bogan, and Geoffrey Hill,
they acquire an authority not usually available to the
novelist or playwright. And so, we should take note
when two of the more prominent, David Lehman and
William Logan, air and air again their complaints about
the dangers literature faces in the contemporary
English Department and treat their posts as critics as
one that reacts against rather than capitalizes upon the
most prestigious academic criticism in our time.

They and others have spoken in defense of *belles lettres*
against the tatters of high theory, by which they mean:
Derridian deconstruction; the political regimentation
that reduces every poem or novel to a series of
contradictory reflections of cultural assumptions about
race or gender (or perhaps, unfashionable a subject
though it is, class); the priggish disapproval of all
literature that does not answer the Left's simple, often
psychologically desperate, need for affirmation of the
self-fashioning of one's identity as the highest good—
the one and only heaven; worst of all, perhaps, the
amnesia of many professional scholars of literature
regarding the basic terminology and history of genres
that make education in literature possible in the first
place. These are realities worth reacting against. They

have been with us for long enough now that some of these trends (deconstruction in particular) have dissolved into the background noise of academic chatter, while others, such as the hunting for "ideology" in every "text," have become so conventional and ubiquitous that most professors can no longer imagine what "criticism" would be if it were not that.

To offer an exemplary catalogue of these curious developments: at a recent convention of the Modern Language Association, one scholar presented a paper on the Anglo-Irish novelist, Elizabeth Bowen, of which the main point seems to have been a defense of Bowen's status as an only child. The scholar prefaced her remarks by suggesting her main ambition was to justify her own, identical status. Her targets were those "purveyors of hate," such as Patrick J. Buchanan, who have dared observe that large families are usually the happiest families, most obviously affirm the goodness of life, and are conducive to a flourishing society. Another scholar at the same session spoke of Bowen's "late-modernist" novels, but, when questioned, could provide no account of what made Bowen's novels, as novels, particularly modernist, much less "late." Elsewhere in the echoing halls of the convention center, an angry young critic used the famous inaction and infertility exhibited in the plays of Samuel Beckett to complain about the Catholic Church's past discouragement of "disparity of cult" marriages and encouragement of big families. Much like the Bowen scholar before him, he seemed interested in his author primarily as a means of striking a blow against birth. The Satyr's secret that "never to be born is best for man" whispers through the corridors of academic discursive power. This will not surprise readers of Roy Campbell's *Flowering Rifle* (1935), whose poems

16

delighted in mocking the culture of sterility that had penetrated the English intelligentsia back when it was gravid with Bloomsbury and the Auden group. Campbell will "flaunt" Truth,

> Before the senile owl-roosts of our youth
> Whom monkeys' glands seem powerless to restore,
> As Birth Control was profitless before,
> Which, sponsored by their mockery of a Church,
> Like stranded barbels, left them in the lurch,
> Whose only impact on the world's affairs
> Has been to cause a boom in Rubber shares,
> Who come to battle with both arms held up
> And ask to be invited home to sup—
> While back at home, to sound their battle-horn,
> Some self-aborted pedants stray forlorn
> And pity those who venture to be born.

In the pitiable darkness beyond the MLA, lusty for the birth of an article in one of the myriad unread journals stored in the digital heaven of academic libraries, some politicized pedant of Victorian literature writes about novels that feature women and property issues, because said sage believes firmly that contemporary women should—definitely, should— own property. Another studies the relation of Irish nationalist drama to the architecture of maternity hospitals, in the belief that both manifest the same coercive ideology—the forcing of birth upon female bodies, and the birth of status quo ideas upon the minds of potential young revolutionaries. And still another harnesses Latin American pulp fiction to complain about the forced sterilization of Puerto Rican women by the United States' government; lest one confuse this with a defense of fertility, the author emphasizes that sterilization is a good thing, it just shouldn't be forced.

This sampling is selective, of course. It reflects only the most plaintive groaners in the academic waters. The harnessing of "texts" for entirely extra-textual ends; a suspicion of ideas, wherever they are manifest, as mere expressions of a sinister will to power; an individual but proliferating hatred of making and creation itself as a coercive and oppressive regime. The contemporary academy seems to have taken T.S. Eliot's Sweeney at his word when he sang,

> That's all the facts when you come to brass tacks:
> Birth, and copulation, and death.

Against the despotism of fact, their scholarship becomes an ineffectual back-tracking, wherein they seek to rescind the power of created, actual existence, as if they might dwell in a realm of uncreated, pure possibility. Creation is no cause of joy; it is an iron fist; only unbeing, unmaking can set us free.

Perversely, this contempt for the actual weight of the body and its life-perpetuating nature finds much of its inspiration in the work of Judith Butler, the author of *Bodies that Matter* (1993). Like their intellectual father, Descartes, these critics kick that pregnant dog, literature, in the gut to demonstrate that matter does not matter, even as, contrary to him, they do not believe in an intellectual soul, but merely in the "possibility" of the body's absolute liberation from the conditions of its existence—beginning with those ties that do, but should not, bind: body, form, truth, goodness, self-diffusiveness, fertility, and life. Proud of having passed beyond the limitations of modern liberal democracy, these advocates of freedom from the determinations that compose actual existences have

18

really just pushed the doctrine of "self-determination" to its absurd limit, that of self-fashioning as pure promise. They are ahistorical anthropologists of the possible; they aspire to subsist in that state of pure indeterminacy J.V. Cunningham neatly summed up in the professor who grew "so broad-minded he was scatter-brained."

Contemporary Marxist scholars react violently against the social concern for the human body, what they call "biopolitics," as a salacious and seductive front in their war against the persistence of political bodies. Following the writings of Jacques Rancière, Giorgio Agamben, and Slavoj Zizek, they insist that any stable, self-affirming, and slowly self-cultivating political system disguises an oppressive regime under the appearance of discursive tolerance and the idea of a "loyal opposition." Such a system is mere "meta-politics." Politics per se entails the cataclysmic conflicts that determine whether and how these systems exist in the first place. The body politic, to be truly political, must therefore also remain indeterminate, a politics of pure possibility, a prospect of violence. Political form forecloses politics; conversely, politics is the cracking of all forms. Hence the Victorian novel becomes the subject of study to show how our present regime of "post-liberal" state domination came into being through the insidious discourses of the earlier liberal society of the British Empire. Because English liberals used the law as a means to increase their power, such political critics contend that legality *per se* is mere ideology. The lesson of bad laws is not to make good laws, nor to abandon law altogether; the lesson they learn is to resent what is and what has been, and to move according to an intellectual quick-step of infinite regression beyond the horizons of what is possible (what might actually be) to, again, possibility itself (the "mightness" without the actuality). The only politics they could approve would be a liberation so absolute that even autonomy—the "possessive individualism" of a self that generates its own law even against nature's law—will appear quaint. True political freedom is to be aswim in the coming-and-going tide of evanescence that never has to settle for mere being.

While every once in a while one is shocked by a real insight in scholarship of this nature, it does not want for absurdity. It was one thing for Plato to criticize his imperfect world; he did so because his intellect already dwelled in the knowledge of the ever-present, real existence of ideas, of which human society and the world at large could from time to time become a fine expression. It is another for those wounded by and disaffected with birth, their families, society, and the gallivanting of global capitalism—for those, in fact, too wounded to believe in the reality of anything except physical matter subject to the amoral voluntarisms of power—to "critique" out of existence our few cultural achievements along with human nature and the human condition itself. The academy *after* Plato, as it were, has expelled poetry and poets for a reason Plato never dreamed: not because poetry is mere *imitating*, but because the individual it makes always imitates a *universal* model, a truth, and every truth stands in the way of the march toward a utopia of pure possibility.

Academics will not settle for their own sterility. They would unmake the particular by first denying that there is anything universal for it to imitate. So they would both un-make human experience and un-world the *cosmos* in which we live. They would replace the real world with one of pure possibility, and deny Plato's plain of being and truth, which is most real and always present to the intellect, in favor of a utopia located somewhere beyond the edge of history and never to be seen.

Or, they would, if only they could. Instead, they settle for disenchanting the literary and encouraging in their already disengaged students an ignorance of literary and poetic form in favor of a paranoid sensitivity to the forms of political power. The poet and scholar Helen Pinkerton has summarized the literary theorist's will to dominate the literary work well, deploying the most appropriate metaphor possible, that of rape. For, like the hypothetical rapist, many of these theorists seem set on domination of the text as compensation for failings elsewhere:

> Abusing its otherness, its soul and wit,
> He rapes the text, claiming its benefit—
> And that, inscrutable, it asked for it.

Sharp and just though Pinkerton's accusation is, we should note it is not the use of literary theory per se that rankles. *Theoria* is itself the contemplative and speculative activity that makes possible our coming to know the rich particulars of a literary text. To read literature is already to have a theory of it, however unformed, and many persons have found postmodern theory rewarding precisely because it helped them come to an explicit knowledge of beliefs that had been implicit hitherto. That said, it is necessary to suggest what is so terrible about these academic trends as a kind of propaedeutic for what I consider the much graver purpose of this book: to address and correct the embarrassing failure of most contemporary poets to write something that can, if we are to speak with integrity rather than compassion, be called poetry.

Most recent poetry resists, or simply embarrasses, any attempt to ascertain a definition of what poetry in fact

21

is. Analogously, most recent literary criticism decries the "essentialism" of the "imperialist metaphysics of the West." Both these acts are founded on a shared revolution against the notion of reality as an intelligible whole wherein to be means to be something in particular, and to be something in particular means to be knowable. It is remarkable that many of the same poets whose poetry illustrates what an unintelligible world might sound like are among the first and most zealous to declare English Departments as their overly intellectualized enemy. The anti-intellectualism and anti-humanism of much contemporary writing owes a great deal to the prior rejection, in literature departments, of knowledge as "oppressive." What but the "liberating" loss of a compelling notion of *what poetry is* has made possible the proliferation—not to say flourishing—of contemporary free verse with its splattering of phonemes across the page? If much contemporary poetry paints the human person as a traumatized, debased, and mutable body stuck in a history of shapelessness and violence, the literary theorists were there before them and provide to that poetry its only sympathetic audience.

That is, contemporary poets and contemporary critics are up to the same thing even if they do not always know it. They are the vanguard of a race that discounts as oppressive the hypothesis that there should be any formal value or inherent meaning in a work or in the world, and they have the additional kinship of being, by some cruel fate, engaged in two of the few enterprises that should require, as the price of admission, a belief in just such value and meaning. Poets currently do not believe that their poems need to make any intelligible contribution to our understanding of reality, but merely insist that they float upon it as reality's superfluous metaphors, like medical waste improperly disposed of off the Jersey shore. Scholars, conversely, do not believe that a literary text can be anything more than an accidental expression of ideology; in consequence, literature *qua* literature has nothing (wise or valid) to say to its readers; its form and figure cannot be a revelation of truth made incarnate, but merely betrays in its details those historical conditions external to, yet inscribed unwittingly within, it. Poets and scholars in our day do not create or produce so much as reduce—to text, to bodily sensation, to matter, to power, to history.

To put this another way, contemporary literary criticism generally acts as a crude psycho-analysis of a work's author and its first readers, divulging their hateful complexes in order to condemn them, while contemporary poetry often sounds like the leftovers of a world devoured by such critique. John Crowe Ransom's complaint, in "Criticism, Inc.", about the literature departments of mid-century America remains apt today:

> English might almost as well announce that it does not regard itself as entirely autonomous, but as a branch of the department of history, with the option of declaring itself occasionally a branch of the department of ethics. It is true that the historical and the ethical studies will cluster round objects which for some reason are called artistic objects. But the thing itself the professors do not have to contemplate . . .

Contemporary literary studies generally amount to a historical debunking and an ethical denunciation performed by those convicted of historicism (the belief that all knowledge is historically conditioned and not reflective of some actual and unconditioned truth) and voluntarist amoralism (that is, the belief that ethical judgment can never be more than the expression of a historically conditioned drive for power).

Ransom, of course, spoke on behalf of poets who were fast becoming professors against the professors who, in his view, had long since reduced art to pedantry. In the process, he helped in the ascent of that once familiar creature, the poet-professor competent to exercise both functions. In our day, I would claim, certain poets and academics are up to roughly the same thing as the historians and philologists Ransom opposed, but with one crucial difference. The old style of English professor was merely a sifter and note-taker who sought positive knowledge but deprecated critical judgment and creative activity. In our day, the aim is total deconstruction: the poet un-makes rather than makes, and the professor exposes discursive power rather than cultivates literary wisdom. And so, while I have frequently heard and been tempted to join the chorus of poets denouncing the academic critics, I cannot. What I can do, however, is step back from this ruined colonnade that once constituted the large, informal academy of literary culture, of artists and critics, in order to make a formal tabulation of our loss.

And so this book aims to do. But, not that only. Its roots go deeper than a splenic reaction to decadence, incoherence, and *Thanatos*, and lie rather in a sense of the fundamental goodness of things. What is good seeks always to become actual, to become as real, as fully so, as it can be; this involves not the eschewal of all definition and limit, but the embracing of precisely that shape, that form, suitable to one's nature. It began in the conviction of the goodness of poetry, and the desire to have more of it. The death wish of the contemporary world extends far, far beyond the literary cabinet, but a world of creativity, a world given over to the slow cultivation of craft, of form, and invention, that leads to growth, self-giving, and new life is one worth defending. As will become clear in what follows, the seeds of such a literary world have long since sprouted, or re-sprouted, and where I can I would help them to flourish. New poems appear in our magazines almost daily that testify to the ineradicable goodness of verse, of rhyme, of poetic form in the truest sense, and it is in the writing of more such poems that much of the hope for our literature lies. Each day, some young or old scholar arises and realizes he reads books for the sake of wisdom and contemplation, not for that of a professionalized gesture of political loathing. We must document the decay of literature's edifice; that is one significant function of criticism, and the purpose guiding much of what follows. But we will also do as much as a small critical book can to aid in the reconstruction, by preparing an outline of poetry's enduring life and form—to show why it is, simply, good.

2/ CRITICISM, INC. IMAGINED AS A FRENCH HOLDING COMPANY

Against the poets their own arms they turned,
Sure to hate most the men from whom they learned.
—Alexander Pope

In the middle decades of the last century, criticism inside and outside the academy flourished as a compound chiefly of evaluation and exegesis, and, secondarily, speculation and appreciation. One explained what a work of literature meant in order to justify one's judgment about its quality, or one made a judgment about a work as a departure point for exploring what it meant. One might also speculate on literary theory to establish principles for judgment and interpretation or offer appreciations of a work to draw the initial attention of readers and scholars. General theories of literature, history, and metaphysics often emerged, though tenuously and with more than a hint of philosophical pragmatism, because evaluation and exegesis remained primary. Those theories that did emerge almost invariably came grounded in larger critiques of culture and civilization. This was the case with T.S. Eliot, John Crowe Ransom, W.H. Auden, Marianne Moore, and Yvor Winters, all of whom tended to be particularly "practical," because their criticism was written out of, or in response to, their own practice. It was no less the case with W.K. Wimsatt and Cleanth Brooks, who felt morally obliged in their critical work to understand what a poem actually *does* as a poem, even if they were chary about its connection with an actual poet. Because of this practical orientation, much of the criticism during this period served brilliantly to illuminate the actual dimensions of the poems and books investigated even as it often revealed and supported the deeper philosophical commitments of the critic.

In its first decades, before the New Criticism became an institutionalized title, these practices developed and massively improved the *ad hoc* cultural-critical tradition founded by Matthew Arnold and other formidable Victorian sages. In brief, criticism during this period combined a pragmatist's modesty with a Platonic conviction that literary form resonated with, resembled, and reflected upon the forms of culture or even of reality as a whole. The reader in search of what a John Donne poem simply means *in itself* did not go away disappointed. The searcher reading to find out what that poem means *in the cosmic and total scheme* of things also found that hunger addressed, for the first implied the second. The modesty of such criticism did not reduce literature to a mere language game, but it did insist on grappling with the words themselves, approaching them with critical reverence, all the while allowing the work of art to open on other and larger wholes. In an age when metaphysics and theology were in retreat in many parts of the West, such modesty and openness seemed to make their stakes and spirit available in a form palatable to the rising generation.

There can, however, be no substitute for real theology or real philosophy. These same critics, in consequence, sometimes seem childish in their fumbling flights of abstraction, overly content to make judgments based on distinctions sometimes tenuous, sometimes too superficially comprehended, like that between romanticism and classicism, reason and emotion, science and poetry, use and beauty, prose and verse, form and content, knowledge and experience, myth and history, ethics and art, genius and talent. They took dualisms of recent—romantic—vintage as the natural categories of thought not because those formulae were adequate to the reality under discussion, but because they were unaware of any other possibilities.

Ransom, for all his essayistic brilliance too often the most childish of them all, freely confessed this fault and blamed it on the failure of English departments to educate students at something other than philology and literary history. He wrote in his manifesto for literary study, "Criticism, Inc," that the only true literary critics, before the New Criticism, had been "home-made critics. Naturally they are not too wise, these amateurs who furnish our reviews and critical studies. But when they distinguish themselves, the universities which they attended can hardly claim more than a trifling share of the honor." In their pragmatic ambitions and fervor to correct the errors of civilization with the achievements of high culture, ethics and aesthetics, religion, poetry, and politics often got messily rolled into one.

Now, I should note that the usual dismissals of the New Critics on account of their "religious" obsession with metaphor and paradox, their obscurantist hunting after the "heresy of paraphrase," or because their apparent formalism closed off literature to the deeper exigencies that explain why we read it and why some of us write it, are mistaken. As their Arnoldian pedigree suggests, few authors have ever so persistently insisted on the importance of poetry as a mode of discovery and critique in religious, political, and other cultural fields as did Ransom, Tate, Brooks, and, especially, Yvor Winters. Far from erring on the side of isolating or eviscerating the aesthetic, these practical critics only failed in articulating the profound and convincing relations between the aesthetic, cultural, political, and religious spheres of thought and activity with a nuance and sophistication that could remain permanently satisfying. Their practical successes were real, they just did not always arrive at a fullness of *theoria*.

It is hard not to blush at some of Ransom's efforts to take on John Dewey, his hillbilly Kantianism in the defense of art as something more than a chemical or natural "reaction." All men of good will root for him, as they would root for Winters's more accomplished attempt at a Thomistic criticism, if they ever read it, but they must acknowledge such arguments are neither as cogent nor thorough-going as they ought to be. But let us at least cite Francesca Aran Murphy's ground-breaking study, *Christ the Form of Beauty* (1995), which draws Tate, Ransom, and Caroline Gordon into dialogue with the theological aesthetics of Jacques Maritain, William Lynch, and Hans Urs von Balthasar; in doing so, she demonstrates how important the New Critics become when we move beyond the horizon of the contemporary English department into the cosmos of modern theology. Their naïveté, clumsiness, or whatever, becomes secondary to the insights they have to share in that much wider world.

Nevertheless, one can see why professional scholars in the last few decades, once they got a loose grip on certain minority trends in Continental philosophy, with its pseudo-scientific jargon and parody of technical complexity, felt their intellectual moment had arrived. Confident in the rectitude and genius of postmodern semiotics and the efficacious explanatory power of the latest "hermeneutics of suspicion," most influentially expressed by Michel Foucault, the professor could shed his pragmatic, hokey subservience to the great work of literature and hierophantic poet, and claim a certain autonomy—an autonomy that has been *sometimes* unfairly brow beaten as "Theory." The form of a poem must appear minute—literally—when one judges it in proportion to the forms of civilization and human experience, and so Continental literary theory seemed to debunk the figurative grandeur of literature. If one can wield that axe, the literary scholar *qua* amateur philosopher came to think, no tree will be left standing —except my own. As such, literary theory promised to wrest the importance and prestige of art from the author and put it in the hands of the scholar. Unfortunately for the scholar, grandeur is not fungible; the head-scratchers of the western world, who had at least stared confused at the poetry printed in the margins of their favorite magazines, cast their glance on academic literary criticism only once a year, as *The New York Times* published the most absurd paper titles from the annual Modern Language Association convention. The age of Hitler Studies had arrived, but its practitioners would receive no laurels. *Sic transit gloria mundi.*

As I indicated above, the age of "Theory" has passed, and has left us *not* junior American Derridas mouthing "*Quoi?*" with pursed lips in the salons of academe. What it has left us is a sense of the scholarly-critical enterprise entirely given over to different, ever-subtler variations of "reflection theory," where the scholar's chief aim is to prove how the historical ideology of a period informs a text, or how the text reinforces the ideology of its age. This does not make such scholar-critics bad teachers of literature in comparison with those of the past. Rather, it literally makes them professors of a different, incommensurable discipline from that of the poet-professors and New Critics of the past (the break between earlier philological scholars and the New Critics was not nearly so great, because the latter drew on the researches of the former, whereas responsible "close reading" actually gets in the way of most postmodern scholarship). It also almost

31

ineluctably binds them to a set of political principles as the ransom for freeing them of any sense of obligation to a certain body of literature or canon of aesthetic standards. I say *almost* ineluctably, because the fate of scholars like Frank Lentricchia and Terry Eagleton has been to be branded "reactionaries" by their colleagues for their attempt to find a way out of such a bind. They believe, or would like to believe, that literature still has something to give us that we cannot spin for ourselves out of the threads of theory.

In general, though, academic scholar-critics are now trained to sniff out ideologies and classify them according to certain gender or racial nomenclatures. To their graduate students, they may speak of the indeterminacy and historical contingency of these and all ideologies; for such trained academic specialists, the chief task of literary study is to show how the instability of cultural forms goes all the way down to the foundations of human experience, and therefore might as well be manipulated (by whom?) in favor of selected liberal truisms. Astonishingly, this voluntarist pursuit of one liberal platitude or another is now most frequently couched in a critique of liberalism itself. (Jeremy Bentham and John Stuart Mill get martyred for ideals they helped formulate. This revolution, like every revolution, culminates in the burning of those who started it.) Meanwhile, to their undergraduates, such professors recuperate this nihilistic news of "cultural relativism" in a form of neo-liberal diversity and civil rights discourse intended to impart a spirit of non-judgmental tolerance. Such an education inculcates the students to question the reality of binding moral claims so that the freedom of an ever-multiplying number of identities may be won. They are taught to doubt their ability to know truth as such for the sake of the one truth no one is allowed to deny: that freedom, including the freedom to become whatever one wants, is an absolute good. They are taught to love the Good less so that it may be remade more easily in the image of every individual soul's private perversity. In sum, identity politics never looks so superannuated as it does in the graduate seminar, and never appears of such urgent political importance as it does in the undergraduate lecture hall.

The first practitioners of critical theory were really just trying to introduce Continental philosophy into an institution formed on principles of literary evaluation and exegesis that were themselves founded on a fairly robust, but inadequately articulated, set of philosophical commitments. However awful much of theory was, it nonetheless marked an honest attempt to flesh out literary criticism with a philosophical method that could stand up to scrutiny. These aims have gone into the dark long since, in part because the philosophy itself was just too hard, and in part because, once one had penetrated its long and whimsical periods, it brought one to an intellectual dead end. (That dead end was soon labeled *jouissance* and enjoyed a rather sterile and un-joyful resurrection.) What theory's dainty French footprints have left behind of the English Department is an institution fanatically closed to new philosophical thinking and equally fanatically committed to rehashing ideology-critique-after-ideology-critique with ever more minute refinements of vocabulary. The same assertions made thirty years ago appear incessantly and ever more nuanced, each new monograph just one more teratoma in an endless, pointless, finally monstrous project.

It is worth pausing here to state the obvious: this need not have happened. Had the frequent efforts of early-twentieth-century critics to ground their ideas in realist metaphysical systems been performed with more rigor, an alternative and altogether happier path might have opened up. Had R.S. Crane and the Chicago School been more limber in their adaptation of Aristotle's *Poetics* and more open to developing aesthetic theories and criticism in continuity with the broader Aristotelian tradition, their influence would have been much greater than it was. Had Ransom never read Kant and Hegel, or had other New Critics like Allen Tate and W.K. Wimsatt been better able to harness, correct, and expand upon the Thomist philosophies of art and beauty Jacques Maritain outlined in *Art and Scholasticism* and *Creative Intuition in Art and Poetry*, their already deeply metaphysical sense of aesthetic form might have endured and flourished. Indeed, the New Criticism might have forged a rich and compelling meeting of Thomistic judgment and poetic contemplation, even though the neo-Thomism that informed it fell out of fashion in the 'sixties. Then again, perhaps it is too much to hope that anything rich or good or intelligent could have survived the upheavals of the 'sixties, when American therapeutic religion, Marxist historical necessity, and a drug-addled populism joined forces to injure slightly a few persistent evils and destroy utterly a great many (until then) perennial goods.

In any case, the union of philosophy and English Departments came in the form of theory, and theory remade those Departments so that they only seemed to be performing their proper function if they were tearing down the screens of received ideas of what was true, good, or beautiful in order to expose the usually (dead?) white, mad male imperialist wizard-monkey operating his ideology-machine just behind. This does not necessarily mean English Departments are bad things, even now; they are capable of producing interesting analogies between high and low works of art that help us understand more deeply some of the forces that shape our culture. Further, even the post-humanist English professor is still human, and, despairing of his mediocre students, will often enough settle for just teaching them about how pretty the close of *The Great Gatsby* is. More than one professor has complained to his confreres about feeling like a high theorist in the bedroom but only a New Critic in the classroom. It does entail, however, that the underlying principles of such culture critique are other than those of traditional literary education and should be understood as such. And, further, the explicit politicization of modern literary-cultural research makes difficult if not impossible the nuanced discussion of any aesthetic question independent either of its immanent political implications or a very limited set of ideological commitments. If ideology means simply "a system of often irreconcilable beliefs held together by force of will and purporting to explain reality, when in fact it screens the reason from a clear vision of it," then ideology critique, whatever its merits, has become the greatest ideology of them all. As Eric Voegelin famously argued, ideology functions as a critical tool or method, but its central characteristic is that it makes impossible the asking of certain, fundamental questions, such as whether the ideologist's tools are adequate to reality.

Before turning from recent institutional history to contemporary poetry, let me suggest that the corrective to the deficiencies of the contemporary academy is not a turning back to the more reductive institutionalized modes of the New Criticism. Plot summaries of *A Chaste Maid in Cheapside*, followed by glowing recommendations of its structure, or catalogues of the appearance of anapestic substitutions in late-Victorian verse, constitute an essential element in good literary criticism. They do not exhaust it. Rather, we need to look back to how the best New Critics developed their practice within the tradition of cultural criticism that sprang up in the nineteenth century. This fast and loose, omnivorous tradition believed criticism (contrary to Samuel Johnson's definition) could apply itself to any facet of human life—that it could in fact help find and evaluate the connecting veins that spread through the tissue of our culture. I have mentioned Arnold, but consider also the shelf of books that constitutes the complete work of G.K. Chesterton and Hilaire Belloc. Think of Ruskin and Carlyle, of course, but peruse also the works of Hannah Arendt, the literary remains of T.E. Hulme, and all the prose of W.H. Auden. Here one finds a genre of writing of inestimable importance that gains in value because it knows no institutional boundaries; the only boundary is the breadth of human reason and love.

These redoubtable figures are the ancestors and heirs of the greatest New Critics. What Eliot and Tate wished to do was refine that critical reason so that it recognized poetry as poetry rather than something else, and so escaped the error of confusing it with a political pamphlet, a totem, or a whiff of opium. They refined literary criticism within cultural criticism; they did not seek to amputate it as one sometimes suspects the conservative decriers of the modern academy would have liked. To the extent that one suspects William Logan of meeting up with William Bennett in admonishing literature professors to keep their heads down and stick with teaching the greatness of Shakespeare, his anger is misguided. The critics' embrace of Continental theory was not a sign of ambitions too high for their office, but too low and lazy.

Logan's celebrated proclivity for the biting, negative review is not most important for reminding us that literary criticism should criticize, that is, should evaluate and, more often than not, berate. Many writers today think that the return of the barb to review columns would save poetry and criticism (admittedly, it would help), by bringing it back to its central cultural function. But, to the contrary, what Logan's negative reviews demonstrate is how bad literature can prove an occasion for great, instructive criticism, for the writer with a capacity to think theoretically. His snarls often bring good from bad, sound sense from fuzzy writing. The New Critics understood this. Indeed, Milton got off badly in the writings of Eliot and Ransom in part because these poet-critics wished to show that no literary great was beyond reproach. Those truly deserving of reproach certainly have something to teach us, if only by the incompetence of their writing or the blindness of the worldview they express. As the seventh chapter will show, the conventions of English poetry only came into being through a fruitful response to the practical missteps and theoretical exaggerations and misperceptions, of the first modern English poets. We need to be something more than evaluative critics and readers, however, if we are to learn such lessons.

I am calling then for a criticism far broader and richer in interest than that which now predominates. The return of evaluative criticism and positive arguments about the contents of the canon—by all means! But there is nothing wrong, and a great deal right, with my colleagues' frequent interest in abominable works of literature; we can learn a great deal from the clumsiness of lesser artists. Those of us who have an interest in the totality of human experience and wish to come to a rational understanding of it will naturally find much for study in bad works of art—and that includes, but is scarcely limited to, what can be learned about the great from what is absent in the bad. The error so many of contemporary scholars make is to justify their interest in minor or bad authors by categorically dismissing the identity of an art work as art, and so pretending as if aesthetic evaluation were irrelevant except as an ideology to be studied.

And so, what we need is neither the perpetuation of the ideologically stunted scholarship of many contemporary academics nor a cozy book club for the appreciation of how "classic works warm hearts," nor finally an endless chronicle of disapprobation. Literary criticism should be what its best New Critical advocates hoped it would someday become: a robust venture that appreciates and explores the distinct attributes of the aesthetic and the poetic, and in two ways beyond traditional exegesis. First, it should bear down on the practice and craft of literature after the fashion of the serious artist. Second, it should also recognize that every artist and reader is, before all else, human; as such, properly literary attentions must extend into those larger conversations about human nature, history and culture, and, finally, being and the ground of being, metaphysics and theology. Eliot recommended something like this when discussing the virtues and limitations of Johnson's *Lives of the Poets*. He observes,

> Criticism of poetry moves between two extremes. On the one hand the critic may busy himself so much with the implications of a poem, or of one poet's work—implications moral, social, religious or other—that the poetry becomes hardly more than a text for discourse. Such is the tendency of the moralising critics of the nineteenth century, to

which Landor makes a notable exception. Or if you stick too closely to the 'poetry' and adopt no attitude towards what the poet has to say, you will tend to evacuate it of all significance. And furthermore there is a philosophic borderline, which you must not transgress too far or too often, if you wish to preserve your standing as a critic, and are not prepared to present yourself as a philosopher, metaphysician, sociologist, or psychologist instead. Johnson, in these respects, is a type of critical integrity. Within his limitations, he is one of the great critics; and he is a great critic partly because he keeps within his limitations . . . For Johnson poetry was still poetry, and not another thing.

The necessary but limited role of evaluative and exegetical criticism subsists within a larger unity of human inquiry. The critic performs a distinguished service by examining a work of art as just that; but his queries should awaken us to the whole field of human experience. The most enduring New Critics practiced just this. The academy rarely allows for it now. Its professors mostly rush past poetry altogether in order to shred to tatters the more easily "sociologized" blocks of prose novels and thought-bubble comic books. Poems and novels become incidental bodies of evidence to be dissected that some blue vein or proud stilled heart of ideology might be extracted for our— our what?—our assurance that there is no truth these professors have not killed.

Outside the academy, the sort of criticism Eliot describes is more common, but less sophisticated than it once was (in part because its practitioners are given little space in print to spread out their thinking properly, and in part because they respect too tenaciously their limitations as critics and ignore too easily their responsibilities as intellectual creatures). We live in a twilit age of dull philistines and crusaders of resentment, and this does not admit of easy solution. Because the philosophical foundations that recognize beauty as a transcendental property of being, alongside goodness and truth, have become unmoored, the critic who believes in these things and makes judgments according to them, must also perform the task of explaining and justifying the foundations of judgment. In this sense, we must move against, or rather beyond, Eliot's praise of Johnson.

The literary critic must also be, at least, a metaphysician, but not just any metaphysics will do. The long theological-metaphysical tradition that begins with the ancient Greeks and careens smoothly on through history until the modern philosophers tried to shipwreck it, must be restored its deserved authority. Only in that tradition, the Christian-Platonist tradition broadly construed, where beauty is understood as knit into reality, perhaps even constitutive of it, can literary criticism flourish. And only, to repeat, if critics have the intelligence and education to argue persuasively within that tradition, can their practices have any claim on our souls, can they worthily support our incontestable and insatiable vocation to the contemplation of the Real.

In the chapters that follow, I shall attack much of contemporary poetry from a critical position firmly if usually implicitly Christian Platonist, to suggest how the art form could be better than it is in almost every respect. I hope also that, in the performance of such a critique, the value of realist metaphysics and the theological presuppositions from which it is inextricable may become apparent. I have written about these matters more directly and systematically elsewhere, but here, I shall for the most part presuppose them and proceed to practice the sort of unified inquiry that I find otherwise wanting in both academic and non-academic criticism. If the hunters of ideology have taught us anything, it is that Aristotle was correct when he claimed that inquiry into the nature of even so ethereal and minute a thing as a poem or word must be grounded in reasoning that extends back to the first principles of being. To write of contemporary poetry, or of any matter, will summon us also to ask what it means to be a thing. To judge what kind of poetry is good will lead inevitably at least to our touching on questions of how a human person—not just as a reader of poetry, but as a person —can and ought to live in the world. *Poiesis*, the science of making, leads eventually to *genesis*, the science of creation itself. Before we are done, I shall show that this insight has not only been present from the beginning of the poetic tradition, but has defined it. We need not begin with such a big bang, however, but only with that most whimpering of phenomena, the modern poetry reading.

3/ THE HALF-EMPTY AUDITORIUM

Those who love literature, or at any rate have a vested interest in making sure great works of literature are taught at universities and that radical politics are not, could only find the conquest of the English Department by "post-liberal" liberal ideologues distressing. But complaints on the hijacking of the academy by "tenured radicals" too often lead us to overlook more pernicious problems. For a literature professor such as myself, the spectacle of some of my colleagues tends to induce fits of speechless exasperation, followed soon after by the writing of polemical essays. But there are worse scandals to which no response on my part could be effectual. From time to time, I have found myself slumped as one soul among dozens, in a large, third- or quarter-filled auditorium, and listened to a renowned poet decry the decline of English Departments, only to look about me and see nodding "fellow poets," and the recently published Cornfield State University or SUNY— Milltown Press books of those poets, as greater threats than any bizarrely and narrowly trained academic.

If literature is to persist as an interest of honest men and women in the decades or centuries to come, it must be good enough to withstand the assault of any, and every, English Department. That poetry should be primarily read in the classroom is a bad thing, whether or not the professor teaching it does so badly or in the interest of forwarding bad ideas. That poets should cultivate productive and intelligent conventions of their craft; that they should understand the traditions in which they write, and treat them with deference and care; that their poems should be quite simply good— these are far more essential matters than whether some

43

aesthetic deaf-mute should "out" a woman novelist of the nineteenth century, or whether some brash assistant professor, with complacent zealotry, should denounce Ezra Pound's politics for the one-millionth time.

I have little reason to believe that poetry can long continue to exist outside the academy, however, because I have observed that the vast majority of publishing poets have abandoned or betrayed everything that makes poetry a valid and valuable art form. They do so *not* by entering the academy, but through a far more basic, bizarrely deliberate, lack of competence in writing. The academy should help sustain poets and poetry. It should initiate students into the study of that art so that the students may go on to enjoy it freely over the course of their lives. That is part of its mission as an institution of culture. But, to complain about its poor stewardship in that purpose as the singular cause of literary decline ignores the essential passivity and marginality of academic criticism and exaggerates the reach of those incompetent malcontents who feed upon it. It mistakes an easy target for a moving one.

I read a generous handful of new books of poems and new issues of poetry journals every year. The few journals to which I subscribe and re-subscribe include an impressive number of great poems in their pages alongside many bad ones; the books I buy, as opposed to those I thumb through in stores or some of those I receive to review, offer extraordinary riches. Indeed, if I were careful, or just more selective, in my reading, I might almost think contemporary poetry was flush with imaginative vitality and formal accomplishment. Some of Geoffrey Hill's work, most of Dick Davis's, all of David Middleton's, nearly all of Mary Jo Salter's, Timothy Steele's, Catharine Savage Brosman's, and

Dana Gioia's; the lyrics I have seen of Leslie Monsour, Bill Coyle, Joshua Mehigan, Amit Majmudar, Paul Lake, Maryann Corbett, William Connelly, A.E. Stallings, Alfred Nicol, Peggy O'Brien, Ernest Hilbert, Jennifer Reeser, and Adam Kirsch; the translations of Rhina P. Espaillat, Len Krisak, and William Baer; the fractured narratives of Brad Leithauser, Ned Balbo, David Mason, and William Logan; the weird classicism of Fredrick Turner's lyrics and epics—these constitute remarkable achievements. The selected and collected editions of Helen Pinkerton, John Hollander, Elizabeth Jennings, Donald Justice, Anthony Hecht, Derek Mahon, Derek Walcott, Gjertrud Schnackenberg, and Richard Wilbur suggest no less that some few titans still walk among us, or did until yesterday, and have perfected and extended their medium over a lifetime.

But too many times—too many cringing, aching times —have I sat in some cool and shabbily furnished auditorium, with its burnt orange curtain and wood-paneled podium, set like a soporific discotheque in the heart of a Stalinist slab of concrete poured out for the training of the State's industrious wards, only to witness a ragtag bohemian army. There they sit, the piercèd ones, the assembled mass of a generation of well-published, would-be poets who simply do not know what they are doing, crowded by their well-disposed sycophants, even now conceiving non sequiturs in lines, waiting to hear something they may steal, waiting to hear the next new thing. In their quest to be original, inventive, "experimental," and above all, published, they have repeated and repeated the mistakes of their slightly elder elders and their illiterate classmates in myriad MFA workshops.

By "mistakes," of course, I mean "present poetic conventions." Do I ask them to cease being

45

conventional in order to become great poets? Not at all. Every poem is written within conventions, even when it is explicitly against them; it is a new whole of which conventions are the parts. I ask rather that they ask themselves why it is they write what they write. I have noticed that very few poets enjoy sitting and reading other poets' work. This is not because "most of the poetry in any age is bad," but because most poetry written and published today is produced within a body of conventions that guide poets in banal, opaque, nonsensical directions—directions that no one, save another poet looking for something to copy, would willingly follow. It is the hack work of the incompetent yet ambitious, a professional parlance with nothing amatory about it suitable for the amateur: but literature is *for* amateurs or it is for nothing.

When someone (in this instance Wayne Koestenbaum in *Fence* 17) publishes disjunctive declarative sentences followed by an extract from Theodor W. Adorno as if it were poetry, one understands that certain conventions are in place. They are simply bad conventions that manifest a theory of poetry entirely conformed to the practices of a modern consumer society, even as they pretend to move against them:

> I might benefit from supplemental testosterone.
> My arm is missing a wedge.
>
> My girlfriend had a much-touted abortion.
> I'm not emotionally expressive.
>
>
> Adorno: "He who offers for sale
> something unique that no one wants to buy
>
> represents, even against his will,

freedom from exchange."

The reasonably intelligent reader would be unlikely to spend much time puzzling out the connection between the first lines and the quoted passage from Adorno. Granting that he could, he nonetheless is not meant to do so, because poetry of this nature is constructed according to conventions that have nothing to do with the craft of poetry and everything to do with the publishing of poetry as an event, or rather, as the proof-of-purchase of itself as an event. This poem was intended to appear in a journal, perhaps to be glanced at by other young "poets" of certain ambition so that they will know it is there. It serves to reaffirm for them that poetry consists of little more than a series of ill-configured disjunctive sentences; so affirmed, they will proceed in manufacturing their own formulaic variations to appear in future issues, other magazines.

The compositional practice here derives historically from the surrealists but, as we shall explore in a later chapter, it has only the most superficial connection with actual surrealism. Such a practice is usually justified implicitly—though in the present instance, it is explicitly justified—according to a Western Marxist conception of art as resisting the reifying logic of modern capitalism. By refusing to be absorbed in the marketplace, art in its very uselessness and apparent ugliness enacts an isolated liberation from the "exchange" relationships that dominate market societies.

I do not like having my life reduced to its economic value any more than the next guy. But, unhappily, this poem and the thousands like it published each year attempt no such liberation; rather they serve as counters of cultural capital with no more intrinsic value than a dollar bill. This very "valuelessness" makes them available for ever-quicker consumption, as poet after poet skims journal after journal, in the impossible hope of keeping ahead of the market and, through imitation, getting another, similar poem published. This is what I mean by the poem as a kind of proof-of-purchase of the event of its publication. The poem is never meant to be seen in itself, and it will not be. It is meant to indicate that so-and-so has been published and this validates the continuation of publishing just this sort of thing. It is a species of that academic specter called a "credential," a line on a CV.

Such a literary culture neither resists modern market culture, nor merely subsists within it. Because of the absolute marginality of contemporary poetry to that culture, it perversely exaggerates the inherent instability of the marketplace. The old Marxist saw that, in capitalism, "all that is solid melts into air," seems an understatement here. Contemporary poetry of this sort was never solid to begin with; it was never meant to subsist and is already out of date the moment of its appearance. No one but the poet's classmates, students, and imitators would shuffle into an auditorium to listen to such a poem. And even they would consider it a burden, for all talk of pleasure, interest, appreciation, or, in Adorno's terminology, "shudder," is beside the point here. The poem exists solely to be accepted by an editor and to reside unread on uncut pages of one journal or another. A poetry reading would merely slow down the rate of consumption, and one's time is better spent either mailing out one's own poems—or, perhaps, skimming a "post-avant" journal in search of something to steal and reformulate as "post-post-avant." If poems were worth money, one might have to think about them awhile; but, as it is, the only sign of a poem's value is its publication and the publication of more like it.

If penurious hyper-capitalism drives the small heavens of contemporary poetry in their ambit, this need not be so. An abundance of polemical essays in the last two decades have explored the importance, fate, and material of poetry in hopes of saving it from its practitioners. Dana Gioia's *Can Poetry Matter?* (1992) is perhaps the most concisely perceptive and is certainly among the most well-known and unjustly maligned. William Logan's prose, especially in his volume, *The Undiscovered Country* (2005), offers a copious supply of sharp (if not always as sharply worded as one would like) insights on the nature and failure of recent poetry. I hesitate therefore to suggest that the small readership of poetry criticism needs mine. At the risk of appearing to claim an authority I only doubtfully possess, I would nonetheless like to catalogue a handful of the losses from which poetry currently suffers. Because I so much enjoy reading poetry, perhaps my account will indicate what at least one enthusiastic reader looks for when he opens a book and what, to his disconsolation, he so seldom discovers. We shall move from a reflection on the failures of contemporary poetry to a defense of the new formalism, a movement that has helped revive our tradition. In Part II, we shall undertake a more systematic critique of modern poetic theory and practice, praising where we can, condemning when we must, before concluding with a series of seven definitive notes on what is the art of poetry and why it has mattered and should matter.

4/ ERRORS AND WRECKS LIE ABOUT ME

> I would shake off the lethargy of our time,
> and give
> For shadows—shapes of power
> For dreams—men.
>
> —Ezra Pound

Two poets I have long admired, John Matthias and Robert Archambeau, have justly charged contemporary poets with falling into two unsatisfactory camps. As Archambeau once expressed it in a self-deprecatory little essay, "We're still swamped with the poem of the semi-confessional backyard epiphany . . . poems that focus on the exquisite sensitivity of the speaker, caught in a meditative moment in an ordinary American life." He was probably thinking of pretty much any poem by Charles Wright, who has become the paradigm of the backyard lyricist in our day and to whose work I shall attend in a later chapter. But, the bulk of poets could fit this description without too much modification. (Some poets, for instance, do not have yards and still others show themselves to be positively insensible to anything but the electric shock of scandal.) On the other side of the wood fence, one finds "linguistically hazy, indeterminate, pseudo-sophisticated nonsense verse that has emerged from the wreckage of language poetry . . . Poems about nothing, doing nothing that hasn't been done before. This emperor has no clothes, and we're all too cowed by Charles Bernstein-quoting associate professors to say so!"

Indeed. For these two worthies, the passage out of this suburban poetry of *l'homme moyen sensuel* in his garden or the unformed and fragmented simulator of revolution seems to be a close development of what

one might call the "impersonal historical poetics" of
Ezra Pound. By this I would indicate those who take
the modernist (Eliotic) call for "impersonality" as one
for a poetry that rejects the lyric mode in favor of a
collage of learned lines drawn from the public and
arcane materials of our history. They draw
considerably on the emotional expressiveness of
Pound's *Pisan Cantos*, where the high modernist's
method boils down to a refracted but no less personal
or heart-rending variation on the traditional lyric (a
lyric "fugue, or frog," as Pound might have put it), but
the heart of their method does not lie there. Likewise,
they are suspicious of the pagan, spatial vision of
history Pound advocates in the *Cantos*; for that matter
they are suspicious of Eliot's advocacy of the
permanent and universal *Logos* of which history is the
incarnation, which is the essential principle that guided
that poet's complex theory of the "impersonal." And
yet, we still hear echoes or intimations of such grand
mythical structures.

The main aspect of Pound they emulate is the wide
swipe of his paw in search of subject matter, and the
refractory construction of the poem itself that allows
us to get history without narrative; after all, if one just
wanted to tell a story, novels would do fine. What they
are after are emblematic patterns, archetypes, spatial
forms for contemplation that nonetheless remain
immanent to history. Where Pound promised an
epiphany that issues in ideology (a new political order)
rather than religion (an eternal order), they, more sober,
promise only a momentary crystallization of the
contingencies of history. In his essay, "Roads Less
Traveled: Two Paths Out of Modernism in Post-War
American Poetry," Archambeau has described
Matthias's poems as the enactment of "postmodern
intertextuality." By this term he appropriately highlights

the "inclusion" of history and archival materials in Matthias's works, while acknowledging that it lacks the search for an absolute, whole, or organic culture against which a chaotic modernity can be measured. His poems therefore may resemble *The Waste Land* in some ways, but they will forego the deep structural anthropology that gives shape to that poem.

Matthias's *A Gathering of Ways* (1991), for instance, offers three poems reminiscent in style and method of Pound's Malatesta or Jefferson/Mussolini Cantos, with their fragmented and leaping historical accounts. Matthias, in representing the histories of East Anglia, the Midwest, and the France and Spain on the path to Santiago de Compostela, moves temporally back and forth, from the pre-historical geology of the places to their early-modern and contemporary conditions. This movement within history demarcates the horizon of the poems, so that the grand transhistorical or absolute vision Pound sought is refused, is put beyond use, even as it (admittedly) sometimes creeps back in the form of an ethical judgment. It will do little good to quote the poems, for their effect derives primarily from the slow-developing patterns of leaping between proper nouns —between toponym and toponym, between historical figure and historical figure. But, we should at least offer a few passages. This comes from "An East Anglian Diptych: Ley Lines, Rivers":

> *Extensio.* Eastern point
> north of Southwold on the Easton Ness, now lost.
> *Portus Adurni.* Was the Deben called Adurnus
>
> by the Latins here and on the Alde?
> Harbour, temperate climate, sheltered creeks—
> and vines growing high above the cliffs.

Counts of the Saxon Shore constructed here
their fortress where they failed to hold the tide
against the kin of those first called

by Vortigern to fight his wars against the Picts.

Here is a humorous passage from "Facts from an
Apocryphal Midwest":

The old Sauk trail, they say
still runs under U.S. 12
north from Niles to Detroit.
U.S. 20 takes it west through
Rolling Prairie to Chicago.

You can drive a car that's named
for Cadillac up U.S. 12
to Ypsilanti, turning north
at 94 to a port named for the Hurons.
You can even drive
your Pontiac to Pontiac.
But only trickster Wiske's brother
Chibyabos ever drove
in a Tecumseh to Tecumseh.

Perhaps the most impressive of these poems for
quotation purposes is, "A Compestela Diptych," as
with this fine description of one dreaming of the
apocalypse in France:

From Mont Saint-Michel to Sens,
from Besançon to Finisterre, a darkness fell at
      noon,
the walls of houses cracked, down

from all the bell towers tumbled bells.

In the encampments, flames leapt from spears of
    ash & apple,
hauberks buckled, steel casques burst,

bears and leopards walked among the men in
    Charles' dream.
For so he dreamed. Dreamed within
a dream Roland's requiem . . .

In each of these, different rhetorical tones lead us to
the same basic encounter: with the material history of
things. Only in that context does Matthias allow
himself something of the refracted lyricism of Pound's
Pisan Cantos. At the end of the last, for instance, we
hear,

Towards Pamplona, long long after all Navarre
was Spain, and after the end
of the Kingdom of Aragón, & after the end of the
    end,

I, John, walked with my wife Diana
down from the Somport Pass following the silence
that invited and received my song

This adds to the poems a lyric beauty, but, overall,
one comes away with a sense of the vastness of the
historical stage, the strange, clotted linguistic beauty of
the prosaic, as well as a sense that one will never learn
what was the meaning of the play acted upon it.

Without rejecting this solution, I would nonetheless
like to get back of it. Consider the dichotomy
Archambeau has constructed. One side of the
unfortunate fence cordons off poets categorized
according to subject matter, poets who expatiate upon
the gentle numinosity of things or their lurid

bankruptcy, all of which returns to one persistent subject—*the subject*, the Cartesian "I" (or the Lutheran or Freudian "I", which comes to the same thing). On the other side, are those corralled primarily by the "form" in which they write. And this form is disjunctive, highly fragmented—it portends to be shattered like a television screen or the glaring mirrored surfaces of a corporate tower, though we might suspect it is broken like the back of a dead horse. Dropping the hammer again and again until the fragments are as dust, such poetry preempts our asking what it means by refusing to give us even enough coherent language to begin the inquiry. What does it mean that, nearly a century after the supposed fusion of form and content in the aesthetics of modernism, we can still effectively group poetry (and other arts for that matter) according to those who write about something (content-centered) and those who write in a certain way (form-centered)?

Well, one lesson may be that modernism *per se* had to fail because form and content cannot ever fully converge for the obvious reason that they are not the same thing. A work of art is a unity, certainly, but what is one in being may be diverse in reason, and the best reasoning we have acknowledges that a work of art can adequately be understood if we recognize form and content as distinguishable. When they pretend to fuse in an absolute identity—as in the poetry of Gerard Manley Hopkins or Emily Dickinson—one soon discovers a limited repertoire of subjects has fallen upon an even more limited range of rhetorical styles and formal gimmicks. Form becomes a special kind of content, which means that the form will only be adequate to the representation of certain aspects of reality. This is obviously true if one understands form as having a modal quality to it; that is, that some styles, meters, and other qualities will be suitable for the treatment of certain themes and not others. But the Hopkins or modernist experiment conceived of form as purely expressive of, and one with, its content so that whole aspects of experience and reality can simply no longer be admitted into poetry. If one's form is that of "God's Grandeur," then only God's grandeur can be expressed by one's form. This is a costly curtailment of poetry's traditional terrain. But, to shrink it still more, as Timothy Steele has argued, poets have repeatedly embarked on the fool's errand of compensating for deficiencies of subject-matter by repairing to formal "experimentation."

As Pound's early poem "Revolt" exemplifies, most modern poets at some time or other become aware that what they are writing about is old hat (or old "dreams" in Pound's case). They merely iterate the conventional subject matter of a given time and therefore, while desiring to speak about some matter of reality, perhaps even the heart and light of Being, suspect all they have really offered is a rhetorical formula. If the only suitable subjects for a poem are accounts of "prowess in arms, kindling of love, [and] rectitude of will," as Dante once claimed and as even the mature Pound seems to have believed, then perhaps the subjects themselves may become so embalmed in conventions, become conventions themselves, that it may seem that the only terrain on which the individual poem can strike out in order to become *this* poem rather than an imitation of poetic themes long since expressed, is that of experimentation with form.

Sometimes this can be all to the good. Wordsworth felt that the Augustans had cut poetry off from the most intimate subject terrain of the heart, and so he changed the subject matter of poetry radically under the guise of formal innovation. The "real language" spoken by men that he purported to write really provided him occasion to justify a little poem about a leech gatherer or a woman singing as she reaps in a field, or a big one about the plight of the rural poor. We should not be fooled by the preface to *The Lyrical Ballads*, which Coleridge coerced him into writing and then judged misleading, that Wordsworth was nearly as concerned with diction (as a formal attribute) as he was with subject. Indeed, the Miltonic element in *The Prelude* and the new titles he stuck on his poems late in his career (e.g. "The Leech-Gatherer" becomes "Resolution and Independence") should suggest that he embraced the notion of poetic language as an august enterprise, so long as he could apply it to the intimacies of the countryside and native feelings. Similarly, "The Solitary Reaper" evidently deploys the stock language of eighteenth-century travel writing without irony, because it was the experience of hearing a beautiful woman sing as she reaped a Scottish field that mattered most to Wordsworth. If conventional language could replicate that experience, he would retain the language. We have taken Wordsworth at his word and too often ignored his practice, although both Coleridge and T.S. Eliot warned us against it. His apparent formal innovations served largely as excuses for the further cultivation of conventions of subject matter. The former never served as a panacea for the failure of the latter, but rather they formed a virtuous circle, where changed diction made possible the representation of new subjects, and new subjects occasioned the development of new linguistic and prosodic practices.

Pound was among the first poets to put his trust in formal experimentation as a substitute for lively content. In the years before World War I, he saw that the Wordsworthian conventions had shriveled into Georgian pastoral lyricism; they had become so desiccated, in fact, that poetry could then worthily take for subject a much more contracted range of matter than it could before Wordsworth's day. Students and the poorly read seem to assume Dryden and Pope could write nothing but the sententious or the satirical. Indeed, their range was immense and their work is appalling—if for anything—for its narrow rationalism rather than for any narrow neo-Classical matter and manner. Can any intelligent person read *The Rape of the Lock* and contend that any poet in our day could spin such a well-wrought tale? Similarly, Dryden's *Religio Laici* exemplifies a mastery of discursive verse sorely wanted in our age; problems in the poem arise only when one tries to resolve the contradictions in his epistemology, ecclesiology, and soteriology—none of which need detain us here. Their strength, following their interest, was not in the lyric mode, though lines such as the following suggest lyric genius was not entirely lost in their long and elegant age:

Thou treacherous, base deserter of my flame,
False to my passion, fatal to my fame,
Through what mistaken magic dost thou prove
So true to lewdness, so untrue to love?

Wordsworth did well to recuperate the interior monologue (which Pope's *Heloise* might otherwise have ruined beyond repair) and the intensity of the meditative lyric, in the wake of the Augustans, melding the two in the process into the convention of the narrative-lyric. But Wordsworth's successors, we know, clamped onto his conventions of the poem as expression of pastoral landscape and sincere, often warmly affirmative, emotion—and they ran it into the ground.

When young Pound came to poetry, he believed fully in the emotional power of the art. He believed in it at least as strongly as did Wordsworth. He could not immediately see any way to escape the general round of fit subjects for poetry that the late romantics had canonized, because only those subjects seemed to guarantee to the poetic the emotive power he craved. His response was to fasten on a still narrower range of emotions—those pertaining to "world weariness" and an exasperated elitism—and then to "renew" poetry by propagating a new form of free verse distinct from any other seen before. With some help from T.E. Hulme, in other words, Pound invented a poetry that broke with formal conventions *in response to* dissatisfaction with prevailing conventions of subject-matter.

I see this as a grave error. Not because I despise free verse, though I do not like it much. Rather, to correct a poet's failing of subject with a panacea of form reminds one more of the compensatory role alcohol plays for unhappy, failed men, than of a serious innovation in the history of poetry. Instead of confronting and solving a problem, Pound pickled it. Only the pungency of the brine increases as we move from his *Personae*, those early works where he fiddled with free verse in otherwise quite conventional late-Victorian lyrics and monologues, to *The Cantos*, where he remade the subject matter of poetry and ostensibly made the poet the historian of the modern age, as Homer had been for his, simply through committing himself to a poetic form of the chopping knife. Early Pound simply toys with the form of familiar lyric conventions; later Pound largely substitutes form for subject matter.

Pound would understandably reject the "cream puff" early work, in favor of this new Homeric epic style that promised to extend the range of poetry as Wordsworth had. And yet, *The Cantos* does not quite return freedom and variety to the subject matter of poetry—certainly not to the extent Pound had hoped—precisely because that gain seems a footnote in comparison with his offering of formal innovation as an answer to what was fundamentally a problem of content. The fragmentary mode of composition there deployed allows for many kinds of *disjecta membra* to be represented on the page—whether it be late-medieval correspondence, Chinese characters, or moments from early American or contemporary European history. But the form itself is so imposing that it folds the different matter together into a kind of gravy: what was, before the poem was written, an impressive indeed commanding range of materials, has all been subjected to too much heat until all that is left is a burned crisp, a rhythmic monotony. The fragments of which it is composed are not identical but they are certainly fungible; in large doses, the poem seems like an excited redundancy. The real subject of the poem, then, might merely be that persistent lyric "I" recording the experience of a broken history and his failed attempt to put its fragments into order:

Tho' my errors and wrecks lie about me.
And I am not a demigod,
I cannot make it cohere. (*Canto* CXVI)

Pity those who ever mistook Pound for Plato's demiurge. The demiurge made the *cosmos*, that is, the world-order, a content brought into being with its form. Pound, in contrast, tried to correct subject-matter deficiencies with formal innovation, as if you

61

could change the world just by rearranging the parts. In his case, the form itself so filtered the matter that he did not really make poetry much more capacious or varied than it had been before the death of Swinburne. Pound did not have the artistic ability to write a poetry that embraced such a wide range of materials without rendering it a pile of interchangeable lyric fragments. He could have failed in a number of other ways, less interesting ways, because any poet who corrects subject-matter insufficiencies with mere formal tricks will fall into some kind of error or another.

This leads us back to the limitation I see in Matthias's and Archambeau's work—even as I profess to include them as among the better poets writing in our day. I am frequently astounded with the range of materials Matthias draws on, but I have noticed that in his longer poems he is overly concerned with breaking them into *Canto*-like units, whereas in his best poems he has allowed the subject-matter to predominate, or rather, to determine the form. See for example the breathy nostalgic lines of "Swell" or the paternal incantatory magic of his "Variations on the Song of Songs," both of which appear in a recent chapbook and the first of which is in his *New Selected Poems* (2004). I might also mention his "A Note on Barber's *Adagio*", which like many of his shorter poems is deliberately prosaic in every formal respect, allowing the power of its material to draw forth in a long, sustained note.

Thus, Matthias's work is certainly nowhere so limited by formal procedure as Pound's *Cantos*, having some of the more controlled capaciousness of the welsh poet David Jones. But, I would suggest that where he transcends Pound's limitations he also confirms them as limitations, that is, deficiencies. Beyond this, I must also protest the immanence of his historical vision, which I discussed above. His poetry is impersonal because it remains in the realm of historical things and events with remarkable, austere consistency. For the typical "postmodern" theorist, this would seem a virtue, insofar as it takes for granted the "prison house of language" and the "nightmare of history" in which we are all trapped. But, for one aware that a fragment always signifies the reality of a whole, that the relative always implies the absolute, that contingent forms, whether those of poetry or history, always participate in, and yearn for, a wholeness beyond themselves, the abandonment of the "modernist" search for (an unachieved) totality so evident in Pound's poetry, strikes me as an impoverishment in Matthias's. Pound's error, a common one since Hegel, was the attempt to make history do the work of theology and metaphysics. Matthias's is to recognize only that Pound errs in the ambition without abandoning the practice. The constant moving back and forth along a historical timeline in which one is trapped, but in which one can play no meaningful part, proves a vertiginous experience for this particular admirer of Matthias's work.

Let us return to the more general point that lingers behind my historical digression. Failures in the conventions of poetic content cannot be fully compensated by ingenuity with form. Nor for that matter can formal inadequacies be *fully* healed by turning to interesting subjects. Between the two, however, the latter is more excusable. Everyone at one time or another has said a poem, a novel, a film, or a painting had an interesting subject that merited one's attention, even if its formal execution were egregious. Contrary to Pound's claim in one early essay, it is not inappropriate that women meandering through an art gallery should happen upon a portrait and naively ponder, "I wonder what this person should have been like to know?" A portrait should always make one wonder just that; but if it is a good portrait, it should shock us into asking all kinds of other questions as well, including, "How does such a thing of beauty exist here before me?" "How does this picture manifest reality—including realities that cannot be *seen* though they can in some sense be painted?" At that moment, the "transparency" of the portrait that leads us to its subject fuses with the "opacity," that is to say, the form of the work as a work, and one has worthily entered into the union of form and content that we call the aesthetic.

The aesthetic is a destination, and one frequently follows many ostensibly trivial paths on the way to it. Modernists erred in identifying form and content too readily—prematurely, as it were, as if they were not just one in being but in concept. The contemporary avant-garde to which Archambeau refers has not only identified the two, but taken one as a substitute for the other, in the process strewing impassable rubble on the otherwise inviting paths to the aesthetic.

5/ THE NEW WORLD OF NEW FORMALISM

Marble staircases climb the hills where derelict estates
glimmer in the river-brightened dusk . . .
And some are merely left to rot where now
broken stone lions guard a roofless colonnade . . .
—Dana Gioia

The sudden—though long foreshadowed—demise of the important literary journal *Edge City Review*, in 2006, first afforded me occasion to consider the ways in which some contemporary poets have sought to escape the practice of prescribing formal experimentation as a treatment for a dearth of content. Consciousness that other poets' frequent obsession with experimental form was a panacea for deeper problems with the scope and interest of contemporary poetic subject matter inspired what has become known as the new formalist movement in poetry. *Edge City's* former editor, Terry Ponick, retails a curious history of the movement in his magazine's signing off:

The poetry constituency we once mainly served, in spite of our efforts to publish a literary publication embracing many of the written arts, has been slowly imploding. This constituency generally came to be known as the "New Formalist" poets. Early pioneers in reviving meaning in poetry as well as traditional form, included Fred Turner, Fred Feirstein, and Dick Allen. To oversimplify somewhat, these poets preferred to dub their movement "Expansive Poetry," preferring to emphasize the return of their poetry to real meaning while not focusing it strictly on their

65

secondary concern of promoting a return to the poetic traditions of meter and rhyme.

As he would have it, beginning in the early 1980s, "expansive" poets sought to enlarge the audience for poetry by recovering once flourishing but largely disused kinds of poems: satire, light verse, and epigram, for instance, but more importantly, narrative, whether in the guise of the modern narrative epic or the relatively new form of the verse novel (the first verse novel, to my knowledge, was Alexander Pushkin's *Eugene Onegin*). By restoring variety to the art form, these poets hoped to recover also the prominence in high and popular culture that poetry had once commanded. They wanted to show that the short, often fragmentary lyric-narrative of autobiographical experience was neither the only form poetry could take nor even the most important form within the hierarchy of poetic modes crowned by the epic and descending to light verse. But, as he tells it, the "new formalist" movement existed in close but ill-defined relation to the "expansive" movement, setting off myriad internecine discussions and arguments, of which Ponick's farewell was but a belated instance. The suggestion is that something multifaceted dwindled to something simple; a recovering of the full poetic tradition became a recovery of modern English verse elements only.

Ponick's story does not quite correspond to what happened in the 1980s. True, Turner and others were early practitioners of a revived narrative poetry, and Turner's important career comprehends a massive recovery of the riches of western and eastern cultural, biological, anthropological, religious, and poetic traditions; his has been a truly polymathic, "expansive" adventure that deserves more extensive consideration than I can provide here. But there never was a publically known "expansive" movement that was somehow diminished or coopted by the New Formalism. Turner argued for a scientific basis for metrical verse in his influential article, "The Neural Lyre," in 1983, but the term "new formalism" was probably in circulation by then and became an object of controversy as soon as 1985, when Ariel Dawson used it to smear what she called the work of "The Yuppie Poet," in an essay of that name. Dawson was only the first, as we shall see, to identify the return of poetic form with the revival of political conservatism that had led to the election of Ronald Reagan. In contrast, the first mention I have found of "Expansive Poetry" comes in 1989, when Wade Newman took stock of Turner and other likeminded writers, whom Turner had published during his tenure as editor of the *Kenyon Review* from 1978-1983. In brief, there was a widespread revival of metrical, narrative, and other traditional genres of poetry in the 1980s—one much too wide to be attributed to any single movement or small club of poets. To account for it all in terms of the rivalry between two camps, one expansive, the other merely formal, would be misleading.

If Ponick's history is doubtful, the problem its narrative conveniently outlines is nonetheless real. The clamor for "expansive" and new formalist verse manifested itself most auspiciously as a call for the return of poetry as a truly omnivorous medium. As I said in the last chapter, Pound sought to expand the material that could find its way into poetry, much as had Wordsworth and others before him. Eliot wrote, late in life, that one of the goals of the modern movement had been to discover "a form of verse in which everything can be said that has to be said," while Winters spoke approvingly of the ambition for a "carry-all meter." The moderns wanted to get more of life into poetry, but, in the event, modern poetry has shown itself significantly less equipped to carry, or rather, to give form to, a wide range of experiences. It tends, rather, to melt them all down to that fool's golden nugget, the fragmentary narrative lyric.

The new formalists and those who followed them did their best to produce poetry that could take on—once more—a wide variety of subject matter, but rather than dissolve formal conventions into the formless possibilities of free verse "experimentation," it sought to recover the various conventional types of verse, with their specifically *modal* characteristics. The differences in kind of human experience are better preserved when the poet has not to pour them all into one capacious "carry-all" meter, but rather can choose among a wide variety of different forms with established associations, significances, and rules of decorum.

To repeat a point for which Dana Gioia argued in "Notes on the New Formalism," more than two decades ago, it is essential to recognize that poetry is a genus of which there are many species. Formal conventions, genres, and modes make such diversity possible in the first place. Thinking of form purely in experimental and expressive terms tends to undermine it. The poets who recovered meter and narrative in the 1980s clearly appreciated that the lyric holds, at best, the third rank in the great hierarchy of these species. Narrative and dramatic verse, historically, and even in the present estimation and inevitable prejudice of most literate persons, rank above it. And so, Frederick Turner's *The Return* (1981) helped return the epic to our tradition, while a poet like R.S. Gwynn revived satire and light verse, Paul Lake renovated the dramatic monologue, while Gioia's work highlighted the value of non-iambic meters to restore to poetry its role as performed song: not lyric in the Renaissance sonnet-tradition sense of a narrative of private meditation, but in the sense of John Dowland and Thomas Campion —words to be sung.

Contrary to Ponick's implication, it hardly seems that the expansive movement was the campaign that failed, dragging his magazine down with it. Brad Leithauser and Glyn Maxwell published successful verse novels just a few years ago that were of significantly greater ambition than Turner's early work. And Turner himself, in *The New World* (1985) and *Genesis* (1988), has attempted to reclaim the sublime scale and historical significance of the heroic epic—an attribute inevitably missing from his first "novella" foray into the genre. Consider that *The Return*, though about the aftermath of the War in Vietnam, focuses on a sense of personal loss. The more recent books are far less inward, after the fashion of both ancient epic and modern genre fiction. Turner has in fact rammed epic narrative into science fiction, a practice that may be inevitable if the traditional martial and heroic components of the epic are to be present and if the novelistic obsessions with interiority and character development are not.

David Mason's *Ludlow* (2006) exhibits still another successful reclamation of story-telling for verse, taking on as it does a historical moment and conflict of great power, while refusing to surrender the attention to richness of character one expects of non-cinematic and non-"genre" narratives. Mason paints a picture of early-twentieth century Colorado, while telling the story of Louis Tikas and Luisa Mole during an infamous chapter in American labor history, when coal miners struck and, after a prolonged stalemate, were brutally assaulted by the Colorado National Guard. At least two dozen people were killed in the massacre.

The verse novel, for good and for ill, unfolds as if Mason were a postmodern Steinbeck. His evident natural sympathy with the strikers and hostility to John D. Rockefeller, Jr., and the management class are subtly brought into question as the story unfolds and are interpolated by scenes of the author himself considering how he came to imagine his subject. He describes himself as among "the ungrounded ones," that is, among those suspicious of the foundations of their beliefs and sympathies—but who know they maintain them in some qualified way nevertheless.

This complex relation of author to his subject matter bears fruit in the frequent formal movements of the poem, where meter serves sometimes an expressive function, but in the context of what the late John Hollander has called a "metrical frame," or contract function, like that of the disciplined blank verse of Milton's *Paradise Lost*. Written mostly in eight-line stanzas of iambic pentameter (that's the "frame"), Mason sometimes slant-rhymes entire stanzas to give them a subtle didactic and conclusive quality (that's the "expressive"). His pentameter line is loose, but never more so than at moments of dramatic tension, where repeated headless lines serve to telegraph details of the action. This is most impressively displayed at a key moment, when the mining company's hired guards erect a machine gun in range of the striking miners' tent camp, and terrorize the families living there with random volleys of shot (metrically interesting syllables are in bold):

> **Bull**ets cut the tent. Across the field
> the TAK-TAK-TAK was hardly noise enough
> for all the havoc in the camp, **bull**ets
> **hit**ting cookstoves, knocking stovepipes loose,
> **toss**ing coffee pots and china urns

in pieces everywhere. And then the screams
were coming too from other men in tents
not far away. And then the shooting stopped.

A final-foot trochee and three headless lines convey
the pounding pulse of fear and confusion, as the
"TAK-TAK-TAK" wreaks havoc in the camp.
Elsewhere, the shifts are more dramatic. Ballad stanza
takes over briefly as Christmas carols are sung and
answered by the (thematically and generically out of
place) caroled religious skepticism of the poet. As the
story moves toward conclusion, one of three author-
interludes breaks free of verse altogether, the prose
lines reminding us we are outside the plot of the poem
but inside the poem as subjective creation. Most
interesting of all, in the central chapter depicting the
battle and massacre, Mason expands from pentameter
to hexameter in imitation of classical epic. The
resonance with Virgil's style is especially powerful, and
becomes most obvious in Mason's depiction of the
camp as it is destroyed by machine gun fire and
conflagration:

Canvas burns and wooden platforms burn, and
    Bibles
burn, and furniture, beds and dressers burn, and
    clothes
and picture postcards burn, and gnarled walking
    sticks burn,
hats burn, old protest signs, sheet music, violins,
guitars burn, boots burn, and money burns,
    though troopers
liberated money where they found it, taking
chairs and glass lamps, anything that looked worth
    keeping

for themselves, and Louis saw this looting and kept on walking.

Mason's handling of the episode is at times inexpert. One senses that *Ludlow* has benefited from the earlier attempts to revive story-telling in verse, but that it remains a first effort to recover the genre of American social realism for poetry. The most accomplished passages are those of lyric description rather than of dramatic action. And yet, the book as a whole is a serious achievement and alone suffices to prove that that movement that never was, expansive poetry, has succeeded marvelously and, under whatever name, is with us still.

The edge in *Edge City's* retired editor's tone is in one respect warranted, however. In the arts, coherence and consciousness of being part of a "movement" tends to calcify rather than fructify. Robert McPhillips' delightful *The New Formalism: A Critical Introduction*, after the fashion of contemporary academic argument, attempts to differentiate the subjects of his study along lines that will be of immediate and obvious interest, but which, in the process, truncates the history it retells. He follows an early Gioia essay, "The Poet in an Age of Prose," in arguing that, if free verse narrative lyrics have become the norm in our day, indeed the "hegemonic" convention, the new formalism transgresses current poetic ideology and practice by reviving rhyme and meter, but doing so in a popular, democratic way rather than by a mere repetition of the "elitist" irony of the post-War academic formalism represented best by Richard Wilbur and Anthony Hecht.

As one can imagine based upon the description of the academy I provided in the first chapter, nothing gets the atrophied veins of the English Department flowing like chatter about "transgression"—especially when it can be convincingly deployed with the word "democratic." But to have to be "transgressive" in this way, while it may ward off some slurs from hostile critics, imposes an extra-aesthetic limit on a movement that was aiming to recover breadth and depth.

The same might be said of David Caplan's fine study of formal verse, *Questions of Possibility: Contemporary Poetry and Poetic Form* (2005). As I contended years ago, Caplan is all too aware that the crossroads where homosexuality and sonnets meet is just the place for a young professor to play his fiddle for a large right-thinking audience: identity politics rushes in to justify the apparently otherwise unjustifiable acts of writing and reading poetry. Perhaps Ponick finds the focus in such critical writing on rhyme and meter, especially when it can be "ironized" for some political bent, to the exclusion of narrative, an unfortunate reduction. Perhaps he finds it a scandal and a disappointment that one should feel the need to justify poetry that deserves to be read on its own terms by couching it in the jargon of an utterly politicized imagination.

I should point out, however, that neither McPhillips nor Caplan has written a merely "scandalous" or intellectually dishonest study. To the contrary, McPhillips' book is concerned chiefly with mentioning and characterizing the work of as many contemporary metrical poets as possible, while also suggesting the broad themes that guide their work and the context in which it first appeared. Again echoing Gioia, he shows us that, in an age where free verse is the norm, it would be naïve to characterize the absence of meter as a rebellious artistic strategy; to the contrary, a sonnet or stream of heroic couplets should appear much more "subversive." Caplan's study, building upon this observation more pointedly, demonstrates that within

73

even the narrow, monomaniacal political orthodoxies of the contemporary academic milieu, formal poetry is still important. Their books are supremely readable in comparison with the vast majority of contemporary academic criticism and are no less sophisticated for that (although they deliberately forego the appearance of sophistication).

I would, however, offer a reservation—one after which Ponick also seems to be angling. New formalist poets may have been aware of the decimated poetic scene on which they tried to improve, but in emphasizing the recovery of poetic genres in addition to the resuscitation of formal prosody, their work seemed benignly and irenically to restore to contemporary poetry the variety and power it should always have possessed. And yet, the new formalism, whether in its earliest practitioners' critical prose, or the later academic arguments of McPhillips, seems still to rely at times on the "shock" formal verse provides in an age of bland, prosaic free verse lyrics—and this reliance is bound to limit the kinds of achievement contemporary formal verse might make its own. As Kevin Walzer's path-breaking *The Ghost of a Tradition: Expansive Poetry and Postmodernism* (1998) disturbingly suggests, it might be impossible for such work to break free from its "dialectical" entrapment as a sort of heresy always griping against the louche orthodoxies and loose prosodies of Charles Wright, Louise Glück, John Ashbery, and Jorie Graham. Contemporary readers may well find it incomprehensible in any other terms.

It is thus to be feared that, because the free verse orthodoxy is so widespread (its domain extends almost as wide as does the narrow terrain that is contemporary poetry), even if they wanted to, metrical poets could not indulge in simply getting buzzed on the sweet liquor of poetry, because they are already punch drunk from the barbarous ham-hands of free verse. Such being the case, the formal poet seems almost compelled to posture, to keep the gloves up, as it were, lest someone accuse him of "pretending modernism never happened." "We know it happened. We are past it. A return to meter is a post-modern act, untethered from those modern prejudices about history having an inevitable and irresistible power over artistic and other choices." And so, the significance of the formal poet's work remains tied to the free verse totalitarianism against which it has rebelled. When, Ponick seems to plead, can a poem just be read as a poem?

For many poets who fall under the category of expansive or new formalist, the purpose of the return to form was—*ancillary* to the rejuvenation of various subject matters and poetic genres—to free poetry at last from that suicidal dialectic between subject dearth and formal experimentation, to free it indeed from an obsession with novelty at the expense of refined achievement. Expansive poetry was not supposed to be a permanent reaction, but, as I said, a benign recovery of good things that had been lost. Ponick thus warns us that "new formalism" may provide a hospitable label for a supposed revolution that in fact results merely in blank verse renditions of Carl Dennis or W.S. Merwin, or anapestic cross-rhymed quatrains relating the mundane sexual voyeurism that, for the time being, oozes through the loose lines of Sharon Olds.

One concedes that just this has occurred. Kim Addonizio's poetry, for instance, relies on a kind of "shock" to the sensibility that has become the most typical convention of the conventional verse of Olds and other belated, reader-inuring "confessionalists." Most confessional poets, like the realist fiction writers of the early twentieth century, offer in their work that mild *frisson* contemporary persons have come to identify as the controversial power of "progressive"-minded art. When we read details of some sexually abusive midget uncle on whose life a poet's eyes have lingered for a free verse strophe or six, we are intended to experience both indignation, uncomfortable arousal, and finally a warm sense of self-congratulation that we can stomach the "great art" of a tortured modern poetess. Addonizio complicates this slightly by throwing in the bonus shocks of, first, frequently writing in form, and, second, frequently adding in metrical substitutions that "subvert" that form. My complaint here is not that Addonizio's poetry is bad; it often is much more interesting than that of other confessional poets, and even simply good. Rather, this complacent rehashing of the kind of poetic "shock" tactics that have become so familiar and unshocking over the last few decades is surely far less significant, artistically and historically, than were the bold ambitions of expansive verse. Most confessional poetry had to "shock" by subject matter because it had lost the formal interest and integrity provided by meter; so, the recovery of meter should conversely free poets to move beyond such cheap and provisional conventions. If it has not, if the ambitions to re-expand poetry have been in some ways foiled, then Ponick is right to mourn.

Properly conceived, the new formalism offers freedom: the freedom of poems to be poems again. It does not necessarily constitute an apolitical or genteel turn in our literature, but it does seek to relativize and unshackle us from the aesthetics of shock and the hermeneutics of postmodern ideology critique. Rather than encouraging critics to group its poets under yet another ephemeral manifesto, or categorical grievance, and thereby rev the engines of the cultural hyper-capitalism that masquerades as radical identity politics, expansive poets would seem to have insisted that the notions of "experiment" and "revolution" have no proper place in the practice of an art. We must free ourselves from the traumatized and trembling historical consciousness that leads poets to produce poems so that they are "contemporary," "current," "avant-garde," or (Lord, have mercy) "post-avant," rather than simply good and worth being read today, tomorrow, or—the greatest test of all—yesterday.

Dana Gioia's second and third collections of poems exemplify this with force; and, his resistance to both the "expansive" and "new formalist" labels should admonish us to care less about claiming a historical narrative and more about what good work poets in our day actually do. He moves from free to formal verse (though his free verse is always metrical in the way Eliot's was) and from elegy, to satire, to ballad and song, to extended narrative, dramatic monologue, or brief lyric, without making any great fuss about these formal and generic gestures as gestures. *The Gods of Winter* (1991) displays this combination of formal variety with metrical virtuosity, and in total constitutes a sustained elegy for the loss of his infant son, Michael. "Planting a Sequioia," the best known poem from the book (and rightly so), is written in stanzas of five, long, slow-moving accentual lines, while "Veterans' Cemetery" is written in elegiac quatrains:

> The afternoon's a single thread of light
> Sewn through the tatters of a leafless willow,
> As one by one the branches fade from sight,
> And time curls up like paper turning yellow.

Anchoring the book are two stories in blank verse. "Counting the Children" is a restrained narrative detailing an accountant father's fear for and love of his daughter that echoes in subtle ways the anxious philosophy of death and immortality found in Plato's *Phaedo*. The father, Mr. Choi, observes near the end of the poem,

> We long for immortality, a soul
> To rise up flaming from the body's dust.
> I know that it exists. I felt it there,
>
> Perfect and eternal in the way
> That only numbers are, intangible but real,
> Infinitely divisible yet whole.

"The Homecoming" is less haunting but more striking in invention. An escaped murderer seeks the home of his foster mother, and this fateful encounter occasions an interior confession to her, recounting his childhood and sense of being destined for damnation. Early in the poem, the narrator recalls hearing rumors of a boy who had fallen down a boarded-up well: "One night I started whispering down the well. / What was it like, I asked him, to be dead?" By the end, he has shared a last meal with his mother and, in a moment of elation, kills her. The final lines suggest how inescapable and possessing the desire for what we have lost can be; the poem as a whole offers such an ingenious imaginative projection of what Gioia's grief for his son must have felt like that it ranks among his best poems, even if it is less accomplished in voice or imagery than most of his lyrics.

His *Interrogations at Noon* (2001) achieves a similar coherence-in-difference of several modes of poetry, though they are less insistently fused by a single emotion. As with his previous volumes, *Interrogations* shows Gioia's appreciation that the lyric is, and probably will remain for some time, the dominant poetic mode in our culture, but that lyricism is most effective when complemented by songs and ballads, and when given a context of dramatic occasion with narrative verse. Further, the most polished lyrics in the collection show Gioia perfecting the more public, less autobiographical, voice that was present even in his first book, *Daily Horoscope* (1986), and which predominates in his most recent, *Pity the Beautiful* (2012). We see this in the opening poem, "Words," whose unrhymed hexameters begin,

> The world does not need words. It articulates itself
> in sunlight, leaves, and shadows. The stones on the path
> are no less real for lying uncatalogued and uncounted.
> The fluent leaves speak only the dialect of pure being.
> The kiss is still fully itself though no words were spoken.

The noon of the book's title does not designate the present historical moment of artistic fashions or "advances," but those moments of scrutiny under which the soul is cast in bare light ("Just before noon I often hear a voice, . . . It is the better man I might have been"). As if to underscore this, the book contains a substantial number of songs and translations, including pieces from Gioia's libretto, *Nosferatu*, and Juno's anguished opening speech, from his translation of Seneca's *Hercules Furens*. The book thus serves as an exercise—in the best sense—in variation and integrity. It is a library of forms that alternately dramatizes the soul in judgment or summons our own to the tribunal of the dead.

Much the same could be said for *Pity the Beautiful*, though, there, after four collections, it becomes clear that, for all Gioia's variety of form and genre, his poetic voice—the voice of the man one hears saying the poems in one's head—is less varied than the forms in which it speaks. The wonderful spiritual ghost story, "Haunted," for instance, has a blank verse narrator who sounds a little too close to that of "Homecoming." It may be his best narrative, however, in its fluent blend of conventions of eighties realism (Bret Easton Ellis), Jamesian ghost story, and the salted conversion stories of Graham Greene. It is simply a great story and serves as a strong backbone for the entire volume.

Many poets complain, as I have, about the reductive pedantic labeling of academic fads, where a poet's usefulness as a counter in the game of identity politics is more likely to get that poet into an anthology or taught in a classroom than any honest quality in the work itself. Steele has remarked, for instance, that "the absence of agreed upon standards of versification" leads poetry to be "judged exclusively with respect to its intentions or subject matter," i.e. "political views or ethnic backgrounds or sexual preferences." His late friend, Thom Gunn, one of the best craftsmen of the last half-century, received extensive attention in the academy not because of his versatility as an artist, but on account of his documenting of his guilty bystander status during the AIDS crisis, in *The Man with Night Sweats* (1992). But what often goes unsaid is that an obsession with being "contemporary" leads to most poems being of interest only when such topical, often extrinsic, matters are taken into account. The convention of novelty and experiment predominates in both the composition and publishing of poems. That much more humble and fruitful convention, that of craft and tradition, which insists that the best poetry is produced when it merely extends, elaborates, deepens, and renovates what has come before, is deprecated out of hand.

Obsessed with the "now," most poets write with a "technique" that cuts them off from all the poetry of the past and, indeed, from any meaningful understanding of poetry as an art form with traditions, conventions, and laws proper to itself. And so, when expansive verse, with its almost avuncular open mindedness—indeed Odyssean myriad mindedness— to poetic genres aplenty, is eclipsed by the "new formalism" (as Ponick and McPhillips, with opposite judgments, understand it), it may sound as if a moment of great promise has gone into the dark. A generous opening has withered to a narrow coterie.

But I have already shown that this reading of things is doubtful, and I endorse only Ponick's concern, not his history or his despair. When one surveys the masses of poems published each year, one ought to conclude that, if we can have nothing else, then we ought at least to have the kind of narrative lyrics produced by many exemplars of the new formalism. One hears all the time about the dullness of the new formalism; *Poetry*'s 2005 humor issue jabbed it smartly, and others whine about it ignorantly. In truth, the vast bulk of published poetry, these days, inures with dullness. It is so coarsely written, is so transparent as all "prose," lineated or otherwise, supposedly is, that one turns the page from poem to poem as one does the pages of a newspaper circular. Conversely, when a contemporary poem is not transparently dull, it is opaquely so, concealing its absence of interest along with its absence of meaning. This two-headed monotony, to distill it all, is free verse that has neither the interest of compelling content nor that of formal prowess. Since all things are good to the extent that they are (that is, that they *have being*), we can fairly assert that most published poetry clings very tenuously to the coattail of existence. Most new formalist poems I encounter, on the other hand, reassure one that they really are things, because their craft, their form, at the very least gives them an integrity sufficient to keep them in being as wholes not reducible to their (formal, experimental, political, etc.) parts.

Let us turn from Ponick's assessment of the new formalism to one more hostile and embedded in the commonplaces of contemporary academic criticism. The year after Gioia published "Can Poetry Matter?", the most influential essay to come out of the new formalism, Thomas B. Byers took up from the turf the already dusty Ariel Dawson gauntlet and complained about the tedium and conservatism of this movement. In "The Closing of the American Line: Expansive Poetry and Ideology" (1992), Byers insisted that Gioia's award-winning poem "Cruising with the Beach Boys" was not remarkably distinguished from the free verse narrative lyrics that typically populate literary journals. The "major difference I can perceive," Byers opines, "between this and hundreds of skillful but generic— and totally self-involved—workshop lyrics is Gioia's use of meter. But it is unclear why this represents any sort of real gain." Byers makes many such summary judgments in the essay, and they require a tripartite response. For, his essay testifies to the obtuseness of his own reading of this and other poems, to his deafness to the *intrinsic* value of meter and rhyme, and finally to the way in which these things can be generative of formal qualities in a poem beyond themselves.

The fiercest assertions in Byers' attack target Frederick Turner's *The New World*, which he portrays as an obscene Reaganite, neo-conservative, science fiction fantasy. Turner probably would not reject much of that charge, actually; after all, when one traces down whence Byers gleans his information about and interpretation of the epic poem, one quickly sees he has merely summarized the introduction that Turner himself provided. It hardly constitutes a critical insight to paraphrase an author's own words and then shout, "Ah-ha!" One suspects that Byers has not actually read the poem; he never even considers how the genre conventions of epic and of science fiction may transform or complicate Turner's introduction. But that is just the problem—or the point. The truth that the modernists discovered but misinterpreted is that form constitutes meaning, and formally rich works, such as those with the added coherence of meter, may have their meaning woven with complexity in the process of being crafted. Certainly most poems transcend the simple messaging painted by Byers' broad strokes. One would hope that, in an essay contemplating the value of the formal aspects of the new formalism, the scholar would avoid the appearance of a lazy, ideologically polarized plot summary and turn to the poem itself.

He would have found the effort rewarding. Turner has spent several decades engaged on a consciously syncretistic quest to draw the findings of neuroscience, physics, anthropology, and eastern and western religions into a coherent vision of culture and the world as they shape and are shaped by human nature. As Turner argues in *A Culture of Hope* (1995), this quest is neither liberal nor conservative, but one that embraces the best insights of both. He views liberalism and capitalism as indicative of human nature's dynamic, iconoclastic but also inventive, culture-making character, while he believes with conservatives

83

that the cultural productions that most befit human nature will always be classical in character, though a classicism renovated by human choices in every age. The argument for this position was first set forth in the aptly titled *Natural Classicism* (1986), but even earlier it gave life to his epic.

The New World offers an early dramatization of this synthesizing vision, and is at once dystopian and utopian. The quest to exploit natural resources and develop advanced technology has led to the fragmentation of nation states into hostile, tribal factions, but it has also led some of those factions to attain a high level of civilization. As in most science fiction, the primitive and the technically complex blend together in ways often imaginatively amusing and usually challenging in interpretation. The story's heroine, Ruth McCloud, comes to view law as the "frozen, heroic frescoes / of the fought-out wars of desire" that are human culture. Laws permitting "abortion on demand" and euthanasia "constituted a redefinition of what / it is to be human," so that,

> The soul was legally real, but synthetic, composed
> by its culture and in turn composing the culture
>   about it.

To read Byers, one might take such lines for one more shot in the culture wars of the Reagan era in which they were written, but in the poem, their meaning is ambiguous. The legal system, on my reading of the poem, is in some ways a wreck that has led to the denigration of human nature, the decline of the nation state, and the evacuation of civil society. Near the end, for instance, we hear of social collapse presaged in these terms:

. . . the people withdraw to themselves,
And lose that humane and civic nobility which
  stamps
The Free person with higher concerns than his
  own.

Entire segments of the American population, dubbed
Riots, now live as "liberated" crazed addicts of drugs
and violence, others lose themselves in a
fundamentalist Christian Jihad. And yet, it seems that
these developments allow Turner to dramatize a theme
that has come to be a focus of much of his work: the
way in which nature, the material world, shapes and is
shaped by the cultural, made world. In the poem, he
expresses this intrinsically circular relationality as the
"great historical law of beauty" in accord with which
human beings "build the world in the human image."
He recovers the ancient conception of the *cosmos* in the
language of modern physics, where "no / part of the
universe, small though it be, is cut off / from
anywhere else, but is knowable everywhere." All things
hold together, but not in a preordained and static order
which human beings merely receive, but rather as they
come into fertile relation with one another in part
through human choice and action. Turner ably avoids
the nihilistic cultural relativism of the contemporary
left, which is founded on the suspicion that nothing is
true (except power and its use), in favor of a richer
theory of value that conceives of human agency as
participating in and shaping the beauty of the universe,
an open-ended but not ungrounded activity. His is,
again, a "syncretistic faith" that accepts "the beautiful
unbearable tragedy / that all faiths are true."
  The form of the poem puts into practice the ideas it
thematizes. On Turner's view, epic meter is properly
made of enjambed long lines of roughly five stresses.

The English iambic pentameter line is merely a "special case" of this broader cross-lingual phenomenon. Most of the poem is composed in a long, loose line that, contrary to Byer's fear that meter is "illiberal," could in no way be viewed as a "closing" of the American free verse line. Turner's practice is so pliant and variable that most readers would presume it was simply a fairly rhythmic free verse. Consider the lines quoted above, where a sense of order subtly shapes fluid speech. When his hero, James George Quincy, speaks, however, the verse tightens into a regular blank verse. In certain battle scenes, such as James' early match, in the shade of the ruins of the World Trade Center, with a mute, inbred, and obese giant, called the Slob, this comes to great effect. One is reminded of the battle scenes in Allen Mandelbaum's superb blank verse translation of *The Aeneid*, a vehicle well suited to the cinematic, sometimes "comic-book," movements of the story:

> I kicked the knife away. He groped at me;
> I lashed him with my fists. He blinked, and smiled.
> I hit him in the paunch, it was like dough.
> Rioters jabbered in a ring around us.
> Soon he would have me. What of his could hurt?
> I took his right hand in my own, and squeezed.

Turner would later deploy this idiomatic and cinematic blank verse in the twenty-five four-hundred-line scenes that make up *Genesis*.

I remain myself uncertain of Turner's total achievement here. It will be hard for most readers to embrace his deliberate mingling of arcane epic and futuristic fantasy, which is sometimes comic but often serious in intent. He continuously surprises our expectations, both by his willingness to exploit the clichés of genre literature and his paradoxical, because always two-sided, cultural politics. This may perplex even patient readers. Finally, the arc of the plot is so wide and its content sufficiently diffuse that it resembles more closely the form of the science fiction novel than the classical epic. But one can at least recognize his project in verse and prose is a grand one (truly epic, as his new study of the genre testifies), and requires extended and careful reckoning.

True to his intention, Turner opens up new possibilities, intellectual and imaginative, for a "postmodern creative era." They are so multifarious that they require patient thought and an open mind, just as they indicate Turner's simultaneous classicism and openness to the new as a writer. Those like Byers who sought to stick the new formalism in a political pigeon hole thus failed to deal honestly with the work and hastened to foreclose fruitful, new developments in American letters.

This same obtuseness and reactionary impatience presents itself in Byers' treatment of Gioia's poem. "Cruising with the Beach Boys" begins by describing a moment of self-estrangement, when encountering a long unheard, and never openly loved, pop song on the radio:

So strange to hear that song again tonight
Traveling on business in a rented car
Miles from anywhere I've been before.
And now a tune I haven't heard for years
Probably not since it last left the charts
Back in L.A. in 1969.
I can't believe I know the words by heart
And can't think of a girl to blame them on.

Every lovesick summer has its song,
And this one I pretended to despise,

But if I was alone when it came on,
I turned it up full-blast to sing along—
A primal scream in croaky baritone.
No wonder I spent so much time alone
Making the rounds in Dad's old Thunderbird.

As we noted above, in McPhillips's telling, the new formalists' poetry tends most obviously to distinguish itself not only from contemporary free verse but from the graceful, austere style, and high-cultural affinities of mid-century American and British "academic" formalism. Whereas the early poetry of John Hollander, William Bell, Richard Wilbur, Anthony Hecht, Edgar Bowers, Charles Gullans, and others, was frequently urbane and safely distanced from emotion and mass culture by a screen of irony, Gioia's tends to move less anxiously amid the forms of what Theodor W. Adorno called "the culture industry." As Gioia wrote in the "Age of Prose" essay, such poets

> departed from the example of the most influential formalists of the older generation (such as Merrill, Hecht, or Hollander), who saw themselves as guardians of the imperiled traditions of European high culture . . . Having found high culture in shambles, the New Formalists looked to popular culture for perspective. In film, rock music, science fiction, and other popular arts, they found the traditional forms and genres, which the academy had discredited for ideological reasons in high art, still being actively used.

The Beach Boys' music stands out as a quintessential —rather, cliché—example of mass culture; that is, of a cultural semiotic constructed from a compound of primitive sentimentality and ephemeral kitsch, from the immediately disposable and the nauseatingly regurgitated. Gioia's reference to "the charts," the usual economic measurement of the lifespan of pop music, and even his typography in "L.A. in 1969" suggest a fluency in the language and worldview that mass culture provides. The poet can speak of such trivia without an immediate air of condescension. Los Angeles is the home of the movie industry, the source of our consumption and celebrity culture, but it is also a city of immigrants who, like stray airs of pop music, have wandered into a common place. It is also the city of Gioia's birth to a mixed Mexican and Italian family. The unreality of the Beach Boys as a "production" of the culture industry and its reality as music heard and formative of one's mind coexist uncomfortably.

Gioia embraces this as one of the resources of language. Reference to Los Angles and 1969 particularize, but they also evoke: a city every potential reader of the poem will immediately recognize as bearing a certain freight of meaning about American mass culture, and a year so evocative as to be an emblem of an entire epoch in American history. That the Canadian singer Bryan Adams had released a single titled "The Summer of '69," just the year before Gioia's poem appeared in *Poetry*, suggests how evocative it is of a time of simultaneous upheaval, counter-culture, and nostalgia. The familiarity of such language on account of its emblematic power (to provoke specific associations in us) is, on the one hand, essential for poetry, which depends in part on commonplaces in order to communicate, and yet, on the other, it is a sign of language's corruption, of culture's reformulation into a tool of capital—the movie *industry*, the record *industry*, and, again, the culture *industry*.

89

The poet follows James Joyce in maintaining an ironic distance from that refitting of the commonplace to the market place, but it is the same distance of any reluctant singer of a bad song that refuses to come unstuck from memory. For all the sophistication of Adorno's critiques of mass culture, it is in some ways just a sharpening of the duller shame many of us feel when we know we should not like something because it is dumb, inauthentic, or sentimental—but we like it nevertheless. The younger version of the poem's speaker felt even more shame and more pleasure in the Beach Boys than does the older voice speaking to us in the poem, because bad taste has consequences for the young that it seldom does for the old.

The ambivalence between actual experience and manufactured experience, between evocative commonplace and cliché, intensifies in the line, "Dad's old Thunderbird." This may be historical truth, but has also the inevitability of the trite. The poem is formed of the same stock imagery on which The Beach Boys relied for their success and so bears witness to both our resistance to its ploys and its intractable power over us. The Ford Thunderbird could become a cliché, a representative car of a period, only because it actually attained a centrality to mid-century American youth culture that most other models of the time did not. To represent the time accurately, therefore, the poem has to let itself feel coopted by the overly-familiar, the too-easily-evocative. It enacts the embarrassment the speaker once felt and feels again.

Is, therefore, the poem just a Beach Boys song with faint literary pretension or ironic protection? It would seem not. Gioia may show his comfort with mass culture, but the frequently formal voice of his other lyrics, and his easeful allusions to and adaptations from the European canons of orchestral music and poetry, especially the German and the opera, suggest a more complicated perspective. Indeed, Gioia has found a way in his poetry to preserve the distinction between high, popular, and mass culture on which the modernists relied, without indulging in mere crankery or snobbery. One can approve high and low culture alike without collapsing them; one can deprecate aspects of each without surrendering one in favor of the other. The poem acknowledges this distinction and the consequences of it, when Gioia confesses that he had once "pretended to despise" the Beach Boys' song, even while part of his heart indulged it, in solitude.

In our age, it is still common enough for one to cultivate one's sensibility, to come to love the art forms of high culture. But, significantly, one has to confess that the ubiquitous forms of mass culture inform, and often enchant, that sensibility as well. If one's adulthood is formal poetry and opera, one's adolescence still reeks of pop music and the concomitant "freedom" of cruising alone down a coastal highway in a fast car. These generically opposed things tend not so much to fuse as to coexist, like shame and repentance, like humor and seriousness, and like mawkishness and clear vision, in the individual mind.

Gioia's own success in writing opera librettos may remind us that the opera itself is a consummate high cultural form heavily loaded with the adolescent melodramatics of mass culture. It is "strange" to hear the unnamed (does the title of such a consumer item matter?) song, because it comes as an alien sound, representing a way of seeing the world to which the poem's speaker had thought himself superior. But the song is strange as well, because it is eerily familiar, a lingering presence in the mind. The poem contemplates via reminiscence the widespread

91

experience of having a bit of junk culture lying within the fortified compound of one's cultivated personality. It may not keep to itself, but rather leave its grease on everything refined it touches. The later stanzas of the poem develop this guilty mingling of the serious and the kitsch, by suggesting the depth and curious beauty of it:

> Some nights I drove down to the beach to park
> And walk along the railings of the pier.
> The water down below was cold and dark,
> The waves monotonous against the shore.
> The darkness and the mist, the midnight sea,
> The flickering lights reflected from the city—
> A perfect setting for a boy like me,
> The Cecil B. DeMille of my self-pity.

It is a difficult fact that great art and the silliest youthful emotions both find their elemental source in —are different responses to—the encounter with the "cold and dark" of the natural, and the distant lights of the civilized, worlds, of which we are always a part and yet from which we may remain in some sense apart. The Beach Boys are at once alien and natural to the poem's speaker; the world as a whole is caught in a similar ambivalence. High and low, the world and the self, which are both too much with one another, simultaneously erupt in these lines. Gioia mocks the bathos of his teenage self, and yet the tableau he describes seems keenly felt and powerful. Cecil B. DeMille could just be another director within the gigantic Hollywood industry that crowns American mass culture, but he was also one of the first directors to make film into a great American art form. Early silent film cinematography exaggerated emotions to the point of caricature but thereby made film expressive;

we may wince at the gestures even as they still communicate. The rigid distinctions between high and mass culture, which have not quite broken down in the form of the poem, intermingle nonetheless. Gioia acknowledges them as all part of the compound that constitutes a life, writing in the final stanza,

> I thought by now I'd left those nights behind,
> Lost like the girls that I could never get,
> Gone with the years, junked with the old T-Bird.
> But one old song, a stretch of empty road,
> Can open up a door and let them fall
> Tumbling like boxes from a dusty shelf,
> Tightening my throat for no reason at all
> Bring on tears shed only for myself.

As the clichés fall one after another (I count seven in the first five lines), the poem admits that they are not just the adolescent forms that one naturally grows out of and leaves behind. Even our fully formed personalities are informed by them. Consequently, they retain a grip upon us—"Tightening my throat for no reason at all"—and command our attention.

Many occupants of the postmodern academy make their living decrying as "elitist" the very enterprise of distinguishing high from low or mass culture. Some of them, more justly, would note what I have: in our present civilization, mass culture's very ubiquity does not so much put in question this distinction as it does make it harder to sustain in one's everyday life. There is a marked ontological difference between art and trash, and we build different frames for them within our experience, but the *de jure* blurring, even the erasure, of that distinction is the normative experience of early-twenty-first century Americans. We do not always know when we are encountering one or the other and frequently draw the high within the low or promote the low to the high for any number of reasons. (Think, Van Gough paintings on coffee mugs, or the playing of a Bon Jovi power ballad at a wedding.) For many contemporary artists there is joy in this loss; for some few there is pathos. Gioia's poem explores not only how the teenager is "father to the man," but how American mass culture creeps through the cracks of even the most cultivated personality. Byers ignores all this, or perhaps refuses to see it, precisely because that would require subsequently establishing some standards—other than the political litmus test of Reaganite-versus-enlightened-leftist with which his article shows him comfortable—for the judgment of this poem and for poetry as an art form.

A second point: we have still to consider, what is the "gain" of meter? If one enjoys reading poetry, versification becomes its own reward—not separate in being from the meaning of the poem, but so central to the poem that it can become an independent matter of exploration. In the present instance, the "gain" (so unclear to Byers) is that Gioia's poem becomes interesting on account of its craft, even though its subject matter may initially appear tired. The placing of words into syntax, into phrases and sentences, establishes a coherence of sound, rhythm, and meaning. Composition in meter introduces a further refinement and order into language, as Sir Philip Sidney wrote in his classic *Defense of Poesy* (c. 1580), "piesing each syllable of each word by just proportion." Is this a gain? Truly so, continues Sidney, explaining,

> that cannot be praiseless which doth most polish
> that blessing of speech, which considers each word
> not only, as a man may say, by his forcible quality,
> but by his best measured quantity, carrying even in

themselves a harmony—without [i.e. unless] perchance number, measure, order, proportion be in our time grown odious.

To treat the structure of Gioia's poem as a matter of indifference is to ignore the poem as a poem. It is to ignore the way in which the chaos of modern mass culture and the alogical echoing of the memory is given meaningful order, iamb by iamb, line by line. This is a good in itself. But, and here is my third response to Byers' attack, like any good, it diffuses or goes beyond itself. A reasonable mind would appreciate such a gain and seek to see how the good of craft transcends itself to deepen the weave of the poem's meaning.

Byers' article suggests, however, that he is not interested in this kind of reason and that he has not read much of the new formalists he condemns; either refusing or ignoring the craft on which their poems are founded, he is unlikely to be drawn into serious scrutiny of their achievement. But, were he open to it, we would have to tell him, the gain of meter is meter, of rhyme is rhyme, and this is enough—though, as with every good, many other gains follow.

Largely because of Diane Wakoski's unfounded imbecilities two decades ago in "The New Conservatism in American Poetry" (*American Book Review* May/June 1986), the new formalism has been constantly harangued with being regressive, un-American, unpatriotic, etc., etc. While I am sure and pleased that, in a profound sense, new formalism is conservative, it certainly had nothing properly to do with any American political movement. And while I grow almost misty eyed to hear a modern poet concerned with the love of country, I suspect Wakoski's piety is at best opportunistic. She, and those like Byers who followed in her wake, relies on crude television caricatures of the Eisenhower era in order to conclude that the new formalism is conservative, therefore boring, therefore something we need not read for ourselves. She goes further. Radicalism, by which she means simply non-metrical poems, gets strangely confused and celebrated along with the patriotic vision of Walt Whitman. It is astonishing to hear leftists wield that supposed last refuge of villains, patriotism, as a weapon to attack rhymes and prop up an otherwise flaccid free verse—or rather, to undermine the reputation of a few poets who like the sound words make when their syllables resonate.

I think Wakoski asked too much of us for the sake of our country, really. Why must we give up even the most humble or trivial sonnet for most free verse, when odds are it will be a better work of art—will have better attained to "the perfection of the thing made"? Does this advance manifest destiny? Is it meter that stands in the way of the mystic chords of democracy? Do villanelles threaten the union, or sonnets restore us to Her Majesty's empire?

When a metered poem is dull, it perhaps upsets us because that achievement of craft forces us to slow down, to stop and think, and to recognize that we have encountered something rather than nothing—and an unsatisfactory something at that. But even the dull sonnet helps to keep alive a tradition; its small modulations of stress may make some new contribution to the art, however minute, which will bear greater fruit in the hands of posterity. Because its formal elements are made intelligible within the context of a tradition, what would by itself not please may do so there. In that same context, its limitations and failings may put us in conversation with works better than itself.

We dwell poetically in the world with far more wakefulness and light when we read Timothy Steele's plain style lyrics than when we get sandblasted with the dialectical diarrhea of David Antin, the Brooklyn street corner shell game of Charles Bernstein, or the bloodless, shuffled slips of type of Susan Howe. Steele himself has repeatedly noted that the distinction between "verse" and "poetry" generally leads to unproductive and fanciful speculations on the essence of "poetry," and petty dismissal of the achievement of form—of meter and rhyme. Nevertheless, if one must accept the distinction, then we would do better to insist that the art form first achieve "verse" before it aspire to "poetry."

As an intelligent reader, one ought to be capable of appreciating this modest craft with all its potential for ingenuity, even when its subject-matter does not immediately arrest the mind. Why, I ask, would Byers suggest that Gioia's lyric is not a great "gain" merely because it is written in suave, irregularly rhymed iambic pentameter? *I* am the richer for it. In a poem of J.V. Cunningham's, we get a typically dense, terse reflection on this question:

> How time reverses
> The proud of heart!
> I now make verses
> Who aimed at art.
>
> But I sleep well.
> Ambitious boys
> Whose big lines swell
> With spiritual noise,

Despise me not,
And be not queasy
To praise somewhat:
Verse is not easy.

But rage who will.
Time that procured me
Good sense and skill
Of madness cured me.

Consider these claims. Cunningham's poem suggests that his work has been dismissed as mere verse, as if it so far missed the higher good of art that it did not even seem to shoot for it. But the tumid lines of other poets, for all their bluster, have grown as naturally, not as the leaves on the trees, but as the fantasies of the lunatic as he mounts to the interior abyss. Verse, however, does not come naturally. It requires real work. It is a virtue, not a knack.

It is a romantic, a particularly American romantic, convention, to presume that hard work breeds common sense. If that is so, then Cunningham's poem makes a true claim and, incidentally *pace* Wakoski, is a more authentically American work of art than, say, Whitman's "loafing" yawps. The disciplined needle-work of writing verse has punctured Cunningham's spirit before it could malignantly swell, and has made him a more intelligent and sane poet for the deflation.

Ponick certainly touched on a truth in his concern for the vitality of any verse revival to occur only in the context of a larger recovery of poetry's far flung modes and subjects. But it has been my argument here that the new formalism has manifested just such a vitality in the works of Gioia, Turner, Steele and many others. It continues to do so: the main ambitions of the expansive movement are alive and well in the work of poets like Mason, Leithauser, and Maxwell. Even if we could not point to such figures and their successful revival of the narrative poem, we could still insist on the tremendous value of recovering formal verse itself. In my experience, most new formalist poetry offers at least as sophisticated and intriguing content as any free verse (a rather difficult claim to demonstrate, even as I hope to have done so at least partially in this chapter), and so intellectually rewards reading even on that level. Moreover, because it doubles or triples its interest with the presence of verse craft, new formalist writing tends to be both immediately compelling to the ear and mind in addition to whatever second order intellectual delights it affords. If the ambitions of the "expansive" movement had been lost, only to be replaced by versified versions of some of America's more popular free verse poets, then I would agree something has gone wrong with a promising project. If meter had returned only as an adjunct to party politics, we might also think it a raw rather than a new deal. However, even mediocre versified lyrics are *prima facie* better than free verse and they put us in contact with the deeper and enduring traditions of our civilization not the platforms of a party. But, enough of this. Cunningham was right: better all verse and no poetry, than an art of swollen heads and gouty feet.

6/ THE THERAPIST'S COUCH

> O early ripe! To thy abundant store
> What could advancing age have added more?
> It might (what nature never gives the young)
> Have taught the numbers of thy native tongue.
> —John Dryden

We stood in a living room furnished with antiques and, on small tables winging the brocaded sofa, fanned displays of recent poetry books too cute for reading. Behind us, a dining room table spread with hors d'oeuvres, and a sideboard crowded with bottles of wine and bottles of beer, peaking at odd angles over the rim of an ice bucket. It was an early autumn night in northern Indiana, after the slate of academic events had recommenced on campus but before the snow had come to ensure no one attended them. I had just come from the sparsely attended poetry reading whose featured author was the occasion of this reception. When the audience is composed of ambitious MFA students, and faculty members who have long known each other but seldom cross paths, such events invite harmless literary gossip and awkward, circuitous talk about gourmet cooking, and other elements of what has come to be called "private" life. One does not talk about art.

As it happened, the poet was exceptionally talented and, appropriately, a master of impersonal, cinematic blank verse narratives. Perhaps made too boisterous by this rarity of a rewarding and impressive poetry reading, I violated decorum by making my own "new formalist" convictions known. A colleague of mine, himself the author of three books with lines as long as the day, was in turn provoked to make the following two statements: "Whatever everybody says, it's not hard to write formal verse." And, "My students can only express themselves in free verse." My immediate impression was that he must be a lightweight, because only an easy drunk could harbor in the same skull two clichés that so obviously contradict one another. If formal, that is to say, metrical, verse is so easy, why could not his students "express" themselves in it? Is it not only the ones who cannot "express" themselves that find verse hard?

There is a fine convention found in much ancient and medieval verse of stating within a poem that it has been fashioned in "difficult" meter or numbers. These poets did not mean that this difficulty was the only one to be surmounted before one achieved great poetry, but they did want to insist upon the minimum of craft that ensured the identity of the work and the earned distinction of their role at once. Meter forms the poem, but measuring speech is a particular skill, a trade, a craft. The sense of verse as not only a craft, but as one entrusted to a guild with criteria of its own is most vividly depicted, for instance, in Daniel Corkery's history of Irish bardic verse in *The Hidden Ireland* (1924). As Corkery, and the tradition he recounts, suggests, the *file* (poet) is merely confirming that his prominent office in clan society is well deserved and stands alongside those of the warriors whose deeds he is charged with recounting. He has undertaken a training in composition in some ways as grueling as that of those warriors and understands his role as one of a bearer of precious knowledge. We hear identical claims for the poet (scop), in *Beowolf*, in lines Seamus Heaney renders as follows:

> Meanwhile a thane
> of the king's household, a carrier of tales,

a traditional singer deeply schooled
in the lore of the past, linked a new theme
to a strict metre. The man started
to recite with skill, rehearsing Beowulf's
triumphs and feats in well-fashioned lines,
entwining his words.

For those suspicious of either Corkery's historiography, the scop's claims to training and discipline, or the *file*'s shrewd efforts to corner the market on the arts of communal memory, the more mannerly praise of properly executed "numbers" in ancient and Augustan poetry should at least suggest just how rigorous and precise the poets, from the beginning of civilization on to that age of witty generalizations, could be about their versifying. If you doubt the almost supernatural significance of numbers, keep it to yourself, for the *file*'s measured curse was said to have a dangerous power.

These claims for the difficult craft of verse are valid, even if a *file*'s spells were not (I am agnostic on that point). It takes work to learn to hear meter as it does to write it, simply because everyday practices tend *not* to sort out sound from sense or to discern the identity of syllables relative to one another. Our minds are synthetic: they put individual realities together quickly, unconsciously, in order to form intelligible wholes; the practice of verse demands that we continue that integrating practice but do so with a simultaneous analytic consciousness of their audible particular elements.

Not easy, no. But, like grammar, once one gets the hang of it, it becomes as natural as the marksman's eye for his target or the hand of the blind seamstress at her stitching. Let me amend that last statement by removing the simile: versification *is* a branch of grammar. To ancient grammarians we owe our knowledge of classical prosody; it was part of the trivium. Dante referred to poetic composition as grammar *per se* in *de Vulgari Eloquentia*. Dr. Johnson treated prosody as the fourth element of grammar in his textbook on the subject. One must know how to punctuate a sentence to write sound prose. One must know how to pronounce a word—to weigh its stresses —to be articulate. One must know how to write a sentence in meter and, perhaps, in rhyme, to write verse. And, one must be capable of writing verse to be fully literate. But, once one has learned grammar— including the grammar of verse—it becomes quite easy, and one turns not to *other* things, but to *more* things, which is what is meant by developing a style. One may write in form, after a few hard jogs, with ease; but style is the work of a lifetime, and few men truly live.

Does this prevent "self-expression?" I should almost hope so, if only so that it might chasten the proclivities to exposure in our loquacious and therapeutic age. But formal verse certainly does not prevent anyone, student or master, from saying anything that needs to be said. I have always been perplexed by those persons, like my anonymous colleague, who seem to believe that the writing of poetry is primarily about self-expression. I apologize even for noting my perplexity, for I am aware that many others have made the same complaint, and we have *The Mirror and the Lamp* to explain it all in terms of the mutations of literary theory in the romantic age. And yet, any professor of creative writing who believes it is his job to help his students to express themselves ought to recognize immediately that he is less qualified than a trained art therapist to do so—presuming, of course, qualifications obtain in such a neologistic profession. He ought to recognize in addition that art therapists do not have anything *essentially* to do with art. In wartime, one may use a mattress as a barricade rather than as a thing on which to sleep; similarly, in desperate circumstances, psychologists may deploy art as a means to alleviate the murderous or merely "mopey" tendencies of a psychopath. But, no intelligent person would change the definition of "mattress" to "that which is used for sleeping and the stopping of bullets," any more than one ought to change the definition of "poetry" to "that literary genre written in verse . . . and also used for the soothing of backward children" (St. Hilary, *ora pro nobis*).

In ancient Athens, the sophist Gorgias promised that the art of words could not only teach one to make persuasive speeches, but to direct those speeches to virtuous ends *and* to make the rhetoricians all-powerful. So, in our age of diminished expectations, professors of creative writing not infrequently think their life's work is justified in helping a few teenagers get a little angst off their chest. But neither the greater nor the lesser claim will stand. Rhetoric is rhetoric. Grammar is grammar. The art of verse makes possible the writing of verse: however proud its traditional authorities are regarding their craft, they should not follow Gorgias into claiming that meter will enchant the trees, tame the lion, relieve the emotionally constipated, or mellifluously advance the will to power. It may well do these things, but that's not what they can teach you in singing school.

If we look further into his words, still another problem appears. Any statement in words in its essence expresses something, and since only human selves speak, poetry like any verbal artifact cannot be anything if it is not a medium of self-expression. My colleague seems to have been arguing that his students

105

could not get what they wished to express to pass fluently through this medium. If he were an instructor in philosophy, I should sympathize. After all, Kant's obscurities launched a thousand ships of obfuscation from which philosophy in general has never fully recovered. In contrast, whatever the complexities of the reality he describes, St. Thomas Aquinas found a clear and efficient medium to express that reality—and, crucially, it is the workman-like clarity of Aquinas' writing that helped ensure the soundness of the thought within it. If he were forced to write his articles on the Incarnation of the Word in Sapphics, more people might read Aquinas but even fewer should understand him properly. The purpose of Aquinas's writing was to bring others to understanding beyond the words used, and to do so in an efficient manner that might even lead us to leave those words behind. But this was a professor of the writing of poetry with whom I was clinking glasses not, unhappily, the Angelic Doctor. That is, he occupied an institutional position that insisted there was some relevance to the medium of communication beyond its role as conduit of a certain propositional content.

It has been my purpose thus far to resist the reduction of Marshall McLuhan that "the medium is the message." I would not confuse form and content; they are the complementary conditions of each other's existence, forming a composite unity that is the work. But we know from experience at least these two things: a) poetic form can and does add to the "content" of a work; by giving it shape it helps determine its nature and meaning. And, b) apart from this entrance of form into content, poetic form is of its own intrinsic interest, and indeed gains in interest when, by prescinding from the content of language, we consider the potencies—the variety and freedom—possible to form. As I have facetiously suggested, the professor of poetry writing may be professionally incompetent to direct the content of his students' writing (of itself, or to any particular end), but he has failed in the role assigned him if he does not, perhaps through long and tiring effort, impart to them the skills necessary to compose competently whatever thought they may wish to express in well-wrought verse. From an institutional perspective that is such a professor's duty, and in this instance the institutional perspective is in the right. What a dereliction it was, then, to hear one such professor consider the difficulties of formal verse an imposition. If we were to cast off that imposition, there would be nothing left for him to do.

I have taught the writing of poetry for a few years in my duties as a professor, and I have found it easy to bring my students to competence in the reading and writing of metrical poetry in the span of one semester. In the early assignments, it is outright necessary to remain indifferent to the content of their poems, in order to isolate and develop their ear for meter and, eventually, rhyme. It is also necessary to scan and re-scan lines with the students, and to point out to them the choices they could have made, even when the choices they made are metrical. Those students who become good poets—and I have had a pleasing number—do so, in part, because they have matter they deeply and for good reason wish to write about, and, in part, because they have sufficiently mastered the elements of form that they can turn it to the clear advantage of that matter. The former alone will not make a good writer, though, as I have said, it may make for some interesting writings. The latter alone will not make a good poet, though without it one is not really a poet at all.

This is perhaps a good moment to digress by way of protesting against the old canard that meter makes one distort language in order to fit its pattern. If the medium of a poem is nothing but a burden cast upon the Platonic ideal of its content, then I must confess this is a just complaint. Let us, in that case, all pray for the end of all flesh and our restoration to the changeless plane of the exemplars. But we are surely all in agreement that poetry *qua* poetry is in large part its concrete individual expression. If so, we may freely admit that those of limited ability with meter or rhyme will often write sound verse that is bad poetry merely because they are struggling to find an apt polysyllabic to fill out, say, the stress of one iamb and the entirety of the next; or because they have chosen to end one line in "night" and so feel compelled to rhyme it with "light." But quite often someone is accused of writing bad poetry merely because he has made a sentence sound awkward by the standards of a business-like prose in order to satisfy his meter or his rhyme. He sins, it appears, in sacrificing efficiency to formal completion.

But to distort syntax for the sake of rhyme or meter is not a mere disfigurement. Free verse poets no less than metrical poets recognize that the form of a poem is of immense importance. If they did not, then why do they break their prose into typographical "forms" on the page? That may not make free "verse" a *verse* form, but it would still seem to be a gesture indicating that form matters. If one is writing in formal verse, satisfying the exigencies of meter and rhyme is therefore a good in itself. As a good craftsman, at work on the intractable material of experience and language, one should be reasonably content to throw in a trite rhyme, or even a bad one, now and again, purely for the sake of maintaining the scheme. The scheme is good. How absurd to think one would spoil a ballad well on its way to rhymed perfection merely because the only suitable rhymes for "asphyxiate" gnarl and twist the syntax of the sentence. Perhaps the poet would be wiser to backtrack on "asphyxiate" and find a more felicitous pairing, but sometimes *that* is just the word that must be kept, and the poet must accept that limitation and make of it what he can.

The response to this may be, "Fine, but I do not consider rhyme a good in itself." To which I can only say that, in this instance, one has simply confessed not to like poetry. While classical verse did not rhyme, and while much verse in the modern languages does not, poetry, rhymed or blank, makes its form audible—and rhyme is the conceptual paradigm, if not the historical prototype, for poetry's audible form. It is the instance *par excellence* of the various non-syntactical ways in which language can be made to sound and mean. Cutting across the normal patterns of meaning, rhyme suggests that language operates on several different levels at once. In the present age, very few people care that language should mean much of anything. We are saturated by irony and sarcasm, and yet almost no one can *hear* these things. We have become illiterate to our own normal ways of speaking. If that is the case, then it should surprise no one that very few people *do* like poetry. I wish those who mistake themselves for liking it would not tear down the whole craft tradition of a literary genre in order to remake it into something they can like. Perhaps an art therapist could help them with these destructive urges.

The so-called "mainstream" of American poetry has often been derided for writing a mere "lineated prose." This seems a fair criticism, save that in many instances it is not even prose. Even fairly coherent and straight-forward free verse tends to indulge in all manner of "fragmentation," racking words for no good reason across a chaotic grid of lines. Work that responds to the name "avant-garde" usually takes this tendency to a far further extreme and robs words of their status as language by printing them in such random, self-frustrating order that they no longer constitute a statement, but are merely a hunk of jumbled pseudo-subversive phonemes spat upon the page. We see the latter in, say, Lyn Hejinian's senseless, *Writing is an Aid to Memory*, which I quote at random (honoring the fashion in which it was written):

> its consent to time
>   mass perhaps in a form against it
> a cheap reading of what surrounds
>   this taste of opinion
>   it all can be admitted up

Thanks to her collection of essays, *The Language of Inquiry*, which by some hundreds of pages dwarfs her poor little ticker tape of "poetry," I am aware of the radical intent of this work. Above all, I am aware she has succeeded in creating a kind of writing that refuses to be read; it subverts the conditions of coherence that would otherwise insist one be able to abstract some kind of meaning *from* the text, rather than merely holding the text up as exemplary of meanings located elsewhere. She has succeeded well. Who would *want* to read this writing by itself? Graduate students would not, but they may well delight in drawing abstruse connections between its opaque surfaces and the theoretical "depths" its author divulges in her critical essays. One can smell the dissertation topic just coming to a boil.

To repeat in a slightly different manner how her work functions, her "poem" is writing, her criticism is "language." In the former, the characters exist only as objects, in the latter, they fulfill themselves as signs. And so the intent does not inhere in the "poem"; indeed the "poem" distracts me from the essays, which I find idle but can at least engage as if a sentient person had written them. In consequence, we get a "poem" whose obsession with "evading" the (dare we echo her?) patriarchal and capitalistically reified functionality of language has done wonders to ensure that it does absolutely nothing. I have a larger point than condemning Hejinian, and perhaps it will come clear if I quote the following "tercet" from Jorie Graham's translation of *Inferno* XI:

> broken, breaks both that natural bond
> and the created one—the personal, most crucial
>   bond—So that
>
>   it's in
> the smallest, narrowest, darkest spot

By not quoting more, I make the sense of this passage hard to get at, but it is not the sense of it I contest. Her translation is, *qua* translation, a fairly clear, uninspired paraphrase of Dante. But look at the lineation, the "it's in," indented in the fashion traditionally reserved to indicate a spill-over line, where the margins require a verse line to be broken, but where the printer does not want you to confuse *his* break with a metrical one. We have no reason, based upon the erratic lineation of the rest of the translation, to believe Graham has only created such a preposterous line as "it's in" because it spilled over from the previous, but did not belong to the next. She writes in free verse; according to what principle has she arrayed this line thus? To what end? Not one that can

111

honestly be described as *formal*, I should suppose, though that would seem to be the intent.

As free verse has become normative during the last century, its writers have increasingly tried to make the appearance of the words on the page take on *some* kind of significance, even though it has proven impossible to secure a consistent one from poet to poet, or even poem to poem. In formal verse, lineation indicates an order that is present quite independent of how it appears as a text; lineation itself merely aids the reader in finding proper pronunciation by making meter, rhyme, and stanza as visibly prominent as punctuation makes syntax and sentence. A metrical line normally has a syntactical integrity, to be sure, but the two may be made absolutely independent through the use of enjambment without losing their individual identities of sound or sense. But, in consequence of the impossibility of lineation serving such a secondary, heuristic purpose in free verse, it has taken on an ever more unintelligible but prominent position in modern poems. It has encouraged, as Pound's *Cantos* encourages, free verse poets to equate lineation with fragmentation. And so they think of poetry as prose with words, paragraphs, grammar, or syntax, deleted. Poetic diction has come to mean, in many instances, broken words and phrases, isolated morsels of supposedly great "intensity."

Such poets are correct to observe that sentence fragments, which omit the grammatical, can emit rhetorical power. Imagine, for example, coming across some long poem describing the cold, forbidding, obscure peaks of mountains in the Alps, to find a significant "stanza" break, followed by the lonely unpunctuated phrase,

Much suffering

Ah, the power of understatement. Those of us who are parents or have had care over little ones know that, when a child runs into the street, no statement seems of more emotional weight than the imperative:

Stop!

I would never suggest that poets abandon this rhetorical device, or any other. But in the last several decades, poets have come practically to identify such laconic formulations and portentous amputations with poetic speech—poetic diction—itself. In consequence, a poet is encouraged not to make much discursive sense and to do so by way of endless iteration of the same formal property.

Poetry should be, and has always been, composed of grammatical sentences that have the added sophistication wrought by the demands of meter and, sometimes, rhyme. It should be, in that sense, prose with an additional regulatory principle in its marrow. But contemporary poets frequently suggest, by example, that what is to be considered poetic is specifically that which is not prose because it is less than prose. It is prose *without* the grammar. Prose *without* the coherence. Prose *without* the self-evident order of left-to-right progression across the page or the unassuming columns of text. It is prose on the verge of slipping off into non-being and capable of emitting only that last terrible whimper:

I'm . . . melting . . .

Free verse did not, therefore, open poetry to a greater variety of expression, though it probably made it more various of expression than late-Victorian (Georgian) poetic diction and subject-matter conventions *seemed* to allow (an appearance belied by the great Georgian poets Edward Thomas and Wilfred Owen). To the contrary, since free verse robbed poetry of its unobtrusive but commanding requisite of meter, its practitioners were forced to reach ever farther into the darkness for some element of speech that might be distinctively poetic. They hit upon fragments like those I have quoted just above, but since this is to be found as an occasional element of good prose (or as a pervasive element in Hemingway's prose; consider the apocryphal novel, "Baby Shoes"), they had to search farther.

Finally, they grasped some dark matter: the idea of constituting poetry as that which was so jagged and broken and inefficacious at communicating a wide variety of thoughts and rhetorical effects, that which was so useless for any other kind of expression besides emotional portentousness, that it just *had* to be poetry. In sum, with meter and rhyme, many poets also threw away the lot of grammar. I do not call poets to reassume the chains or nets of formal verse as if commanding their return to slavery. Meter is no net; rhyme has sometimes been said to "tinkle," but this does not make it a chain. Rather, I insist that grammar is essential to poetry because it offers real freedom, in the same way our speech offers us more freedom of communication than the grunts of a hog or the barks of a dog. And grammatical poetry, in order not to be merely a lineated prose paraphrase of "ineffable interior states," really does depend on the backbone of meter and, in our language, most often, the forked legs of rhyme.

Mine is no genteel criticism, scolding poets to return to explored and exploded techniques that will no longer harm one's sense of comfort in a comfortable world. I rather have the privilege of proclaiming an invitation to the liberation of well-cultivated grammar and verse. The freedom of free verse is anarchy like any other anarchy, eschewing form for formlessness, language for noise. Liberty requires discipline and rewards the effort of making with the actualization of being. Form *per se* makes things to be something rather than nothing; the richer the form the more real. The art of verse exists not as an exercise conducted on the therapist's couch, but as a whole way of being—difficult, numbered, yes, at first, but then easeful, habitual, and actualizing. Metrical verse offers poets the only kind of freedom that actually *exists*: the freedom to be *determined*.

PART II
NOTES TOWARD A
DEFINITION OF POETRY

7/ THE MUDDLE OVER PURE POETRY

Orléans, Beaugency
Notre-Dame de Cléry,
Vendôme, Vendôme.

—traditional

Aristotle was better who watched the
    insect breed,
The natural world develop,
Stressing the function, scrapping the Form
    in Itself
    Taking the horse from the shelf and
    letting it gallop.

—Louis MacNeice

As Wyatt Prunty, Timothy Steele, and others have observed, the long and turbulent twentieth-century experiment in free verse was just a particularly striking sign or symptom of a larger crisis in the cultural position of poetry. As the following reflections will indicate, it may also be viewed as a minor episode in a larger crisis in the modern West's traditional understanding of human beings as philosophical creatures, as animals with a natural capacity to seek to discover the truth about things. For my part, I have found it helpful to understand the history of free verse and the poetic modernism of which it was a part in the context of the larger shifts in how human beings perceive and ask questions about the world in general. As Erich Auerbach's *Mimesis* (1946) demonstrated in such a compelling fashion, literary style routinely affords us insight into how the society that reads and writes that literature views the world. I argued in the

119

second chapter that good criticism should attend to form and style while also situating literature in broader intellectual contexts without reducing them to one another. In the last several chapters, I sought to suggest why contemporary free verse poetry is unsatisfactory and how the art would benefit from the renewal of its traditional practices and genres.

In this one, I will re-describe how rational inquiry in the nature of things—not just poetry, but anything—has traditionally been understood to function; this will give us a very brief outline of the sort of rational reflection most helpfully exemplified by Aristotle, though certainly not exclusive to him. I will contrast this with the unsatisfactory account of reason and truth implicit to the modern age. I shall do this only in the context of Part II's specific concern, which is to consider some of the more or less insightful results of modern efforts at poetic theory, namely the effort to arrive at a definition of "pure" poetry. Equipped with the account of reason we find in Aristotle, I shall undertake brief examination of the literary theories of Henri Brémond, W.K. Wimsatt, Jacques Maritain, John Hollander, and J.V. Cunningham, all of which will set the stage for my own historical account of what poetry is. This I will conduct in two ways. First, in a series of four short studies that subject contemporary poetic practices to scrutiny to see what of it can survive. Second, in the last chapter, I will conclude with a (relatively) comprehensive account of poetry in its material elements, fullness of purpose, and social, intellectual, and aesthetic functions.

One need only review the major essays of T.S. Eliot, from "Tradition and the Individual Talent" (1919), to *The Use of Poetry and the Use of Criticism* (1931), from "The Social Function of Poetry" (1945), to "The Frontiers of Criticism" (1956), to see that the central questions of modern poetry are in fact the meaning of those two terms. What is "poetry"? What does it mean to be "modern"? Beyond essential definition, what is the contingent place of poetry in modernity? Free verse proposed, in its earliest appearance, to let poetry attain its apotheosis as the antonym of prose. While the distinction between prose and verse is nearly as old as writing, Renaissance literary theorists found themselves reflecting on Aristotle's particular distinction between the two and attempting to give it categorical weight. As Steele's *Missing Measures* (1990) shows us, this led in a misguided but intelligible way to the decisive breach proclaimed by Stéphane Mallarmé, in his essay on the book, in his Oxford Lecture, and by example in his last "poem," *Un coup de dés*. There, we see that modernity, with its etiolating freedom from necessity and secular desire to isolate all human concerns and activities into discrete realms, had at last made the theorizing of pure poetry possible. "Prose" bespoke individuation and form, physical science and functional utility, the hunkering down into matter of thoughts that had no better *or more lasting* purpose than to make something happen. "Poetry," in contrast, indicated that which eternally remains: Mallarmé proclaimed it the one new word come into being, Ezra Pound as "news that stays news." Later, John Crowe Ransom would talk about it in terms of "irrelevant texture," that which hangs on because it cannot be put to some "prose" use.

Here we have two things that differ from each other obviously on the level of composition—prose and poetry. But the obvious was not good enough, and so we are given this far more portentous, much less certain, distinction between that which is ephemeral and that which perdures, the servile and the free, the profane and the sacred. This burying of simplicity in obscurity is just one hint that the question of poetry has been thoroughly mixed up with the question of modernity: those poems were most modern which were so eviscerated of "use value" that they could be described not in terms of what they did or meant, but only in terms of what they were in their rarified freedom. The Renaissance followed Horace in declaring poetry's purpose was to "please and delight," but its modernist successors would find such a claim repellent. Didacticism is useful, it is the stuff of rhetoric, of hygiene and political campaigns, of what Eliot would call "platform prose." Poetry, to be poetry, must be other than that. As Archibald MacLeish memorably put it, "A poem should not mean. But be."

In 1925, the Abbé Henri Brémond provoked an extensive, sometimes furious, debate on "pure poetry," and developed Mallarmé's notions about it, claiming that pure poetry was the absolute toward which all poets strive. Purified of all extrinsic rational contaminants, the poem would serve only the function of its own essential act of existence. It would not inform one of anything, or teach one anything, but would stand forth as its own achieved end. The being of the poem appears as a kind of stasis, preserved from and critical of the world of rationalism and utility glowering all about it. Brémond was primarily a historian of the literature of French mystical theology, however, and the pure poem was not, to his mind, truly autonomous. As his *Prière et Poésie* (1926) argues, the achieved pure poem is the record of the poet's entrance into the perception of that which is most truly real. The poem is a pathway beyond the apprehension of that "painted veil" of worldly facts, leading us "to see into the life of things," as Shelley and Wordsworth had written more than a century earlier. Poetry, in short, is a method of contemplating God.

Brémond had been struck by the continuities between the works of the great romantic poets and those of the mystical theologians of past ages. As well he should have been. We owe to M.H. Abrams' *The Mirror and the Lamp* (1953) the definitive case that romantic poetic theory drew in deep if unorthodox ways on the Christian Platonist tradition. The pure poem became evidence of a long tradition of persons who had pierced beyond the merely use- or power-oriented apprehension of various temporal beings to the vision of the Good Itself, in its simple and eternal unity.

No sooner had he sought out a poetry purified of all merely rational utility, in other words, than Brémond found a use for it higher than many of his contemporaries could credit. The pure poem was either the oracle itself or, more precisely, the record of a poet's experience as becoming himself the oracle that shows forth divine realities. Purity, it turns out, meant beatitude, but few poems indeed shed just the sort of holy radiance upon their readers that the romantics did; some of the best poems would seem to have other qualities, other strengths. Brémond's project, and that of all modern questers after the grail of pure poetry, was both impossible and inevitable, as soon as poetry's definition was asked to comprehend a transcendent glory of the unserviceable that would rebuke by its very existence the peculiar utilitarianism of the modern age. Only that definition could ever *be* pure poetry; every actual poem would come to look like the soul of poetry with its wings clipped.

To get at how this conception of poetry as a kind of pure being came about, let us first pause to consider the history of how human beings understand the act of knowing. I want to challenge the idea of "pure poetry," by first challenging how people typically understand the concepts of nature, essence, or definition in our day. Philosophical thinking up to the modern age had kept at its heart the concept of final causality. The criterion of true knowledge about something was whether one knew what it was *for*, its purpose (*telos*); everything else flowed from this. For simplicity's sake, I will refer to thinking with this criterion as thinking within the Aristotelian tradition. A minimal account of it runs as follows.

The faculties of memory and reason allow one to gather the bulk of our individual experience with that of the experience of others, that of our contemporaries and of past generations, those real or fictitious, and to submit that vast archive, that trove of stories, to sustained reflection. The process of determining the identity of something, of defining its essence, consists of sifting through the various experiences had or reported in order to determine what they seem to say about the function of some particular thing or another. Abstractly speaking, the story of a thing's function, of its purpose and history of success or failure at fulfilling that purpose, leads to the definition of its nature. Knowledge is a matter of knowing what things are for, of how they move toward their end, and we discover the fact or nature of what a thing is for only through reflection on historical experience.

Even now, no one would define a toaster, or a watch, or a bed in terms other than purpose, and no one would deny that we can know that purpose. It is already there, implicit in the name. But our age is full of people longing to know their own purpose or the purpose of human life, and their expressions of anguish and doubtfulness indicate this is not something they believe we are capable of knowing. We tend to follow the Italian philosopher Giambattista Vico (1668-1744) in asserting we can know the purpose, and so the essence, of artificial things, of things we have done or made (hence, of facts, meaning "things done"), while we doubt to various degrees our access to knowledge of natural things. We are skeptical to a small extent regarding material nature, but to a far greater one regarding spiritual realities, such as the movements of the human mind or the movements of creation (the cosmos) as created. Prior to the advent of modern philosophy, this distinction was certainly acknowledged but did not constitute a problem. To the contrary, the traditional philosopher insisted that spiritual realities were in themselves *more* intelligible than material ones. They had a point: matter by itself does not exist and cannot have a purpose; only matter specified as a particular kind of something—a *what*—can be shown to have one, and it is mind, spirit, intention that gives shape to matter. All things must be known in terms of their finality; purpose *for* constitutes existence *as*; more difficult objects simply required a more extensive archive of recollected experiences.

Take the seemingly intractable questions of moral debate for an example. Thinkers in the Aristotelian tradition determined what was ethical behavior by reflection on different narratives of human life, and by subsequently making judgments on what life practices led to goodness or flourishing and which led to evil or unhappiness. Along the way, of course, they arrived at the equation of human goodness with flourishing, evil with unhappiness. As Alasdair MacIntyre powerfully argued in *After Virtue* (1981), the telling of and reflection on stories allowed one to determine what one *ought* to do in light of the flourishing, happy life one by nature desired to live. In the process of formulating a "fact," a more or less precise image of

125

what a happy life looks like, one also discovered how one *should* live, how one ought to think and act, in order to attain it. Conversely, by *doing* or *practicing* one's life, and reflecting on the practices of many different *lives*, the essence or image of the flourishing *human* life tentatively congealed. MacIntyre argued that virtues are those character traits that make possible the practices that must be found in any happy life, and are themselves *signs* of the attainment of the good life. Though, for example, one might be courageous and still be miserable, one cannot be said to be truly happy (truly to live the good life) if one lacks the virtue of courage. The principle of finality thus holds what it means to *do*, the *for the sake of which* one does, and what it means to *be* as nearly identical: form (nature) follows function (doing), which follows purpose (*telos*).

We noted above a common modern objection to this way of thinking. It is possible to know *facts*, but all this talk of "ought" and "should" refers to *values*, which are something else, perhaps something we project onto facts but has no part in them; they are not really knowledge. MacIntyre's account of Aristotelian ethics shows that all supposed values are themselves facts deduced from a prior fact, not alien impositions of the will. Another objection would be that we can know what something is without necessarily knowing what it is for. My knowledge that a sword is made of steel is different in kind from my knowledge that a sword is for fighting. Material reality is other than intention. But this distinction does not hold for a reason we already mentioned. Everything one may know about something follows from the principle of finality; knowledge of a sword's material, for instance, is knowledge acquired by knowing that steel is the material used for the purpose of making the sword. If someone proposed making a sword out of chicken feathers, we would dismiss the notion with a laugh. Aristotle's late disciple, Thomas Aquinas pithily suggests why in his tripartite account of what makes a thing good, by which he means, makes it to have fulfilled its purpose (*telos*).

First, insofar as it is constituted in its existence. Second, insofar as the accidents necessary for its perfect operation are added to it. Third, the perfection the thing has insofar as it reaches something else as its end.

We familiarly call something good when it serves some purpose transcendent of itself, or when it has all those qualities ("accidents") it needs to be fully itself; so much for his second and third accounts of goodness. It is the first one that may surprise. Even the brute fact of a thing as existing is itself the outcome of a prior intention. We know swords are *made* of steel, because steel is what they are at the end of their making. No knowledge comes independent of the principle of finality.

If this classical understanding of knowledge is correct, then we might offer, as a rule of thumb, that one knows sound philosophical reflection when it begins something along the lines of, "Human beings speak of 'health' in three ways . . ." Or, to our subject, "We normally call a 'poem' a written composition . . ." and so forth. Such language bears within it a sense of the permanent and universal as having been discerned by way of the historical and the particular. In a formulation to which we shall return, J.V. Cunningham insists, "I mean by poetry what a man means when he goes to the bookstore to buy a book of poems as a graduation gift . . ." Human experience and commonsense are not a folksy substitute for knowledge of the essence of things; rather, reflection on them is the normal means by which we rise to such knowledge.

As it is in moral philosophy or ethics this narrative method (that is, reflection on shared historical experience as a kind of narrative) remains the norm of every area of rational inquiry, however forgotten that fact may be. We cannot help but determine the essential definition of something by identifying what it does or, rather, for what end (*telos*) it exists. Thinking in terms of finality, or purpose, thinking *teleologically*, is what allows us to determine the nature, the definition, of a thing, and even the most skeptical among us know some things. We must all therefore think teleologically however unfamiliar the notion may sound. When I first heard Aristotle and St. Thomas's definition of man as a rational animal, for instance, I think I snickered. "Not the men I know," said I. Maybe, maybe not. Aquinas does not mean that most men behave rationally, or are always and already reasonable, but rather, that men must use their reason if they are to fulfill the end or purpose which distinguishes their species from that of other animals. Rational animals thinking rationally about the thing to which reason is by its nature ordered are men living fully. Louis MacNeice once quipped, "How nice to be born a man," but that only gets things backwards. When one says that man is a rational animal, one means that one is born a human being because, barring unforeseen contingent obstacles, one's development would naturally lead to one's possessing the adult power of reason. One's essence as human depends not on the daily practice of reason, but only on the ordering of one's being to an end, a *telos*, that (again, barring contingent obstacles) would normally include one's possessing the power of reason.

We define all things by way of the perceptible purpose for which they have been created, not merely by their diverse, incidental states or attributes at a given moment. The seventy-year-old ignoramus and the three-month-old fetus are no less human than the thirty-five-year-old polymath. While only one of these three possesses human reason in the fullest sense, all, by their ordination to the end of rationality, are equally human. One is simply not yet a fulfilled human, and the other may seem to us a failed life, but we can only judge these things in light of the *telos* we have of what it means to perform the act of "humanness," the *telos* of the human being as rational animal.

This pre-modern metaphysics of finality insists that a given essence can only be determined on the basis of our considering what the thing to be defined actually *does* when functioning perfectly. We know, to offer one last example, how a wristwatch works when it does what watches do, and therefore call a watch a small machine that marks the time. If it looks like a watch, but does not and could never tell time, we call it junk. The proper or normal function of a thing determines its essence, and essence determines the identity of any particular being.

As I said, this is, by and large, the metaphysics that subtends the day-to-day life of nearly all persons, however unacknowledged. Consider this old story. In Plato's Academy, a student offered as a definition of man, "two-legged animal without feathers." A week later, another student showed up with a plucked chicken and proclaimed, "Here is your man." A definition based merely on material attributes rather than purposive characteristics seemed silly to the ancients and seems no less so to us. Do clothes *really* make the man? Only if man's purpose is just the wearing of clothes. Is man essentially, as King Lear despairingly opined, just a "forked" (i.e. two-legged) animal? Only if the true human act is the playing of soccer.

The difference between the pre-modern and the more widely *acknowledged* modern way of defining the nature of things is that the pre-modern consciously defines things in terms of their *telos*, the modern does so unconsciously, and grows skeptical, anxious, or contemptuous of any definition as soon as talk of purpose, finality, destiny, or meaning arises. For Aristotle, knowing the *final cause* and thus the essence of a thing was the highest sort of freedom. In our day, we tend to view every statement about essences as a fascist encroachment on our freedom. What made this defensive but nausea-inducing (if Sartre is to be believed) refusal of knowledge possible?

Well, amid the novel scientific spirit of the seventeenth and eighteenth centuries, this equation of function as a determinant of essence was denied. By Francis Bacon, René Descartes, Thomas Hobbes, and many others, who saw the disavowal of finality as a way of clearing medieval speculative "clutter" to make straight the path to human beings' becoming, in Descartes' words, "masters and possessors of nature." This led knowledge to be split in two. We could be said to know that over which we can exercise power or control, or that over which we have no control but which seems governed by an eternal necessity uncontaminated by history. Knowledge was either purely practical or coldly logical, after the fashion of mathematics, but the two could never meet. While the mathematical type of knowledge was the higher or purer sort, human concern was for the useful, even when it was admitted that knowledge-for-use just barely qualified as knowledge at all.

According to the French historian and philosopher Etienne Gilson, this transformation had its definitive success in Christian Wolff's (1679-1764) attempt to resurrect, from the supposed "ashes" of ancient metaphysics, a new way of defining things. He designated as *being* anything that could potentially exist and thereby insisted that to think of being was to think of an essence independent of its actual existence. Wolffian Ontology was to be the theory of determining the essence of what might be and, in Wolff's hands, led to a "dogmatic realism," in which essence was thought ascertainable only if examined in isolation from actual existent things. Its inception was part of a larger trend in western thought that was coming gradually to think of everything temporal or historical as merely "relative." All true knowledge lay impossibly beyond us historical beings, and so the proper sphere of human activity lay in the quest for technical power—for those things subject to our *fact*, our doing, our know-*how*. This was the birth of modern science, which is venerated in our time, despite some misleading rhetoric, not for its disinterested speculative calm, but for its ability to extend our lifespans and beguile our senses with advanced technologies.

Just as a mathematical formula is more easily perceived as true if it is abstracted from our concrete, historical experience, so must be the essence of all knowable things. Actual existence is at best indifferent and, at worst, an impediment to such knowledge. Without going further into the history behind this transformation, we can safely assert that this theory concerning ontology resulted from the loss of understanding of traditional metaphysics with its foundation in teleology, narrative, and function. Thinking in terms of final cause seemed an obstacle to, and a distraction from, the dazzling self-evident usefulness of modern "scientific" knowledge. Metaphysics had traditionally been the first philosophy, because the act of being—to exist and to exist in a certain way—is prior to everything a being might subsequently do or become. But in the modern age, it became a kind of ancillary subject modeled on mathematical theory. Gilson calls this development "essentialism," meaning indifference to actual existence as a way of knowing the essence of things. Essence had always to be thought as a thing apart. But what I see as crucial and troubling in this story is that it has led many persons to the disastrous division of knowledge I defined just above. We come to mistrust the capacity of reason, reflecting on historical experience, to rise up to a knowledge of absolutes. We suspect in turn anything that smacks of being temporally conditioned as not being properly universal, and so the source we require even to arrive at a valid definition or essence has become suspect. And, finally, having doubted the knowability of the historical, and having found "pure" knowledge too precious to have anything to do with us, we give ourselves over to an identification of reason with the utilitarian form of inquiry proper to modern science: only that which gives us power counts as knowledge (to explain Bacon's famous axiom). There may be more to the world than we can control, we may even feel that there *needs* to be more to the world, but the only knowledge for us is the sort that helps us wield power over things. This makes the modern world appear mechanically practical, small-minded and lusty, while it makes real knowledge seem rarified, fusty, and . . . useless.

Modern ontology therefore arose as a marginalized science of essences, and essences must now be understood *not* as retrospective definitions of what a thing does when it exists as it is supposed to exist, but as the identity or definition of a given thing prior to and independent of its actual existence in time and history. This is why a younger me smirked at Aquinas. I presumed he meant *all* men are rational—here, now, and always—by their very existence in the same way a triangle must, in order to be a triangle, at all times have three sides. In this modern anti-historical way of thinking about the world, change and variation appear as cause of laughter and despair, rather than as the conditions that allow our reason to ascend from the flux of events to the permanent ideas that make that flux something we can understand. The rise of pragmatism in the twentieth century sought to rehabilitate philosophy as an investigation of what things actually do, but pragmatists failed to understand that reflection immediately leads us from what things do to what they seek to do: from practice to purpose, from how to why, from experience to meaning. And so, John Dewey and his pards wound up merely extending the practical criteria of control, consequence, and power found in the modern cult of the physical sciences to philosophy as a whole.

It is in the context of this modern stripping of the principle of finality and of historical existence from the realm of knowledge that the quest to arrive at a definition of "pure" poetry must finally be understood. The rise of an ahistorical essentialist way of thinking about definitions guaranteed that any effort to classify poetry would almost certainly be conducted with the goal of arriving at a static concept methodically removed from its various historical manifestations. More precisely, poetry was to be theorized apart from what it *does*, and because so many poems seem to do so many different things, in so many various ways, at various times, and in various social roles, the winnowing down to a poetic essence became so much the more difficult—indeed, impossible. Such an effort was particularly driven by a sense that poetry stood apart in some way from the modern conception of knowledge as power: it was not *useful*, it was not an obvious source of power, and it did not claim to give one knowledge in the sense of a quantifiable, verifiable datum. It was something men wanted to know about because it did not fit in to the stunted modern terrain of the knowable and to which their accepted methods for knowing were not adequate. This explains William Carlos Williams' famous pronouncement,

> It is difficult
> to get the news from poems
>   yet men die miserably every day
>   for lack
> of what is found there.

Poetry was beyond use, and so outside of knowledge and definition. And yet, there it was.

In the Victorian age, poetry was often thought to stand apart from power the way the imperatives of morality and the subtle sway of sentiments appeared to do. Critics such as Matthew Arnold were quick to corral sensibility, morality, religion, and poetry into a common circle, one that stood outside knowledge and reason, but nonetheless had an authoritative claim upon the human spirit. This in effect reduced poetry to a kind of morality, morality to sentiment, and all of it to didactic imperatives that seemed to fly in the face of what modern man really "knew." To be good was to follow your sentiments against the dark knowledge of your reason, your poetic spirit rather than your animal selfishness. By the early twentieth century, literary theorists from Mallarmé, to Brémond, to Eliot, were struggling to free poetry from just this subjacent role as, in Arnold's words, a guide to human "conduct" ("four-fifths" of life is conduct, he observed). But if poetry seemed in itself useless and so did not meet the modern criterion of what counted as knowledge, and if it also seemed condescending to gather it in as just one more sentiment of vague, indirect social use, what transhistorical essence could adequately describe its enduring historical presence, its mysterious prestige, and defenseless but radiant corona of authority?

The answers given to this question explain what I mean by calling this modern ontological quest for the poetic essence impossible. When one boils down all the extant poetry in the world within the essentializing intellect, only two possible elements take the heat, refusing to be melted down as inessential or accidental. These, unsurprisingly, are denominations along the lines of form and matter. Formally, one could argue that poetry is a mode of composition written in verse; and verse is a method of composition based upon generic—audible—principles of meter and, in some instances, rhyme. Materially, that is in terms of content, one could argue that the poetic was a kind of rapture of language—language under the pressure cooker, expression that had attained to a high degree of intensity or insight, or a unity of tropes, or transcendence of vision, where the metaphorical exposes some aspect of reality ordinarily hidden.

One could elect the formal attribute as determining the poetic essence, which has the advantage of being obvious, but then one is embarrassed by the variety of poetic practices. As we shall discuss further on, the Greeks and Romans had no rhyme; more importantly, their meter was quantitative rather than accentual-syllabic, and so their metrical feet determined not the accent placed on a given set of syllables, but rather whether the syllable was long or short. We might understand this a little better if we think back to learning phonics as children and recall the difference between long and short vowels. "I hit the baseball with a bat." The letter "I" appears first in long, then in short pronunciation; the letter "a" appears long once, then in "variant" mode, then long, then short. This is not what Greek prosody measured, but it at least gives us an example of thinking in terms of "long" and "short." In classical Greek, long syllables registered as long because they were held for "twice" as long as short ones. Meter and rhythm, in the musical sense, were thus closely conjoined, because a long syllable might be understood, to put it in our terms, as a half note, a short a quarter note. But even in Latin, accentual stress already appears, and we therefore have a historically constituted difficulty in understanding the relation of meter and rhythm in any terms other than those which we hear as accent or "down-beats" and "up-beats." Which is the *true* unit of poetic measure? Is it the one that we can no longer even hear, even if we learn classical Greek and Latin in school?

In any case, the ancients had a meter that, the resurrection of its nomenclature for modern prosody notwithstanding, operates according to principles different from those of us moderns. We can scarcely conceive of quantity, syllable length or timing, as a principle of meter. Accentual-syllabic seems almost intuitive, because the placement of stress in meter so naturally dovetails with the placement of stress in the rhythm of a sentence, or with the singing of a song to a particular melody. Moreover, syllable sounds, because of the diphthongs with which we pronounce vowels (ay, ey, iy, ow, yoo), seem something we can make long and short arbitrarily, without violating rules of pronunciation.

Thomas Campion's *Observations in the Art of English Poesy* (1602) proposed a formal definition and overcame the historical difficulties simply by denouncing historical practices. He urged a revival of quantity, claiming that modern English meter and especially its use of rhyme were an inheritance from barbarians that perverted poetry in English from its proper conformity to classical antecedents:

> In those lack-learning times [the medieval "dark ages"], and in barbarized Italy, began that vulgar and easy kind of poesy which is now in use through most parts of Christendom, which we abusively [i.e. inaccurately] call 'rhyme' and 'metre' . . .

He advocated our return forthwith to the practice of the ancients, the "right of true numbers." In actual practice, no one could depend on rhyme and meter more than Campion, whose songs are some of our most finely-tuned poetry. His one great poem written in classical "quantitative" meter is perfectly intelligible in terms of the English accentual-syllabic prosody, while his homespun, arbitrary system of assigning "weight" or length to English syllables remains in the background, an inaudible code for his eyes alone. Despite a strong veneration of the ancients, he does not seem to have understood the principles of quantity, or at least could not bring them over into English, as his hostile critic Samuel Daniel readily pointed out in his *Defense of Rhyme* (1603). As one modern editor of Campion's essay puts it, the poet did not convince anyone to take up quantitative meter in English, not even himself. Readers may find the whole project incredible. As Hollander justly observes, in *Vision and Resonance* (1975), Campion's *Observations,* seems pointless to us today. The Elizabethans are, after all, our poetic Greek and Latin poets—the English past is our linguistic and imaginative antiquity, the iambic pentameter our classical verse. But at the end of the sixteenth century, the desire to legitimize a national English literature by giving it good Classical credentials still led some poets and critics to espouse a literal adoption of the quantitative meter of Greek and Latin poetry.

As the great scholar of the history of English prosody, James Thompson, notes, Campions' and others' efforts to revolt against history and distill the essence of poetry as meter by conforming accentual-syllabic English "rhyme" to quantitative Latin "meter" did achieve something, and something vital. It clarified for the age the native principles of English prosody so that they attained the theoretical maturity necessary if they were to serve as normative conventions for a great literature. Campion inadvertently helped make the iambic line our classic. The first lasting fruit would be the poetry of Sir Philip Sidney.

But, Campion remains exemplary of a temptation for the would-be theorist of the essence of poetry. You can elect to define poetry in terms of form, and then get rid of meter's changes from age to age and language to language by insisting that all are decadent save one. Or, you can follow Brémond in thinking of poetry as an august content; he gives us a universal theory, but seems in fact only to be talking about English romantic poets, taking a part for the whole. The theorist of the poetic essence winds up repeating Campion's eccentric prescriptions, claiming perhaps that quantitative composition, or a certain kind of metrical composition, is the only proper medium for poetry, all else being dross. John Milton may not have followed Campion in proposing quantity in English, but he certainly followed him in praising "meter" to the exclusion of "rhyme." To convince himself he was right to do so, he imposed constraints on his blank verse that exceeded those of the matured practice of the Renaissance drama. Once again, history is rejected for a supposedly ahistorical essence of meter.

In the worldview of modern ontology, the historical contingency of metrical practices—not to mention the comparative novelty of rhyme—prohibits one from claiming that verse is the essence of poetry, just because it is so scored by the historical morphological variations of language. I can claim a triangle must, no matter what culture it appears in, have three sides to be a triangle. But I cannot so easily claim that verse must be equally static, because verse-practice is not consistent across Europe, much less across time. Perhaps, we begin to think, there is no irreducible formal essence of poetry any more than there seems to be a universal vocation of the poet to contemplative prayer.

Change and variation *seem* to cow the advocates of meter into a corner. They have usually responded to the fact of variability in one of two ways. Turner's *Natural Classicism*, particularly in "The Neural Lyre," claims to drill down beneath superficial variability to find a common trans-cultural core of metrical concept. His claims are compelling, and I have already defended his sophistication. And yet, as the Enlightenment's inquiries have taught us, attempts to arrive at universal generalities by stripping away historical particulars often leave too little substance behind, or come to appear discreditably selective.

The second and more common response, in our age, is to confess failure to define the essence of poetry as verse. History is relative, and verse is one more

139

historical practice. But one then proceeds to insist on the goodness of meter as a stubborn fact. One is uninterested in poetic essences. What difference do they make? The poet's concern is with the craft and dignity of humble verse as practiced in our tradition. A fine instance of this may be found in Dick Davis' poem, "Preferences":

> To my surprise
> I've come to realize
> I don't like poetry
>
> (Dear, drunkly woozy,
> Accommodating floozy
> That she's obliged to be,
>
> Poor girl, these days).
> No, what I love and praise
> Is not damp poetry
>
> But her pert, terse,
> Accomplished sibling: verse,
> She's the right girl for me.

Personally, I find this one excellent short-cut for a problem that would otherwise require considerable reflection. Those who make "woozy" claims for the content of a poetic essence may make one's head spin with their high talk. Think of Brémond's first auditors, who discovered pure poetry was an analogue for the prayer of the mystics. We could defend the proposal, but can we not just forget theoretical differences and accept that verse is a kind of "common law" and inheritance for our particular linguistic community? In spite of such elevated spirits, or indeed because of them, any person with respect for the perfection of the thing made—for the work in which the artisan rises to fine art without forgetting the craft of making—any such person would rather keep close to the workshop floor of verse. He does not claim to have the truth, but merely to prefer a conception of the art that has centuries of practice in its favor. Though many a romantic theorist might accuse the metrical poet of being an "absolutist," that is, of resisting the tyranny of relativistic "preferences," the poet was merely trying to write a poem.

Davis is exemplary here—and not just in this poem. A prodigious translator of Persian epic poetry into English verse, his books of original poetry sometimes seem afterthoughts of the master craftsman, as if, having completed the most recent translation of a forty-thousand-line medieval masterpiece, his most casual thoughts naturally arrange themselves into epigrammatic little verses, and he, on a scrap of paper he had till then been using as a bookmark, jots the lines down and stows them away with some four-dozen others to await arrangement into his next volume of original poetry. One just gets the sense that he is going to write what he writes no matter what the world "prefers," and how the world receives it is not his concern. He has work to do.

I intend this caricature as only lightly critical: Davis' command of form, as this poem suggests, sometimes is used for off-handed little verses whose interest is exhausted once one has enjoyed the brilliant phrasing. On occasion, pouring a little more potent intoxicant into the glass of his verse would make that girl appear a bit more voluptuous, not just to him, but to all of us. Even so, I consistently prefer to read the slightest of his performances to the unpronounceable dreamscapes of Jorie Graham.

Particular achievements aside, what I have called the formal option for an "essentialist" definition of poetry leads one to verse, and ends by forcing one to concede that verse is distinct from poetry. Some will side with Davis that verse is a good in itself, and good enough, at that. Others will insist that verse is merely ancillary to a greater poetic essence, and the chase goes on.

Few matters in the arts have been subject to such wild speculation as the poetic essence in the modern age of "essentialist" thinking. Millennia of claims about the power of poetry encourage the self-consciously modern thinker to offer his own explanation for why poetry should play the central role it has in every culture. Nearly all such thinkers make reference to Aristotle's claim that poetry is "more philosophical" than history. Given that modern ontology's origin, as I have said, lies in a rejection of teleological, historical, or narrative thinking, moderns have rushed in to confirm Aristotle in this, even as they frequently denounce his theory of catharsis as if it anticipated the mania of the modern utilitarian world. Brémond and Ransom, for instance, praise Aristotle for recognizing a "superiority" in poetry compared with other forms of discourse, but they also condemn his talk of catharsis as an attempt to materialize or "psychologize" that superiority, which is properly understood as spiritual or intellectual, out of existence. They thus put themselves in the position of having to come up with alternate, better explanations, for what Aristotle meant, for what seems to be a universally acknowledged truth.

Those two important figures included, the most interesting modern theories of the poetic-as-philosophical tend to be variations on the theory of the "Concrete Universal." This phrase (Hegelian in tone but far more venerable in fact), was best explored by W.K. Wimsatt, in his essay of that name collected in his great book, *The Verbal Icon: Studies in the Meaning of Poetry* (1954). He observed that the best poetry is rendered in concrete, specific language that seems to embody a truth or reality much larger and more general. The individual incarnates the universal. A particular character represents a type of person, he notes, thinking of Aristotle's *Poetics*, but he finds metaphor to be the finest realization of this principle. Metaphor expresses concretely what is normally understood in the language of the universal. Eliot, lecturing almost three decades earlier on the metaphysical poets had seen just this as their signature achievement, one that, in the minds of Wimsatt and others, makes them the paradigm of the art:

> Poetry . . . is not the assertion that something is true, but the making that truth more fully real to us; it is the creation of a sensuous embodiment. It is the making the Word Flesh, if we remember that for poetry there are various qualities of Word and various qualities of Flesh.

The study of poetry becomes a type of Christology transferred from the realm of being to that of the imagination. Such poetry, one concludes, must be made of highly sensual and detailed language, when it signifies literally, and must be made of highly metaphorical and so no less concrete language, when some un-representable or abstract concept is the matter. In speaking of the "Concrete Universal," Wimsatt meant to indicate the way in which the individual and the universal, the concrete and the abstract, fuse in the "verbal icon" of the poem. He sought to explain why the greatest literature embodied what the ancients called the *sublime*, universality of importance, without the vagueness or generalization of philosophical propositions.

In *The Situation of Poetry* (1938) and *Creative Intuition in Art and Poetry* (1953), Jacques Maritain outlined a theory of "poetic knowledge" that takes the same view, but with greater emphasis on the subject, that is, the mind of the artist, than on the art-object. He claimed that poetic knowledge comprehended, one might say, an intellectual act that discerned the abstract and un-representable (or, indeed, ineffable) without resorting to abstraction, and also the work of art that communicated it. We generally are said to know something when we can formulate a series of accurate propositions about it. Poetic knowledge is not knowledge in this sense at all; it is rather an experience of encountering ideas not *in the form* of sensible things, but *as* sensible things. In poetry, we grasp being's existence without flying up to its intangible essence. To say that Justice is like a blindfolded woman with a sword will not do. The poet's task is simply to give us the image of that woman in so incarnate or manifest a form that we sense in the vision of her Justice as itself an incarnate being. Such knowledge lasts—if it does last—as the memory of an existential experience rather than as a proposition abstracted from that experience.

Wimsatt's argument is a gain to be built upon, not a speculation to be discarded. It confirms and helps us interpret the almost universal experience readers of literature share. So also may we speak of Maritain on poetic knowledge. His philosophy of knowledge includes it as one of the many degrees of knowledge he expertly establishes and classifies, and while there are weaknesses to his tendency to absolutize or overly schematize the separation of art and metaphysics, poetic and discursive knowledge (some of which were worked out long ago in Harold L. Weatherby's invaluable *The Keen Delight* (1975)), his insights are of lasting value and justly reestablish poetry, even romantic poetry, as a way of knowing rather than as a feeling or sentiment.

Wimsatt and Maritain stand out as the greatest philosophers of the poetic of the twentieth century. Maritain's early *Art and Scholasticism* (1920) provides the most complete theory of art as the perfection of the thing made, and of beauty as that which pleases when seen (a unity of integrity, proportion, and splendor), but which is also an ontological reality existentially touching the ground of being that is God, to be found in the long history of aesthetic speculation. We can see how central metaphor becomes for the definition of poetry, and how paradigmatic poetry becomes of literature and art more generally. But, for all that, their theories do not really help us to pin down what makes a poem a poem.

When one tries to take their insights as the very definition of poetry, something bad happens. They wind up as a reductive law of poetic composition. One thinks of William Carlos Williams' kerygma, "No ideas but in things," to which the Irish poet Denis Devlin replied that Dr. Williams had thrown "out all the literary luggage, [and] continues to stand peering, in a mixture of rage and uncertainty, over the threshold of poetry." Maritain in fact considered the "immediately illuminating image" a discovery that, while present in the great poets of all time, had only come to the foreground in modernity. He did see it, as did Williams, as essential to poetry if not always acknowledged as such. But, it quickly becomes clear that there are many works of art and poetry—great works—that he does not include as such. He held the French academic school of painters in contempt, was tepid toward the novel, and at every turn showed himself indifferent to

145

any formal principles of art that belonged to genre rather than to a particular artist's expression of poetic knowledge—meter, not incidentally, included.

Although Maritain cites John Dryden as a possessor of poetic knowledge, and although no one celebrated the intellect more earnestly than did Maritain, he remained deeply skeptical about poetry that strayed from that particularly emotive intensity that Frank Kermode has called the "romantic image." In *The Situation of Poetry*, Maritain warns that "it could happen . . . that a neo-classical reaction would ask poetry to *exhibit ideas and sentiments*, to charge itself with the rubbish of human notions in their verbosity and their natural meanness, and to fabricate *versified discourses* for the delectation of the formal intelligence." Versified discourse, for Maritain as for all who wish to describe the poetic essence as rooted in metaphor, as a concrete knowledge, is not poetry.

Maritain does not intend that some particular sort of language is necessarily more poetic than another. Indeed poetry for him is the creative intuition and actual making of art—any kind of art. He believes that poetry, regardless of its type or medium, must provide a concrete experience of the transcendental richness of Being—of its synthesis of truth, goodness, and beauty. Poetry in its highest form is that which brings us into contact with Being, that which uses the myriad existents of language and image to draw us into the mystery and depths of existence. But the question remains: is Alexander Pope's *Essay on Man*, or any number of other discursive, epistolary, narrative, and didactic verses, an instance of poetry manifesting the transcendentals, or is it merely "versified discourse"? Depending on how Maritain would have answered that question, we could determine whether he has provided an account of how some (modern) poetry works or simply a historically inadequate definition of "the poetic" akin to that we found in Campion. If he would discount the Augustans' poetry, with Arnold, as "classics of our prose," then he has arrived at the essence of the poetic only by getting rid of loads of great poetry. If he would not, then he would have to revise his accounts of poetic knowledge to be, as I said above, less schematic so that the concrete stuff of poetic knowledge could coexist in a poem with the language of dialectic and discursive reason without our concluding that the poem is somehow "impure."

Maritain's linking of art with the transcendental properties of being offers a profound and too oft forgotten explanation of what art actually does. I do not take it up only to lay it by; indeed, I have spent much of the last decade discussing it in print. But, here, I want just to suggest that it is most valuable as a general theory of the fine arts and less so as a specific account of written poetry. Maritain grounds his arguments in the transcendentals, and therefore in the reality of beauty as something to be made and to be encountered in existence. Like most theorists of poetic essence, he abstains from close argument about what constitutes poetry, not as a metaphysical concept of creation, but as a particular genre of linguistic or literary art. My contention is that, if he constrained poetry as a genre to the performance of the task he contends is the essence of Poetry-writ-large, then only a limited number of the great poems of history would any longer still be called poems. Let us presume he does not intend that, but only to explain the metaphysical basis for why the fine arts, as we have come to know them, touch our very sense of reality, of being, without becoming entirely explicable in abstract terms.

A more practical critic, though hardly wanting of ambition in philosophical aesthetics, Hollander sometimes seems to bridge the gulf between those I have designated formalists and materialists by insisting, appropriately enough, on a hylomorphic theory of poetry. By this I mean the conventional theory, common to ancient and medieval philosophy and still implicit in our everyday speech, that an existent material being is one coined, as it were, by the union of the active principle of form (*morph*) and the passive one of matter (*hylo*). Hollander does not outline his position in quite those terms, but they amount to the same thing. Introducing his little guide to verse, *Rhyme's Reason*, he says that it is a guide to,

> the formal structures which are a necessary condition of poetry, but not a sufficient one. The building blocks of poetry itself are elements of fiction—fable, 'image,' metaphor—all the material of the nonliteral. The components of verse are like parts of plans by which the materials are built into a structure [given a form]. The study of rhetoric distinguishes between tropes, or figures of meaning such as metaphor and metonymy, and schemes, or surface patterns of words. Poetry is a matter of trope; and verse, of scheme or design.

Most of what I have said thus far should be reconcilable with this formulation, and so will be much though not all of my concluding account of poetry. From an ontological perspective, verse either is the sole determinant of the essence of poetry, or it is something other but which nonetheless stands in some relation to it. Hollander indicates that he is of a mind that verse stands in a *necessary* relation to poetry; Maritain and others suggest that poetry is primarily a way of encountering reality or being, independent of what most of us would call the formal characteristics of the work of art itself. Hollander stands as one of the formidable poets and critics of our era because he refuses to be taken in by those who would make poetry into a woozy, romantic dose of ether, and because he writes masterful verse in rhyme and meter, without ever indulging what we might call the itch to versify (except, however, when he writes light verse—and it is the lightness of content that defines the genre, for Hollander). That is, some persons, persons who fancy themselves as poets, would not recognize what Davis does as poetry. I doubt very much they or anyone would question the *poetic* achievement of Hollander.

This hylomorphic theory, however, is not without its problems. Of course it is tenable to suggest that verse *formally* constitutes poetry, while the "nonliteral" does so *materially*. But, we have seen, many would say that verse can be verse without being poetry. What shall we call it, then, if it is the formal *constituent* of poetry? Despite Davis's protestations, his scrap of verse quoted above is a nice little poem, but there are other works in verse that might not so obviously qualify, because they do not adequately manifest the nonliteral. Could there really be such a thing as a poem *formally* but not *materially*? Are there really any such works? Might we not just call them *bad* poems?

I am not entirely sure what Hollander means by the nonliteral. The term, "image," he sets in scare-quotes, but an image could just as easily be produced through a literal use of language as it could through a trope. Only if he were willing to suggest that tropes so saturate our use of language that, allowing for its being fitted into verses, our almost everyday speech becomes poetry, could I go along with him. If that were the case, though, his definition would be much too broad to accomplish the task he has assigned it of specifying what poetry is. Hollander's distinction between poetry, rooted in the nonliteral, and verse, risks the same inadequacy Eliot once found in Coleridge's distinction between imagination and fancy. If one simply refers to good poetry as that which shows imagination, and bad poetry as that which merely indulges in fancy, the additional terminology brings one no closer to understanding what is poetry as poetry. As Eliot himself was sometimes willing to do, Hollander either suggests that good poetry is built up of the metaphorical and verse, and bad of verse alone, or (again) he grants us so wide a definition of the nonliteral that its help in understanding the nature of poetry will be minimal.

Rather than dispute the point further, I want to suggest that the plausibility of Hollander's description arises from a refusal of the kind of ontological stasis taken for granted by the first practitioners of free verse. Instead of insisting that a poem must *be*— because the poetic must simply be itself pure and simple, free of all *uses*—he suggests that a poem must do several things, and that, so long as it does them all, it is poetry. So long as the theorist of poetry insists the poem is a kind of self-referential stasis, free from entanglement with the material or contingent, his task will remain an impossibility, because the very thing he would define will keep slipping away into the contingent, the concrete, and the individual. Hollander's account has the virtue of envisioning an end (*telos*) for poetry that must be attained: a union of form and matter, verse and nonliteral language. Fine. We are close to something.

Just as Hollander suggests the fusion of scheme and trope constitute poetry, and therefore refuses one kind of ontological purity, J.V. Cunningham refuses this

150

purity from another angle, and one that comports well with my claim that a good universal definition will derive from reflection on historical experiences, even as Cunningham winds up resisting history in certain ways we shall explore. In his critical volume *Tradition and Poetic Structure* (1960), Cunningham relies upon the aggregate commonsense of readers of poetry over the generations as a practical means to discovering the nature of poetry. After reviewing Aristotle's and Plato's theories of poetry as philosophical, as imitation, or as a kind of fiction (and "fiction" is at least as suitable a term as Hollander's nonliteral), he concedes that, if any of these things are components of the poetic essence, they are *highest* components. That is, they enter into poetry when it is understood to accomplish a distinguished and unique purpose. Poetry as fiction is a final end of the sort we get when we hear that man is a rational animal and discover a handful of men who are particularly smart. Nonetheless, most men are not rational, and most poetry is not a "philosophical fiction" (to conjoin two matters Cunningham treats separately), even though the best poems and men must be.

Cunningham explicitly refuses this kind of teleological thinking, which, with me, he identifies with the Aristotelian tradition. He mistrusts a mode of definition that attends to not what all instances of a case visibly are, but to what they are meant to become when their natures are actualized or fulfilled. Referring, for instance, to the classical discussions of man as essentially rational, but also normally two-legged, or capable of laughter, he writes, "There is not much glory in two-leggedness or laughter" but either might serve the purpose of definition better. What purpose is that? The "common or garden variety of definition," one that does not, as Aristotle would, "distinguish the particular virtue of the object," but one which will simply "mark off the territory" and "describe the thing unmistakably."

What is the one necessary attribute of a poem, "unmistakably" present, that precedes and makes possible this more glorious but less universal final cause? Cunningham insists upon a formal (first cause, as it were, rather than final cause) definition of poetry, which one would expect given the modern "essentializing" tendencies I discussed above. He arrives at his conclusion through reflection on shared experience, and in consequence insists it is a modest, historical claim rather than an ontological one. In "Poetry, Structure, and Tradition," he writes,

> I mean by poetry what everyone means by it when he is not in an exalted mood, when he is not being a critic, a visionary, or a philosopher. I mean by poetry what a man means when he goes to a bookstore to buy a book of poems as a graduation gift, or when he is commissioned by a publisher to do an anthology of sixteenth century poems. Poetry is what looks like poetry, what sounds like poetry. It is metrical composition.

Such a definition does not explain what is good or important about poetry that might make one want to give it as a gift; it does not explain why Plato exiled the poets, or Aristotle credited more to their work than that of the historians. And, it certainly does not explain why Brémond saw the wisdom of the Christian mystics versified in Wordsworth and Shelley. It does not claim to explain these things, all of which may be due to virtues present in all good poetry. Cunningham is more concerned to discover the minimal condition or first cause of what must be present *a priori* for poetry to be poetry in the first place, however it may subsequently ascend, or fail to ascend, the heights of greatness.

A little earlier in the same essay he makes clear this modest but crucial ambition. He begins by summarizing how the word "poetry" has variously been used, in order to establish its primary meaning, from which all other uses derive, it seems, only as sloppily drawn *analogies*. He explains,

> Poetry is regarded as a kind of literature, a quality of experience, a way of knowing. It is contrasted with verse, with prose, and with science. It is defined in such a way as to favor a special view of experience or to promote the writing or approval of a special view of experience or to promote the writing or approval of a special kind of poem. The difficulty, then, lies in the fact that the object of definition is not constant. The hesitations, the scruples, the blurring in the act of definition result from this. There remains, however, a constant point, if not of reference at least of departure, in all these formulations, and this is poetry as it is ordinarily understood: the body of linguistic constructions that men usually refer to as poems.

The deliberately deflating quality of this passage is a sign of Cunningham's typical terse intelligence (one which directly inspired the Davis poem quoted earlier). Modernist efforts to define the essence of poetry *against* the variegated texture of historical experience will not do; they merely ratify the romantic hope for poetry as a new dispensation to replace a failed Christianity, promoting the poetic from a kind of ethical teaching (Arnold's "conduct") to the heights of an aesthetic purity that became spiritual ether (Brémond's "*poésie pure*"). Rather than go out in search of essences, Cunningham points at some poetic objects on the table, and the usual thoughts about poetry had by the average man, and says they all clearly have one thing in common, and that is meter.

We are now in a historical position to appreciate that the efforts of modern writers to redefine the essence of their art under changed historical circumstances may have been inevitable, but they were conducted in a manner that merely imitated the ahistorical abstraction, the "ontologism," the "essentialism," found in other branches of modern thought outside the eminently utilitarian physical sciences. In its opposition to the modern quest to dominate nature by means of technique and technology, old useless poetry is not an archaic residue from an age of speculation and freedom, but rather has been redefined in *typically* modern fashion. It gets praised, again and again, as yet another "not-science" alongside religion, theology, philosophy, and ethics.

The passages from Cunningham will have none of this and will in consequence sound quaint to many ears. Therein lies their truth. Rather than entertain the ever-more-ethereal quests after the poetic essence, he falls back upon the long historical experience—the commonsense—shared by his fellow ignorant men, and it testifies to poetry as founded on metrical composition (regardless of where it might go thereafter). Poetry is a particular kind of composition, whose "propositions are in meter." This distinction in form "tends to beget a distinction in function or purpose," what I have called a material or content proper to poetry. But these "areas assigned" to poetry "shift and vary from time to time and place to place." Therefore, tradition as "a historical process" will lead us to elaborate what poetry does, what matter it treats, and the forms and modes in which it may be written.

But, at bottom, in a sense prior to the tradition and making it possible in the first place, is poetry as metrical composition.

For Cunningham, poetry and the traditions that emerge from it are categorically distinct; metrical composition is poetry, everything else is what is *done with* poetry. The subject of his book is to show several of the ways "principles of order" emerge within the literary tradition, but as such they are inquiries into the history, rather than the nature, of poetry. His modest deference to historical reflection and commonsense has something Aristotelian about it, as I have suggested, but there is also about it something specifically modern, something too much a party to Ockham's razor and the nominalism that Richard Weaver long ago proclaimed a sign of modern decadence. He is thus too suspicious of the deliverances of historical inquiry and resistant to thinking in terms of the principle of finality about his critical position. He specifically contrasts his way of thinking with the Aristotelian tradition, thinking thereby to avoid intractable difficulties. To the contrary, as I shall make clear in the last chapter, I believe this limits the helpfulness of his poetic theory in getting at what poetry in its fullness properly is. Those who have followed in his footsteps, like Davis, have kept the art of poetry alive in our day almost by an act of anti-theoretical stubbornness. For that we owe them thanks.

It now seems appropriate to draw upon Cunningham's observations as a means to reflect on why the modernist quest for the poetic essence has proceeded with a centrifugal energy. It has led much contemporary poetry and literary criticism to still greater extremes of absurd experiments in composition and preposterous ghost hunts after the essence of the poetic, spinning and spinning until almost nothing is left at the center. We shall see, in fact, four of these ghosts, before turning at last to a positive account of what the literary tradition shows poetry to be, not just in part, and not just in its beginnings, but in the fullness of its history.

8/ THE PRINT OF A GREASY FORK

> Yet the fingers on the lyre
> Spread like an avenging fire.
> Crying loud, the immortal tongue,
> From the empty body wrung,
> Broken in a bloody dream,
> Sang unmeaning down the stream.
> —Yvor Winters

Cunningham's minimal definition of poetry as a metrical composition leads us back once again to the essence of poetry. From the modern perspective I have described, content and form present themselves as the two static or constant categories by means of which one could define the poetic. We have seen that Wimsatt, Maritain, and others, in trying to nail down poetry in fundamentally material terms as a kind of knowledge or as a particular kind of language, have borne fruit in providing us insights that help account for our experiences of art and literature. These are no idle discoveries. If my account of the modern person's skepticism regarding historical knowledge is correct, then it will be necessary to remind the reader that, though language is always conditioned by its historicity, signs and symbols function in distinct ways that transcend the vicissitudes of any particular language. We can speak of their *kinds* or types.

A few examples are in order. Natural signs immediately direct us to what they signify—as smoke does fire. Some kinds of language direct us first to a concept in the mind, which in turn enables us to know a thing existing in the world by its species. Referential or vocative words call out to a particular individual—as does the calling of a name ("There fell thy shadow,

Cynera!"). The language of contemplative prayer also points toward something, but without making it into an object known; it identifies, like a finger pointed upward at viewless spaces, without defining. In the last lines of Denis Devlin's poem "Lough Derg," the poet writes of his pilgrimage on that small island, and at last turns away from his overly intellectualized sense of self to observe, "And so, knelt on her sod, / This woman beside me murmuring *My God! My God!*" The woman's vocative, Devlin tells us, is a prayer without content, what is traditionally called *apophatic* speech in which the words negate their normal significance not in order to become empty but to embrace a dark, ineffable fullness.

Wimsatt and Maritain remind us that these and other various kinds of language are really distinct, and that one particular kind of language, a specifically poetic language, achieves what might otherwise seem impossible: it gives flesh to abstraction, it makes present and individual what is universal and elusive. But these achievements have their own names and they should not overwrite that other name, poetry. Let the concrete universal be the concrete universal, and poetry, poetry. Let us grant Maritain his use of the term "poetic knowledge," because he grounds it in the concept of *poiesis*, of making—the made concrete thing, as opposed to the prescinding, analytic act of abstraction in ideas—rather than as an account of poetry as a literary genre. None of this finally will tell us what the art of poetry is, though it may deepen our understanding of what specific poems do. So much for the ontologically materialist approach.

Let us return to the formal answer. Davis concedes that verse may not be that high thing called poetry, but he then half-seriously sets poetry aside as "not his bag." Hollander refers to verse as the necessary condition of

158

poetry, but does not equate the two; and indeed, at least in principle, he is unwilling to equate verse with composition in meter. Only Cunningham, of those we have considered, insists that, while "composition in meter" is not the highest possible element of poetry, it nevertheless is that which describes the common element in the total body of existent poems. His claim is modest, is historical and conventional rather than ontological in nature, and this spares him an untenable position like Campion's, where, in order to keep meter as the formal attribute and highest evaluative criterion of poetry, one winds up trying to undo the whole history of verse and to resurrect the "better . . . custom of numerous [quantitative] poesy." Cunningham establishes no more than that there is a genus called poetry of which—as we all knew until about two generations ago—there are a multitude of species. Things such as "fiction," "philosophy," "imitation," or the "nonliteral" may help describe the virtues a poem can achieve, but meter is the first rule of the "game" in which such achievements are possible. Although to cling doggedly to Cunningham's minimal definition of poetry as metrical composition may discourage us from discovering many richer things about it, his is the most satisfactory account we have thus far examined.

Many contemporary poets would argue that there *must* be limitations to Cunningham's otherwise compelling argument because they do not see meter, verse, as essential to poetry at all. It is certainly possible that such resistance stems from nothing more than a protracted cultural forgetting, where a great number of otherwise literate and literary persons can neither write in meter nor even reliably detect it, but still think they know poetry when they *see* it. For such persons, "verse," in the sense of rhyme and meter, has become so alien to them that it at best seems, not a law threaded through and guiding poems, but some kind of arcane imposition upon it. Therefore, as time passes, it becomes more rather than less difficult to argue for the centrality of meter and rhyme to the practice of poetry. The lesson poets learn from its having once been so central is that poetry may be constituted by any set of apparently arbitrary and senseless rules. Poetry goes on, sort of; meter comes to appear ever stranger, and this strangeness becomes a license to do all kinds of silly things, as we shall see.

It sometimes seems as if contemporary poets and readers of poetry are akin to the population in the cult novel, *A Canticle for Leibowitz* (1960): a curious, post-apocalyptic race that, living in the rubble of western learning, has stumbled upon a book of verse it cannot read, as reading once was done, but which it can venerate and speculate about, free of the historical knowledge that might direct those speculations to the truth. "We can tell this book was important," they murmur, "because it has a leather binding and there is a picture of the author on the jacket. We see the words are staggered on the page in some kind of pattern, and so we will honor it with our imitation." As they scratch and paw at their own "poems," they admire most those that most appear to stagger their lines after the fashion of that runic book, and praise as evolution the addition of even more inexplicable white space—say, a whole inch between words. They take for an identity of essences a mere resemblance of typography. They recognize a poem's phenotype well enough, but dismiss as primitive superstition that real poetry might have a genotypic code as its essence, its formal principle. These belated children of the atom must be made to set aside their *Theological Prosodies of the Moveable Type*, they must be retaught from scratch: first, to speak without the lilting pretension of the "poetry voice" that ruins so many public readings of poems, and, second, to read the form in poetry and not just the visible surface of ink blocks and line breaks.

I said at the outset that the quest to define the "pure" poetic essence within the schema of modern ontological thought was both inevitable and impossible. As I showed, a historical effort was undertaken by those not specifically convinced by the identification of verse and poetry to determine what elusive qualities, then, did constitute the poetic. If the formal definition of poetry has failed, because, increasingly, people who consider themselves poets know little or nothing of traditional forms (save that they do not like them), the quest for some other definition will perforce become increasingly vague. This is what has happened. Since the ambition was to find a transhistorical definition of poetry that was not dependent upon any formal aspect, nor on (of course) a contingent *use* or function, one had no choice but to grasp and grasp after what it might mean for a poem to be. Reason depends on purpose—the principle of finality—to know things. But, for the modern theorist, every assignation of a purpose or use to poetry is treated as a corruption rather than a definition of the art. In consequence, poetry becomes an ever lighter, more elusive—even an impossible—thing.

Mention of Maritain and Wimsatt is sufficient to remind us that some modern inquiries into the essence of poetry have been fruitful, and that they were conducted in the context of a sound metaphysical realism that believed human inquiry could arrive at the truth about being, including the being of poetry. But, at the same time as their great work was being published, the bold pretentious blarney of the poetic theories of Charles Olson and others were also coming into being, and that sort of thing would win the day, at

161

least within literary and academic circles. Since then, we have seen honest ontological efforts flag, and what Hollander calls the pretentious "non-useful fictions" of modernist and postmodernist manifestos compete with each other in becoming ever more unserious and subjective. The essence flees like a will o' the wisp. So much so, that our time bears witness to a profusion of rich language about poetry that tells us nothing about its putative object but serves, rather, as what Maritain called a "reverse sign." It reveals only the eccentricities of its author.

Poets now are always telling us the wonderful things poetry does, but like lovers in a decadent culture, their interest is in seduction and the appearance of earnestness rather than in truth. Their language becomes inversely more rich and lush with affectionate nothings for poetry as it becomes less substantive. Consider, for example, Ethan Paquin's review of Devin Johnston's *Telepathy*, with its well lubricated terminology that lets meaning slide by on grease:

It comes as no surprise that Devin Johnston had to go all the way to Sydney to get his superb first book published. At once casually introspective and rigorously musical, *Telepathy* nestles in nicely with Paper Bark's progressive oeuvre, not to mention that of the Oz poetry scene in general. While many American large presses continue to favor complacently autobiographical verse (much of which pays homage to the self and its travails at the expense of poetic form) and many smaller, independent houses inundate readers with a younger set's vacuous, hollowly ironic mode, writers like Johnston are developing a complex, resonant hybrid of carnival music and classicism. These poems are flashy but not without substance, sophisticated but never distractingly cerebral, painstakingly structured and curious of the world outside the poet-self. Forward-looking lines such as "starlings flock / or skirr / for cockling crust / and pithless hull," "Tract or blade / would scarp a hill / / neither 'mine' / Dear Loss, nor 'made'" and "Sunset, septic rose / Sand would turn to glass / and skies absorb its ash / if sun but chose" hark back to a poetic tradition centered on the sensible, well-turned phrase rather than bland, arbitrarily broken prose. Johnston's centerpiece, the annotated title poem—as well as longer poems like "Commentaries on 'The Witch of Atlas'" and "Molloy and Mollose"—is both lapidary and elusive, fringed with subtle gems ("Three paths were open to me, / all equally impassable") and enigmatic verité narrative ("I hovered in / syringa's meager shade / where the keeper cupped / a little bird"). In one poem Johnston implies the mental process is that of "the dull metal blade / [that] divides, divides," but the poet himself is unencumbered by such mechanism.

It is clear enough that I, too, dislike the bulk of "confessional" poetry published in America, and so I have no argument with Paquin's effort to couch his review within a critical scheme that questions the status quo. But interpolation unsupported is mere posturing, while brave words with only bluster behind them amounts to the dissimulation of a careerist. I have no quarrel with Johnston's book; I have not read it. But this review tells me two things with which some quarrel should arise. First, the passages Paquin quotes are so unexceptional that I can scarcely see what makes them worth quoting, save that they represent the typical "intensely" evocative, pseudo-concrete language approved in the MFA workshop; for nearly a century now, any poetic use of English meets with contemporary approval if it snorts, scylds, scrims, and snuffs like the barnacled scarp of Anglo-Saxon alliterative verse. The institutional Grendels and Yeodans of narrative lyricism must have been on the brink of ecstasy when that bog-slobbering song-weaver, Seamus Heaney, published his translation of *Beowulf*, though surely they were disappointed to find it was not a disjunctive lyric sequence, filled with "septic roses," sand, and glass, but just a story anyone could love.

Paquin quotes these passages ostensibly to establish Johnston's unique note—so unique he had to go Down Under to get it heard! As if the presence of marsupials made the place more "open minded" about the possibilities of form than America, with her dull complacency of horses. But, again, the quoted lines stink of typicality, and this leads me to my second point. If they are so unexceptional, how can we apply the litany of accolades Paquin has assembled? What poetic tradition would not claim to be "centered on the sensible, well-turned phrase"? How exactly are these lines "lapidary and elusive, fringed with subtle gems"? The lithic language, which should call us back to foundations so secure we can stamp our feet on them, Paquin takes in hand and sets aloft to melt into air. The review is a kind of rote recitation. It seems as if the author has selected passages at random and then thrown at them familiar phrases out of the critical lexicon. We learn nothing about the poems, because the critic could not possibly mean what he says.

There is quicksand here. The house's foundation is not settling, it is disintegrating. The practical effect of all this talk is to rob the heretofore undefined essence of poetry of even the possibility of real meaning, until our old friends, form and content, become at last susceptible to a *kind* of moribund definition. We can say that contemporary poets acknowledge a poem as a poem so long as it meets the following definition of form: the lines do not look like prose on the page. Poetry becomes an amateur exercise in text design.

I am not exaggerating. When I first began writing poetry, I tried apprenticing myself to the craft by volunteering to sift the slush pile at a literary magazine. After reading through a great number of manuscripts, in a musty and smoky office, I turned to the editor-in-chief, who was similarly engaged. "I begin to doubt I would know what a good poem was if I saw it," I said. "They all seem the same, or just awful in different ways. It makes me feel like a charlatan that I even try writing." The editor listened and reflected for a time. "Well," he said, "as long as you are not using some loopy cursive font in the word processor, or centering your lines rather than justifying them on the left margin, I'm sure you are doing fine."

Open any page of a prestigious literary journal, and you will be forced to admit the man had a point. I do so now, and see that Thylias Moss has given us this formal atrocity under the title "The Subculture of the Wrongfully Accused":

Ultimately improved by it: slant light
hitting his prison obliquely

near the state bird's pointed head   accentuated
crest, the black-ringed bill

from which *wheat-wheat-wheat-wheat*
from which *whoit cheer, whoit cheer,*   *cheer-*
cheer-cheer

As I always do, when I encounter a Thylias Moss poem in a magazine, I almost skip past it, so anxious am I to flip to the contributors' page to discover what new enormity she has claimed for herself and her work this month. In the issue in which the above text appears, we find the following: "Thylias Moss teaches Limited Fork Poetics, an understanding of poetry based on complex systems, at the University of Michigan." It seems clear that all the centuries of chatter about rhyme and meter just cannot tell us what poetry is. No, we have, at last, the technology to understand poetry through the study of "complex systems," of which the text above would seem to be a bewildering example. Moss might just as honestly confess that she does not know what poetry is, or particularly care, because then it would get in the way of her filling up space on a page with text matter.

This is what "free verse" has become in our time: a recognition that only mechanical margins and taps on the space bar determine the size and shape of a poem. Not words, not meaning, not rhythm or audible order, no, nothing discernably interior to the poem can be said to direct the formal composition. It is typography all the way down.

In "The Music of Poetry," Eliot had insisted that consideration of the "whole poem" was the only manner in which to solve the "vexed" problem of free verse. Understandably, Eliot seems to have taken metered verse to be verse whose order is apparent in even the smallest units of lines and, within them, feet; and in his modernist appreciation for the synthetic operation of fragments within a single integrated poem, he resisted this immanent formal theory of form just as he would have resisted the claim (later advanced by Yvor Winters and Donald Stanford) that *The Waste Land* was not a single poem, but a catch-all

166

bundle and bungle of poems. Eliot was certainly right to draw our attention to the whole of a poem as the way to discern its form. While every poem will have individual lines that shine out, they will not make the poem itself good until they are proportioned or tuned to the whole. In most aspects of art and life we presume a larger order is indicative of microcosmic orders within it, and the microcosmic of the macrocosmic. To acknowledge that line-to-line, or this line and that are but a chaos, and yet the larger whole affirms a certain order is, admittedly, possible. But in a fully realized work, might one not expect order to be immanent to the parts as well as the whole? And that the former would in fact be the building block of the latter?

In any case, Eliot certainly had in mind the notion of "whole poem" as something internal to the text itself. That is to say, the Shakespeare play or Pound *Canto* must earn its claim to order by the language itself demonstrating a form internal to and guiding it. Hence, his poorly expressed complaint about *Hamlet* hits upon an important weakness in the play: the domination by its most gorgeous soliloquies extend and distort the shape of the play as a play. *Othello* is Elizabethan tragedy at its finest formal tautness. And yet, that play of "the beast with two backs" comprises poetic language that is more serviceable than beautiful. *Hamlet*, in contrast, is rather ragged, but as a poem, or better, as an epic poem by circumstance adapted for the stage, it has a grandeur of digression and vivid detail reminiscent of Homer.

Let us contrast the total form of *Othello*, and the imperfect but immanent form of *Hamlet*, with Moss' effusion above. In those plays, we discern an order of verse, an order of rhetoric, an order of plot. Her typographical hijinks, in contrast, bequeath us a text

167

whose order is so arbitrary—and therefore disordered despite itself—that it would not lead us to the conclusion we were face to face with a poem did not the margins of the page intrude to remind us, "This is *Poetry!*" It may not be poetry, but it is *Poetry*. It is a text that appears on a page in a magazine by that name. The text seems to be ordered by no internal principle, as if poetry had no nature, no order and unity proper to itself, but only a tenuous, exogenous, mechanical one made possible by the gift of desktop publishing. Take away the technology of print and the poem as a poem disappears with it.

We could say the same of Joshua Weiner's "Searchlight," which illustrates to even greater degree the formlessness of contemporary poetry, a period style saved from nonexistence only by a firm extrinsic reminder that a poetic essence (guaranteed by magazine margins alone) remains even where form or verse are absent:

> Eye
> turned to see you,
> mind-star, ancient
> beam
>   sharpened to a blade
> by memory
>   cutting a path through
>   many years' midnight.
>
> Tormentor, nurse,
> imp flouting a floral print;
> would that I could
>   ignore you,
> rank, delighted heckler—
>
> *Hey, fuckhead, remember when . . .*

like a lighthouse blinking
open forgotten
regrets; each
              lucent
snake hunts the weedfloor
   of a neglected garden.

This is not ungrammatical in the sense of being full of errors, it is anti-grammatical. The author's use of line seems intended to frustrate our forming words into phrases and sentences, though they finally do resolve themselves into unhappy strands of syntax. My interest here is to ask the question any casual reader would raise on seeing such eccentric spacing and line breaking. "How is this poetry?" It is poetry because the lines evocatively—evocative of what?—tatter and smatter about the page, suggestive of meanings they can never possess. Moss's lines present a clear visual order which brooks no commerce with the words printed; Weiner, in a reciprocal strategy, offers no superficial textual order precisely as if it were an omen of a gnostic or hieratic code of meaning within. There *must* be, we *must* presume, a secret order guiding this ostensibly arbitrary format.

Cunningham offered a perfectly serviceable formal definition of poetry. Poetry is metrical composition, that is to say, a composition realized in verse. Verse is internal to the poem, of its nature. Having refused this commonsense, many poets impose an extrinsic form on their poems, one per se irrelevant to the words or sentences on the page, shaping them from the outside by means that are technological and visual but inaudible and finally unintelligible. They do not mean anything, because they cannot.

Moss is specious, Weiner pretentious. It is as if we have asked them for a fork with which to eat our dinner. Having heard that forks are often set on a placemat before a meal, they hold out to us a white paper placemat besmeared with the greasy print of a fork.

9/ THE DRUNKEN DANCER

> The sea, until she nears her limits, is a
> simple thing, repeating herself wave
> by wave. But you cannot approach the
> simplest things in nature without a
> good many formalities, the thickest
> things without a bit of thinning out.
> —Francis Ponge

In a world that can publish textual "poetics" with a straight face, what is the limit where poetry crosses into prose? Well, that depends. Neither of the poems addressed earlier are grammatical sentences. They do contain words, of course, but the presence of a word or words does not itself constitute language. One must make a *proposition* to meet that bar. Cunningham, in the same essay quoted above, parses "composition," within his definition of poetry as "composition in meter," in order to note that a composition means the *composing* of words into a proposition. When contemporary poets give up typography as a means of "creating" an identity for poetry—which is a brave thing for them to do—they lapse into the prose poem. Now, the interesting coincidence to observe is that, generally, when poets cease fiddling with lineation in the prose poem, they also cease their mutilation of grammar. It is as if the loss of one eccentricity restores to the act of composition its proper matter of logic, grammar—in a word, language.

But, this loss of eccentric lineation poses a greater problem than it might seem. Having lost the "formal" identity of poetry, they are forced to seek after some kind of distinguished content that will be *materially* poetic, that will make a prose paragraph no wider than a tranche of bread appear as poetry. Because of the predominance of prose fiction, with its neo-Victorian emphasis on the *Bildungsroman* coupled with a distinctly post-Freudian obsession with the idea of intense experience as both trauma and release, most contemporary prose poems sound a bit like the early epiphanies written by James Joyce: paragraph-long tales of illumination. Take as one example a passage from Gary Young's *Braver Deeds*:

I was home from the hospital and not expected to survive. My mother had come to visit before I died. She needed my attention; she was still weak. She had tried to take her life again. I have trouble breathing, she said, and tapped a gold coin hanging from a choker at her throat. It's to hide the scar, she said, but the coin was too small. I gave her my hand to sit; I gave her my arm to rise. When friends arrived for dinner, she danced for an hour, beautifully. Everyone agreed she had a talent.

A choicer example could hardly present itself. Our narrator faces death, his mother just has. Better, she is an eccentric failed suicide, whose choice of choker serves a practical purpose, but also suggests in the instance an almost oriental exoticism. Past trauma lives into the present, and in fact defines the present as the moment where one expresses or summarizes—as opposed to resolves—one's past. As if to remind us of the romantic individualism and sublimity from which such privileging of awfulness long ago devolved, the mother is of course a dancer. The dance of the romantic lyric, the dancer as *romantic image*, which Frank Kermode's famous study of that name first described. This is a poem because it contains material elements

172

often found in poetry. It may not dance with the metrical feet of a dancer, but it does have a dancer *in* it.

The little vignettes in Young's book are usually interesting enough to stand on their own, without appealing to the term "poetry" to justify their existence. They somewhat evenly combine conventions from prose fiction and lyric poetry, as does the one quoted here. So, why not simply call them prose vignettes, or short stories? For a reason we will consider in the last chapter, there is something about the word "poetry" that is potent enough to persuade a writer to sell fewer books in order to be considered a poet rather than a fiction writer. What interests me, now, however, is that such a work sustains itself by ginning up a certain emotional intensity within a colloquial and understated narrative. To the extent that one may parse such a thing, it offers us fairly conventional lyric emotions—love, fear, irony— through narrative content and prose form. Emotional intensity, then, would seem to be what distinguishes Young's writing from just any old scrap of prose and has made it, amongst other things, a finalist for a national poetry award.

Prose poetry originates with Baudelaire, but that greatest of modern French poets believed that the only distinction between a poem and a prose poem should be its form. Hence, in a classic example of the genre, "*Enivrez-vous*," he arranges the content of his poem in a manner all but identical to that found in his or other modern poems in verse. Because he has surrendered the great tools of syllable count and rhyme to give his work form, he invokes two kinds of short catalogues— one of intoxicants, one of nature—and repeats both of them once, along with a similar catalogue of verbs, so that—despite the prose—the reader still encounters something like the refrain of a song. David Paul's translation, which is not especially lively, at least makes this application of the formal resources of song to prose evident:

> Always be drunk: That is the whole question. In order not to feel the horrible burden of Time breaking your shoulders and stooping you earthwards, you must be intoxicated without cease.
>
> But what on? Wine, poetry, virtue, as you please. But be drunk.
>
> And if sometimes, on the steps of a palace, on the green sward by a moat, in the dreary solitude of your room, you wake up, your intoxication already diminished or vanished, ask the wind, the wave, the star, the bird, the clock, ask anything that flies, anything that moans, that rolls, sings, or talks, ask what is the time: and wind, wave, bird, clock, all will reply: "It is time to get drunk! So as not to be the martyred slaves of Time, be drunk without ceasing." On wine, poetry, or virtue as you please.

In English, this retains some of the dark velvet imperative of an opium den, but it also gains in power from its resemblance to the balanced parallelisms of the Psalms. My own wonder *at* this poem, which I have always loved, though once for more adolescent reasons than now, hiccups a bit when I wonder why Baudelaire did not simply embed it in his adept alexandrines. Such wonder led me years ago to fit it into a form close to elegiac stanzas punctuated by couplet refrains, so that the poem could at last take its place as a variation on Baudelaire's famous sonnets. I was not attempting a translation, but a version (and so I re-titled it "Drink, Drink" to give it room to breathe apart

174

from its exemplar). The only concession I made to its origins in prose was to allow the first lines to stretch out across the feet in more expository fashion than might otherwise have been desired, and inserting a trochee in the fourth foot of the first line to keep the meter from sounding too much like verse right off the bat:

One must get drunk. One must *always* be drunk,
For in its haze hides every longed-for thing.
To numb yourself to leaden time which breaks
Its weight upon the back, and slowly brings
Your corpse to crawl, mired in the dirt, you must
Come drink without repose. But drink of what?

Of wine, or poetry, or virtue—such
As you prefer, so long as you drink enough.

And if sometime on the steps of Versailles;
Or lounging near some flowered ditch; or closed
In your room's torpid shade, you suddenly
Awake, your mind half-cleared and turned morose,
A furious joy now vanished. Ask the wind,
The stars, the waves, the birds, the clock, and all
That wanders, sings, creates, or speaks or shines.
Ask these what time it is and they will all
Reply. The stars, the wind, the waves, the dark
    birds,
The clock's pinned, grinding hands will answer
    you:
"It's time to drink if you would not be martyred
In Time's dull coliseum. But quickly choose

Your wine, or poetry, or virtue—such
As you prefer, so long as you drink enough."

175

Naturally, if I bothered to put the thing in verse after Baudelaire put it in prose, I must have been convinced something was to be gained. His words fit so neatly in the conventions of the romantic lyric once resituated in verse, that it is clear Baudelaire meant to distinguish it by its prose status and that alone. It is simply a lyric poem set down in prose. Its attributes include the classical tripartite structure of the lyric: a reflective inwardness that begins in an imagined dramatic situation, brings reason to bear upon it, and resolves in a kind of exhortation to the will. Though drama occasions the poem, the refrain prevents the poem from attaining to a narrative structure; it remains always a lyric one, static rather than dramatic. As Cunningham would tell us, these are so many emergent strands of poetic tradition that have been grafted onto the rootstock of "composition in meter." He would take them as wholly outside that root and dependent on it for their identity. I demur. Once these conventions and elements have emerged, they take on a life of their own. They can be detached from verse and yet clearly belong still to the art of poetry.

In contrast to Young, then, he did not intend the "prose" element to indicate one must tell a wee tale, like a novelist with asthma. Though my students seem to call every long book we read, no matter the type, a "novel," it is not the case that writing literature in prose necessitates one's writing a story. Baudelaire's experiment would suggest that a poem, once it has given up rhyme and meter, may still claim in some sense to be a poem, but it may no longer claim to be in verse. It has become prose. Eliot said there is no such thing as free verse for the poet who wants to do a good job, but his master, Baudelaire, suggests by example that there may simply be no such thing as free verse, period. In non-metrical composition, it will not be the appearance of lineation that justifies calling the thing a poem; it will be those other attributes that have become part of the poetic tradition.

In giving up verse altogether in this poem, Baudelaire is still able to give us some of the audible effects of verse along with the reflective qualities of the lyric. In doing so, he shows us that, if poetry cannot be reduced to "composition in meter," it always still depends on it. He shows us also that what makes a poem a poem is not the attainment to a certain "purity" that stands apart from all use, but its having one or more of the sundry attributes we associate with poetry proper to itself. It is more obviously a poem than the typographic hijinks considered in the last chapter, but the source of this obviousness is not in its having been composed in meter but in poetry's being a much more complex and various sort of thing than "composition in meter" expresses. To make sense of this, we will have to sort through the poetic tradition and see how the art form is defined not by a pure and simple essence, but by a composite of formal and material conventions. But, before turning to that positive project, let us explore two more negative, limit cases that reveal how lost the modern revolution against verse has left contemporary poetry and its academic audience.

10 / Outrage at the Vaudeville City Limits

> I want
> a poem as real as an Orange Julius
> —Charles Bernstein

The prose poem serves as one helpful limit case for any consideration of the nature of poetry in the modern context; it draws on a variety of conventions of content that are part of the poetic tradition in general in order to secure its identity as poetry once lineation has been surrendered. It lets us prod and poke and ask what remains once even the last typographical resemblance to verse has been justified away?

The poets quoted in the earlier chapter hold on to lineation for dear life, and so provide us yet another limit case. Without line breaks they would be without resource to show that what they write is meant to be a poem. They engage in a superficial masquerade in their use of the poetic line in order to ensure that, within the pages of a literary journal, their poems will not be mistaken for the book reviews. A fractured lineation goes hand in hand with the fracturing of grammar, so that, on the off chance some curmudgeon such as myself does not believe random or superfluous lineation suffices to constitute a poem, he will be forced to acknowledge, "Well, the language is intense, broken, and incoherent, as I am told poetry must be, so I have no choice but to call this a poem."

Defenders of this kind of writing would, of course, make a more positive case. It progresses, innovates, experimentally tests, and, above all, *transgresses* the limits or horizons of poetry. It stretches and tugs at the poetic essence in order to arrive at an ever deeper understanding of its nature. The future always looks strange to the past, and this is the future. In truth, they have so long ago left behind poetry, left the real thing *to* the past, that they are but grasping at the shadow of a shadow. It allows them to claim to be artisans of a craft, when they are but half-unwitting salesmen of snake oil. While I think most of this is insincere posturing produced in part, as I have said, by a peculiarly impecunious parody of capitalism, it has also led to a fascinating phenomenon: the idea of a "pure poetry" persists and yet thinks itself, refines itself, out of existence—sometimes inadvertently, but, as we shall see here, sometimes methodically.

Most of the poets I have mentioned continue to depend on an untenable concept of the poetic as some indefinable flight of, perhaps, the imagination, but more likely, of the text across the page. They need to keep before us the idea of poetry, that shadow's shadow, because, without it, they would not be engaged in fine art, but simply in setting text. Sometimes, however, the "transgressive" setting of text seeks not only to hold onto the pretenses of poetry, but to turn against that pretension as well. It draws on the cultural prestige of poetry even as it calls out the whole thing as a crock—itself included. Such is the supposedly radical intent of the work of the so-called Language poets (or, L=A=N=G =U=A=G=E poets, as they put it, but having acknowledged the typography I do not intend to repeat it). In this chapter, I want to consider the way in which such poets embrace poetry's historic reception as divinely inspired, prophetic, and transformative. They seek to dissolve the pretenses of poetry as a fine art; they do not ask our deference to their work just because it *looks like* poetry on the page.

Rather, they reimagine in entirely political terms poetry's supposed extraordinary kind of power, the *vates* authority of the ancient Roman poet, for instance, or the curse-effecting magic of the Irish *file*, which seems to stand outside the regimes of power as normally understood in our world. This political poetics of revolt or resistance can only be realized, however, if it is first turned against traditional claims for poetry as something distinctive, as an art form, as something at once a part of our culture and yet something heightened, set apart from and above it. For, poetry is language and language belongs to the Man. Poetry becomes, in these writers' hands, an act of transgression—first of all against itself—in order to attain a shocking wakefulness and provocative power that stands in contrast to the ideologies of a society in which, they admit, it is nonetheless embedded.

The historical avant-garde—Dada and surrealism being the chief instances—sought to reconnect art with life by collapsing the former into the latter. They were as disenchanted as I with the hollowed-out and rarified modern conception of poetry, which they saw as so many shades of social pretense, and so they shed as many unkind lights upon it as they could until it took on all the whiteness of pure experience. One was not supposed to admire Duchamp's signed urinal; one was supposed to laugh at it, and the concept of the signature, the author, behind it. The creative process, deflated thus, would no longer be a thing apart, to revere and admire as the stuff of high culture; it would rejoin us in the flux of everyday life, just as everyday life would be submerged, as they thought it should be, in the flux of dreams. Only there do we feel free. The historical avant-garde was not an advanced movement of artists, but the end of art. Rather happily, art and beauty are such certain truths of our experience that

181

the avant-garde could not dissolve our ideas of them. It did, however, cooperate with the rise of mass culture to persuade our desire for these things to look elsewhere or to remain altogether unsatisfied.

In the poems I have discussed above, one can detect skin and hair off the corpse of the historical avant-garde slapped onto the skeleton of poetry as a nice little art form that seeks to "express" "intense" "emotion." But the Language poets wanted to revive the avant-garde's spleen, its potential to annihilate art as a means of exposing the way incoherent ideologies rule social life with often undetected power. By intuition or book-learning, they tried to deploy some aspects of Foucauldian ideology critique and Derridian deconstruction to the writing of poetry, and in doing so, sought above all to reveal that art and even language itself is caught up in the vile corruptions of the western capitalist machine. Their poetry protests against that machine, but also theorizes its own participation in it. I have quoted Hejinian above; let me now cite a poem, chosen almost at random, by Charles Bernstein, which exemplifies this "procedure":

> I died in chance abandon, made the clearing
> tough to take, or went to meet a bleat of
> feigning belly crates, to fly by number to
> render coil. By bait the trough of
> toil, or tender mute the silent, shrill
> the shorn, and bear a coal to castle's
> glare. Less 'parent than 'prehended
> shakes time to bugger oil (the bellicosity out
> (of). Sponge season, or fretful tongs with
> claws.

Right. I detect an echo of "Prufrock" in that "claws," and everyone will sense the aphorism, "bringing coals to Newcastle" behind "a coal to castle's." One hears something like a principle of order emerging in the repetition of plosives (p-), s's, b's, and the rhymes on "-oil." This writing wants to make us expectant of poetry, to be sure. But its ambition is to defeat those expectations. To toy with us a moment, as if to convince us to enter into a sophisticated act of exegesis, but then to frustrate that act, to stay ahead of meaning, to escape interpretation, to evade the rage for absorption. It is to be a poem that resists becoming POETRY, or worse, LITERATURE, and so it momentarily stands apart from the white noise produced by the gears of that teratological machine, democractic capitalism. But just for a moment. The white noise is already mingled with his music, Bernstein knows.

The violent assault on art for the sake of life of the early avant-garde becomes, here, the Vaudevillian plea for freedom by someone so knowing that he certainly knows there is no such thing as freedom. There is only absorption by mass society and the passing resistance to it; a resistance made possible only by incoherence, an insistence that reality as such is floating, indeterminate, and grounded not, as we thought, in the generous light of the Good, but in the manipulative machinations, the sophistry, of the powerful. It is a poetry of political outrage that shows as much contempt for the licensed poetry of Moss and Weiner as it does for the entire world system and linguistic ideology that keeps the human mind in a condition of insoluble slavery.

How could it be solved? The poem's clearest protest here is that language itself is complicit in ideology. It is ideology. To make sense, to appeal to logic, reason, proposition, or language, is to reinforce a Leviathan so grand it does not merely blot out the sky but holds the word "sky" in its claws. In brief, the Language poets

183

tell us that the poetic is a mask, a deception, concealing poetry's effective identity with other kinds of discourse; a poem, a love letter, and a bank statement are all one. They assume that a poem no less than a stock certificate convicts one of complicity in the capitalist system, in the commercialization of the aesthetic as well as the unconscious. Art is indistinguishable from a television commercial or a commercially sold AK-47, and since the poets lack influence with Madison Avenue or Vladimir Putin, they assert their own power by standing apart in the bare light of confusion.

We say, "What is that?" not out of wonder but out of the absence of wonder. Not because we are drawn by desire to understand what we do not yet understand, but because we have no desire to know, and so are taken aback that someone should have made such a thing in the first place. Not "What *is* that?" But, "What is *that?*" Not, "Tell us what this means," but "Why would anyone want to know what that means?" It does therefore accomplish what it sets out to accomplish, if not for the purpose it intended.

Such a poetry acknowledges it cannot escape absorption, but it must resist as long as possible, and perhaps even destroy the organism of which it is a part. One begins to sense the pathos of *any* poetic ambition when confronted with one so outrageous as this. The *a priori* assumptions necessary for such a poetic to operate are as follows:

a) language is not a tool of the reason adequate for the gradual discovery of truth;

b) this is so, because language along with everything else is part of the structures of power that inform— that are the form of—society;

c) truth itself is but the form of power;

184

d) therefore human beings can neither express their thoughts in order to seek and ascertain the truth, nor can they stand in any relation to truth, because truth itself is just an immanent construct shaped by power;

e) human beings can know nothing, because truth as an object of knowledge does not exist;

f) but they *do* allow themselves to be embedded in and shaped by ideology ("truth" shaped by power);

g) and they *can* momentarily resist that shaping, though that rebellion can issue only in a shock and stillness before the sky clouds over once more.

This is the clear-eyed commonsense my colleagues invoke, when they claim to be post-humanists. To be "human" is just a social construct—a convention, not because it is a truth that has come to be held in common through experience, but a convention in the sense of something that is held, quite arbitrarily, through the invisible but tyrannical grip of ideology's artifice. But, wait. The bread and butter of poets like Bernstein lies in the academy; no one would read them, were it not for the "post-humanist" professors. And here I detect not the inescapable and nihilistic contradictions gleefully played with in Language poetry, but a more everyday, humdrum sort of contradiction, called hypocrisy.

The existence of universities can only be justified, can only be a good thing, in a humanistic society. The only genuinely humanistic societies have been those that shaped, and were shaped by, the broad tradition of Christian Platonism. In this tradition, the fundamental principle of reality is the Good whom we have come to know as God, preceding all things, producing all things, and directing all things to return to itself. Reality as a whole is formed as the good-world-order, the intelligible beauty showing forth from that cosmic circle of procession and return. Though human society consists of many and mighty struggles for power, power is relative and finite. Those who take it for the highest reality are either deceived or perverse. Through the cultivation of the intellect, the human mind can free itself from such chains, can transcend that finitude and contemplate the Good, that world-wielding Beauty of the Infinite. This is what it means to be human: to have a vocation to the knowledge of the beautiful. The university is one of the three institutions of culture that helps us to live it out, to become ever more fully human. The nature of the university is to *humanize*.

Without these propositions in place, the university cannot really be a university. It might be a habituation factory for the insignificant bodies of men who live out their days as "productive" functionaries in the social hive. The university might be a ladder of advancement to help the wealthy realize their dreams of self-fashioning and possessive individualism, and to allow a few token creatures from the underclass to share in that dream to boot. It might even be just a half-star resort for late adolescents. But in these cases, the university would be an evil thing in a worthless civilization. It would not, really, be itself. It cannot be, unless there is a Good, and unless it treats as a solemn duty the initiation of its students into the contemplation of that Good and a life of action lived in its light.

So, here lies the hypocrisy. Bernstein's project is inherently anti-Christian, anti-rational, and anti-humanist. It seems wise to the university as a factory for a technocratic regime, and yet it requires it as a place of contemplation. Language poetry would seem to depend upon the Christian Platonist understanding of the person and of reality to make sense—according to its own terms. To read and scrutinize a poem is, after all, a speculative act: it presumes that the mind at leisure can rise up to a truth beyond itself and that this is in itself a good thing. Thus, Bernstein writes his poem, and a squad of scholars engage in *theoria* about it. Are they not, in principle, taking joy in this contemplation? Is the freedom such poems promise not only available in the Good's generosity of being? Do they not sense this despite themselves?

Well, perhaps. Let's consider the only alternative. "Bernstein" exists as a kind of social-function rather than as a poet-philosopher or object of philosophical study. "Bernstein" does "work"; he produces material that seems to resist or revolt against the regime of capital and power in order to be productive. His specific productivity is the provision of fodder for that down-at-the-heel marketplace of the production of scholarship. The production of scholarship exists for the appearance of expertise. Expertise exists for the sake of official credentials. The credentials of an English professor exist to show that everything can be measured and certified, and so to justify the credentials of the professors of business and engineering. And those professors exist to show that human life may be without actual purpose, but that is no excuse not to spend the entirety of one's own life working for the making of advanced technologies or the selling of them, the consuming of new stuff and the extension of the lifespan. In a world where no one believes in an actual "better," "longer" and "more" rush in to take its place. People read Bernstein not to contemplate him at leisure, but to perform the remunerative work of interpretation that will earn them, at the least, a little social capital for being clever, or, at most, an endowed chair at one of the campuses of the State University of New York. "Bernstein" knows what he is about—I just do not think he or those who abet him know the truth.

But if this is so, there can be no "shock" of confusion produced by a Language poem—not even a momentary one—because it is already absorbed in the machine it pretends to loathe. Indeed, it is made by the machine.

What a testimony to the state of society that, only in the academy, where faith and reason ought to be cultivated by the human person for the contemplation of the Good, have Bernstein and his ilk received a serious hearing. This tells us that those academics who support and promote his work by writing books on Language poetry for the sake of tenure are in fact engaged in an enterprise (academic writing) whose proper presuppositions (such as the rational communication of truth) they do not accept, but rather dismiss as one more formal manifestation of ideological power. Those academics therefore support ideas hostile to the foundations of the university. Though they would be the first to protest the reduction of the university to an instrument of corporate and technocratic power, they are one of the most definite signs that this has already been accomplished.

Our age has quite a stable to clean. All signs point to its just continuing to dig down in the muck.

One would not need to call for a purging of books by the likes of Bernstein, of course. There can be little consequence to the ideas that subtend his work or to the publication of the work itself, except in the academy. It is very unlikely that any wide mass of people could understand his work, and it is even more unlikely that they would be convinced by it of the untruth of reality and the ideological machinations of power. Mass media and the Supreme Court suffice for that.

Language poetry provides us yet a third limit case in the attempt to sustain the life of useless poetry in a utilitarian age. In its ineffectual and purblind strategies of outrage, it shines a light on the shadow of "pure poetry" by purposefully "transgressing" the horizons of the aesthetic. It therefore achieves something— albeit something opaque and unhappy. It reveals that modern thinking about art, along modern ontological lines, has ended in the evangelical proclamation of the existence of Poetry even as the thing itself comes to appear an ever more weightless gossamer of pretension and self-deception.

For some, poetry seems to retain its identity only in the performance of external, typographic tricks, for others poetry is what it is because of certain conventions of feeling, voice, and mood derived from the modern lyric mode. But, for Language poetry, a poem is that which seems to interrupt the discourse of capitalism for a moment before lapsing back into it. It tries to remind us there is a power outside the power of this world—but the reminder lacks conviction and tells us so, because its chief technique is the production of nonsense. We have seen, in brief, three limit cases: type, tone, and transgression. Let us turn to one last, in the search for a poetic essence—one we might best call, trope.

11/ What Wyatt and Surrey Left Around

The headless men wait patiently in line.
—Alfred Nicol

In considering Language poetry, I brought my argument to that margin where poetry becomes another mode of politics—a decisively irrelevant one, perhaps, but one that has at least the virtue of reminding us of poetry's traditionally-acknowledged power that stands apart from worldly powers. It may be useless, but it can still "transgress" the regimes of use. In glancing at the prose poem, we encountered a less troubling perimeter, where all pretensions of poetic form are dropped, but where the accumulated attributes of the lyric tradition are left in place. The poem remains a poem because it retains qualities that first came into the art as ingredients of the tradition founded on the writing of verse, but which, in the course of the life of that tradition, have attained a certain independence. It retains a poetic, or more specifically, a lyric tone and mood. The other poems we have looked at suggest still another margin of formal practice: where form is everything, and yet in reality is nothing, a clashing cymbal. The shape of the poem on the page remains, or rather *something like* the shape of a poem, imposed as it were by force and not by nature. That is all.

So much for the margins; what lies at the sinking center of contemporary poetry? The answer is twofold. As Robert Archambeau observed in the passage quoted in Chapter 4, the bulk of published poetry continues to do what poems have done *en masse* for the better part of a century. It may present a short anecdote in free verse about an intensely rewarding experience, or an intensely traumatic one. It conceives of poetry primarily in terms of faintly lyrical content, adding only a greater bulk of narrative detail than one would find in the sonnets of the Renaissance, whose conventions could leave the dramatic occasion almost entirely implicit. It is fair to note the continuity of content between these poems and those of earlier periods in our literature, where intense emotion provides the occasion, concrete language whether figurative or literal (more often figurative of old, more often literal now) provides the means, and a realization of subjectivity—of a conscious experience of personhood—remains the end. What has changed, of course, is that form grows flabby, declines from meter to arbitrarily lineated prose, and the focus on intensity and subjectivity increases to keep the work recognizable as a poem. In Tom Sleigh's poem "To the Sun" we get all these qualities and even some signs that his free verse still remembers poetry's origins in metrical, real verse. He apostrophizes with the best of them,

> X-ray eye penetrating to our souls,
> show us to ourselves as we bullshit and scheme,
> help us to survive our own stung minds
> swarming day and night with cock/cunt
>   dreams . . .

In this stanza above all, but the rest of the poem as well, I hear an accentual pentameter occasionally complemented by end rhyme. But what makes the poem recognizable as a lyric to most of its intended readers is Sleigh's concern for the bestial honesty hidden in the ecstasy of our deceived and wounded experience. Lust is coupled with "disillusioned" self-

analysis; Baudelaire echoes here, or perhaps just Edna
St. Vincent Millay:

> oh blinding father, enemy of blight
> who drives us to the shade, give us this hour
> to hang by the river and pass around the wine
> until our minds buzz like hives of honeyed light.

Many poets in the romantic-macabre tradition echo
here, because Sleigh has whittled them down to the
toothpick formula of the emotional intensities of self-
contempt (we are less than we appear) and pompous
hedonism (if you get drunk enough, you can still feel
as if you were more important than you appear).

The poetry of Charles Wright, with its backyard
epiphanies, serves as a more typical example of this
school. In Wright's work, we see confirmed time and
again the searching for intensity in a dogwood tree, the
incense of *Cathay*-style Asiatic mystical indifference, or
Cantos-style erudition, followed by a retreat back into
the familiar leaves of grass. Here is how "Disjecta
Membra" starts, set, I presume, at his home in
Charlottesville, Virginia:

> Back yard, dry flower half-border, unpeopled
> landscape
> Stripped of embellishment and anecdotal concern:
> A mirror of personality . . .

Here is an excerpt from a poem set in, I believe,
Rapallo, Italy, and depicting the aged Ezra Pound:

> And now, under the fruit trees,
> the olives silver then not silver, the wind
> In them then not, the old man
> Sits in the sunfall,

Slouched and at ease in the sunfall, the leaves
    tipped in the wind.

  Here is another, set at Laguna Beach. The details
differ, but how much remains the same:

I've always liked the view from my mother-in-law's
    house at night,
Oil rigs off Long Beach
Life floating lanterns out in the smog-dark Pacific,
Stars in the eucalyptus,
Lights of airplanes arriving from Asia, and town
    lights
Littered like broken glass around the bay and back
    up the hill.

In summer, dance music is borne up
On the sea winds from the hotel's beach deck far
    below,
"Twist and Shout," or "Begin the Beguine."
It's nice to think that somewhere someone is
    having a good time,
And pleasant to picture them down there
Turned out, tipsy and flushed, in their white shorts
    and their turquoise shirts.

Later, I like to sit and look up
At the mythic history of Western civilization,
Pinpricked and clued through the zodiac.
I'd like to be able to name them, say what's what
    and how who got where,
Curry the physics of metamorphosis and its
    endgame,
But I've spent my life knowing nothing.

194

I read these poems, initially, with pleasure, but it becomes a bit like shopping in bulk after a while. I have my scoop, and there, down the aisle, sits the Wright bin, filled to the brim with interchangeable units of thought, scenery, and melancholy. Such is the inevitable weakness of the method: a certain kind of conventional content has taken the place of meter, of form, as the foundational principle of poetry, and so the subject matter, modes, style, and idiom that can be admitted as properly poetic all shrink, however various the geography.

These sorts of poems display a concentration, intensity, or even just a gentle reflectiveness on experience as ends in themselves and as the whole purpose of poetry. They circumscribe any significant implications to those experiences by guaranteeing they remain a hedonism confined to a handful of conventions thought proper to the narrative lyric. Whatever references Wright makes, for example, to the annals of learning, the ideas are always safely tucked back on their library shelf by the last line. One poem, which begins by telling us "The Buddhist monk hears all past / and all future in one stroke of the temple bell," concludes,

> Are those lights stars or the flametips of hell?
> Who knows. We dig in and climb back up.
> Wind shear and sleight-of-hand, hard cards, we
>   keep on climbing.

None of these poems seem to be about knowing anything; they are about their own process. They are settings whose small variations of detail from one another ("wind shear") set the poet's mind in motion and give it an excuse to climb, and climb again. There are no "hard cards"; every poem deals us roughly the same hand.

And yet, there is an attractive portentousness in a Wright poem that rewards study and contrasts favorably with the increasingly common free verse anecdote about how unexceptional and banal everyday life can be. Now, the supposed pathos of modern life is that boredom itself seems to be a modern invention; the times themselves are boredom, punctuated by exploding bombs and repeated genocides, but boredom nonetheless. It will not go away unless modernity goes first. The great poem of this genre remains John Ciardi's "Suburban," and it does too much credit to later practitioners of this mode to let them share in Ciardi's wounded reputation. And yet, the suburban school of poetry is prolific indeed; if one wishes to discover what mediocre minds think about mediocre experiences, one need only turn to the epigones of Ciardi for . . . consolation? Confirmation of one's own benign insignificance? Maybe just confirmation of one's prejudices. Let's give Ciardi himself the last word, as he carries a misidentified clump of dog manure from his neighbor's garden to his own:

> I bore the turd
> across the line to my own petunias
> and buried it till the glorious resurrection
>
> when even these suburbs shall give up their dead.

One trouble with this whittling down of the poetical to the narrative lyric is how susceptible everything becomes to paraphrase. I am no believer in the strict dispensation of Cleanth Brooks' "heresy of paraphrase" (of course, neither was he). If a poem is grammatical, by which I mean if it is actually constructed of language, some kind of paraphrase can always be made. The narrative nature of all the arts makes them "paraphrasable," so that the best critics of, say, Rothko's painting understand that a particular narrative crowds the margins of the canvas to make the paint upon it meaningful, intelligible, even if the painting itself is non-representational. All art works can in some sense be expressed in paraphrase. But the Wright and Ciardi types of poetry (with due deference to the work of their eponymous authors) always seem *less* rather than *more* interesting than the brief prose summary one might give of them. Life is intense! Sex and Nature are Good! Sex in nature better! Mowing the lawn is dull, as is my consequent alcoholism! I'm divorced, therefore I chocolate! (Chocolate is a verb now.) Poetry becomes variations on a few themes, but the themes and variations themselves all blend together until it seems that each poet is the author of—at most —one poem. All the rest is bulk.

If the narrative lyric occupies most of what space there is at the center of contemporary poetry, it has been increasingly crowded out by poets descended from what is often called the New York School of poets, including John Ashbury and Frank O'Hara. David Yezzi, in the *New Criterion* (April 2006), diagnoses this mob as practitioners of "unrealist" verse. Yezzi defines "unrealism" as poetry written in the "tradition" of surrealism long after that French avant-garde movement—its high ambitions and the historical conditions that made those ambitions seem desirable—has disappeared, leaving only the exoskeleton of its supposed "style." Indeed, the moment surrealism could be said to have a style, its manifestos and dreams failed. Nothing could have proved it more dead than Dana Gioia's essay, some years back, on the American contemporary "surrealist" poet, James Tate. Gioia saw in Tate's work a poetic expression of the scene from *Dumbo*, when the wee elephant with the big ears drinks big from a barrel of alcohol. Tate is a hilarious poet, but, if he is a surrealist, it is in the tradition of Walt Disney rather than André Breton.

Yezzi's article compares these superficially similar traditions by holding up older surrealist verses, quoted from Mary Ann Caws' *Surrealist Love Poems* (2006), alongside recent poetry from Michael Dumanis and Kate Marvin's anthology *Legitimate Dangers: American Poets of the New Century* (2006). One sees that the surrealists of fifty or eighty years ago, like the contemporary poets in the anthology, exhibit an obsession with novelty that leads merely to repetition. They pursue it by combining words so as to defy all logic. Usually, as in many of the poems I have quoted in this book, they break down grammar so as to free language for curious juxtapositions. A lover's heart compared to Jell-O in a Child's hand; a half-century long list of incomplete, telegraphed declarative sentences; playful uses of parentheses and other punctuation. Yezzi writes, "The sad fact is, it wasn't all that great the first time around, but at least then it had a certain amount of energy and subversive humor. Now it just seems like watery gruel served up by a stern and superior matron." What sets it all apart from the conventional narrative lyric is that no scenario or speaker, at least not usually, can be distilled from the poem. The mind of the poet, as it were, behind or above the poem is simply mixing strands of language into concoctions and betting that some of them will surprise.

For the reader of the English poetic tradition, such poetry will seem more alien, at first, than the narrative lyrics we examined just above. My interest here is to show that this is not exactly the case. In George Puttenham's *The Art of English Poesy* (1589), a book that draws together much of the poetic theory of the Renaissance into an intelligible whole, he divides his subject into three parts. The first, on the role of the poet and the kinds of poetry. The second, on prosody as we now typically conceive it: meter, rhyme, and stanza. The third, and longest, on "Ornament," by which he means the two main sorts of figurative language, scheme (syntax and phrasing) and trope (metaphor and other types of analogical language). In Aristotle's *Poetics*, the philosopher had reserved much, but not all, of this third part for discussion in the *Rhetoric*. Metaphor, or trope, alone had to be discussed in both the context of poetry and oratory. But Puttenham would restore all to poetry. The poet is the most august maker, the primeval philosopher and priest, the originator of law, politics, and society, the first musician, and, last but not least, the first orator in the world. He therefore makes the poet the authority of figurative language and above all of the trope. And the trope, the making of analogies in the form of metaphor, simile, allegory, or otherwise is indeed central—at least to lyric poetry.

It is so central, indeed, that the term "poetic" is used colloquially in our day to designate the use of figurative language as such. Puttenham would not complain; the poet is a maker of metaphors. Two hundred years later, at the dawn of the romantic age, this capacity for metaphor came to be identified explicitly with the poet as a visionary or oracle. To make metaphors was to show that one was inspired, that the imagination was a spiritual faculty that set mankind above the material universe, and the poet was the first man. Trope therefore became associated with the self-expression

199

of all authentically poetic activity. As the various modes and genres of poetry retreated from public culture and the lyric became the most prestigious, even the exclusive type of, poem, this focus on the figurative only intensified. The popularized form of surrealism is just one modern evidence of this; a surrealist poem is one in which the unconscious power of the mind to "dream" fuses the incongruous together into a metaphorical unity. The belated heirs to the surrealists seem therefore to be experimenting to determine how far the act of drawing analogies, of likening things within a trope, can go in serving as the essence of poetry.

As Yezzi suggests, they have probably passed the limit. "Unrealist" verse seeks to build poems out of comparisons that are more like spatial juxtapositions than conceptual analogies. Unrealists are to trope more or less what "typographical" poetry is to metrical, stanzaic form. The way a trope properly works is to state what is literally an incongruity but, upon reflection, reveals itself as a figurative identity. Take, for instance, Thomas Campion's great song:

> There is a garden in her face,
> Where roses and white lilies grow;
> A heavenly paradise is that place,
> Wherein all pleasant fruits do flow.
> There cherries grow, which none may buy
> Till "Cherry ripe" themselves do cry.

Her face "is" a garden, made of pale white teeth (lilies) and red lips (roses and cherries). One may buy the cherries, or kiss those lips, only when the lips themselves cry, after the fashion of an urchin at the marketplace, "Ripe cherries for sale!" Put abstractly, A

200

= c, and B = c, with c being some particular attribute, but A ≠ B.

The unrealists, for the most part, engage in nothing so complex. They simply stick A and B on the page together and let them jostle uncomfortably. Let us look at a few instances. Here is the beginning of a poem by Kelly Smith:

Beach tar on the soft
humidity of bruises a passing wave lifted me
face flush with its surface
I woke early   without memory   a doll's face
I woke early   I remembered
the morning changed color on the wall
and the others also waking
         noise from the dumpster
         an arm wrapping on a spool
      how in the market
tones raised themselves in helix, stacking

Here are a few lines from David Berman:

Announcement: All pupils named Doug.
Please come to the lounge on Concourse K.

Please join us for coffee and remarks.

Dougs: We cannot come. We are injured by golf
      cleats.

And here are a few lines from Yezzi's particular *bete noir*, Dean Young:

How could I not?
Have seen a man walk up to a piano
and both survive.

201

Have turned the exterminator away.
Seen lipstick on a wine glass not shatter the wine.
Seen rainbows in puddles.
Been recognized by stray dogs.
I believe reality is approximately 65% if.
All rivers are full of sky.

Young cannot seem to help but sound like some corporation's resident motivational speaker, dispensing axioms like placebo aspirins. These poets have swallowed a few pills themselves. They have heard from John Ashbery that all poetry is a self-portrait in a convex mirror, and they are at least willing to go along with the mirror part. They are with Ashbery,

> . . . sitting in the yard
> To try to write poetry
> Using what Wyatt and Surrey left around,
> Took up and put down again
> Like so much gorgeous raw material . . .

The aggravating thing is that the only "raw material" they have discovered in Wyatt and Surrey is the trope. In the case of these early English adaptors of Petrarch, the oxymoron and allegory played a distinguished supporting role in the lyric depiction of interior states; in the case of the postmodern unrealists, however, the inert, discontinuous juxtaposition is a trick and their only one. Aristotle gave us the final verdict on this way of writing more than two millennia ago. Writing of the use of figurative language and "unfamiliar terms" in poetry, he observes that they are necessary:

> But a whole statement in such terms will be either a
> riddle or a barbarism, a riddle, if made up of

metaphors, a barbarism, if made up of strange words.

Unrealists are the mad barbarians of modern poetry. They give us what appear to be riddles but are in fact primitive noises whose convergence is just coincidence. If surrealism was a higher realism, descended from the heaven of dreams, the troping of the unrealists never arrives anywhere. It just keeps starting over, like a machine programmed to generate superficially different but substantively identical, and utterly meaningless, verbal objects, and left running with no one to direct it or, at last, pull the plug. Its authors will not do so, for, as we observed in Chapter 3, whether their work is good or bad does not figure. It is just something they produce in order to publish, perhaps to secure a position teaching creative writing, and to excuse their thinking of themselves as poets.

Let us draw together the points we have considered in our five-chapter inquiry into the modern muddle over "pure" poetry. The endeavor's greatest success was in making possible the metaphysical accounts of poetic language found in such theorists as Wimsatt and Maritain. One striking and mysterious aspect of many poems is their incarnational quality. They embody a concrete universal at once highly particularized and of general significance; further, the making and perceiving of poetry, in the broader sense of the fine arts as a whole, constitute a particular kind of encounter with being in its existential dimension, so that those arts are not just things made but a way of knowing reality that does not resort to abstraction. While this conception of art clearly has the metaphors of the seventeenth-century metaphysical poets close to its heart, it does not really help us specify the nature of the art of poetry.

Hollander's hylomorphic theory moved us in that direction; verse is of scheme, poetry of trope, and the poem itself a composite unity of the two. This claim does not so much break down as become overly diffuse on inspection. We gave therefore stronger approval to Cunningham's minimal account of poetry as "composition in meter," and his recognition that an elaborate and extensive number of conventions spring up from the founding principle of verse, and the sum total of those conventions constitute the poetic tradition. One strength of this theory is its reliance on formal rather than material characteristics as primary to the art *form*. Another is its reserved historicism and speculative modesty. But Cunningham's attempt to stand outside the kind of historical reflection we have described as proper to the Aristotelian tradition by definition keeps his theory from becoming complete. By dividing poetry itself from its traditions, he recuses himself from having to account for what poetry does in its fullness. But, if we are to learn what poetry is, and understand why it is a good worthy of our attention and our defense, we have to account for just this. In consequence, he leaves open the possibility that "composition in meter" may wind up being to poetry just what a "plucked chicken" is to man.

Turning from qualified approval of these mid-century theorists to the demolition of more recent poets, we saw that they, after abandoning meter, have sought to define the integrity of their art form as an art form by means of at least four ill-fated strategies. Most embarrassingly, they have tried to maintain the appearance of verse by constituting their "free verse" as merely typographic oddities on the page—ungrammatical phrases or perfectly prosaic sentences sliced and scattered in various shapes. This shows they believe that verse matters, but they have only a residual, external understanding of what verse is. They either do not understand or do not care what were the internal metrical principles that led to the lineation of poems into lines and stanzas in the first place.

In the prose poem, we see that it is possible for a work to seem poetic, even to be a poem, though it has lost even the residual visual appearance of verse. This is so, because of those various attributes, themes, and patterns of expression that emerged within the tradition of writing in verse and, as it were, took on a life of their own. In the politicized obscurities of language poetry, we found that even a group of poets who think all talk of aesthetics and the fine arts is reducible to the ideology of capitalism and the disciplines of administered society nevertheless think poetry has a momentary power to transgress, if not escape, those forces. Poetry retains a prestige even for those who think prestige itself a social construct and a cheat. In one sense, theirs is the highest realization of "pure" poetry, because it is a poetry that has been purged even of itself. It at once protests against a society given over entirely to the harnessing of things for use, for the exercise of power, and yet it does so by reducing poetry to one more thing to be harnessed for a particular kind of use: resistance and protest. Finally, while much of the mainstream of American poetry continues to cultivate lyric moods in free verse, the "unrealists" try to found poetry exclusively as a hyperactive generation of tropes. This would be too narrow a ground for poetry to occupy even if the poets were willing to use the whole range of tropes, but the unrealists exploit only a simplified, literalized kind: the spatial juxtaposition of the incongruous that issues in no deeper, intelligible common quality.

Meter, universality and particularity, being and knowledge. Type, tone, transgression, and trope. All these attributes have something to do with poetry, more or less. But our modern way of looking into things tends either to hunt out ahistorical essences, simple, clear, pure ideas, or to presume that all is merely historical and so is without lasting significance. We demand the absolute show itself, or doubt that anything at all can really be known. This leads us to settle for a kind of pragmatic view of truth that equates reason with technical expertise and knowledge with power. And, then, we see that poetry neither conforms to this sort of reason nor gives us the usual sort of power, and we wonder what it was all about. How could there be so many poems, if poems are useless? Why do so many of us keep writing them even when we no longer see the point in reading them? Why do college professors continue studying the art form, even as its practitioners have found ingenious ways to ruin it, and the professors themselves demonstrably no longer respect it?

We have considered all these questions in the context of critique. Now it is time to offer a more positive response; to recall for the reader why poetry is the highest of the arts and why the arts are among the highest realizations of culture. All this will become clear if we just ask not, what is *pure* poetry? but what—finally—poetry has been for, is for, can be for.

12/ THE PART THE MUSES GIVE US

> The mighty power of poetry and art is
> generally admitted. But where the soul
> of this power, of this power at its
> best, chiefly resides, very many of us
> fail to see. It resides chiefly in the
> refining and elevation wrought in us
> by the high and rare excellence of the
> great style. We may feel the effect
> without being able to give ourselves
> clear account of its cause, but the
> thing is so.
>
> —Matthew Arnold

"The future of poetry is immense," wrote Matthew
Arnold, in "The Study of Poetry" (1880), more than a
century ago. In poetry, he predicted, "our race, as time
goes on, will find an ever surer and surer stay," in
inverse relation to the dogmata of religion, which
seemed to be dissolving before his eyes and coming to
appear as a mere "divine illusion." For poetry, "the idea
is everything," the idea and its attached emotions, that
is, and these will endure while all our beliefs dissolve,
and life itself is "materialized" into brute "fact." It is
hard to credit such sanguine pronouncements in our
day, when, at best, a small percentage of Americans
read in the art at all, and the majority of them do so
under the rarer and rarer compulsion of school studies.

Arnold saw, as clearly as anyone could have, the rise
of mass culture in its two chief components. The
spread of democratic equality had enfranchised ever
wider swathes of society and, as it did so, the masses
had lost their respect for and deference to distinctions
of rank, intellect, custom, and tradition. Freed from
the order and restraint of such institutions, this
unformed populace was increasingly deluged by the

207

early forms of mass media—in his day, the press, with its countless newspapers, magazines, and advertisements. No longer to be ruled and guided by prescription, the people were now to be influenced and swayed by tide after tide of widely dispersed, published passions.

What both old prescription and the new manipulations of mass culture had in common, he understood, was their operation on the "unconscious"; they soaked themselves into the mind without the mind's active consent. Arnold believed that this was necessarily so. His long campaign in support of poetry, to promote "culture" as an antidote to the "anarchy" a passion-governed ochlocracy would otherwise bring, was intended to be one that would elevate the life of the unconscious in a time that had lost all sense of religious, moral, and intellectual authority. Poetry seemed a paradigm in this respect. We read it innocently, and though the poem makes no claim to material authority, it exercises a power on us nonetheless—one that Arnold believed was civilizing, cultivating, and edifying. Sidney had said one may never call a poet a "liar," because the poet makes no claim on the truths of fact, but only on the beauty of ideals. Arnold believed this was indeed the very heart of poetry, and so also believed it could continue to exercise its traditional social role in forming the spirit and imagination even if no one believed a word of it, even if in fact its readers did not *literally* believe in anything, not even the spirit. Poetry would attain religious authority and power without asking for us to assent in faith—all we had to do was "make believe," to let literary form work upon us.

If Arnold's prophecy was wrong in the material way I have mentioned—the audience for poetry has dwindled massively since his day—he erred, on the whole, in a formal sense as well. He believed that the way in which poetry gives itself to us unconsciously could not only continue, but grow, even as our conscious beliefs withered. It was not necessary to know what poetry did or why it was important, but only to receive it passively—and, evidently, he believed all important things were received in this way and that that was just as well. It was, to be sure, necessary to educate the individual in a conscious manner so as to build up a class of intellectual leaders; that was just what he intended by his main activity, the art of "criticism." But, beyond the elite, the forces that move an entire populace must be diffused by other, less exacting means. Poetry was just that part of culture —"the best that had been thought and known in the world"—which could form a wakeful elite with its serious study and the somnolent but restless masses with its beautiful dream.

As we shall see, poetry is in some ways a matter of the unconscious, not in the manipulative sense Arnold intended, but insofar as it is something given to us. The making of a poem always involves a cooperation of the writer and a gift from beyond, a discerning openness, while the practice of listening or reading involves, of course, a kind of receptivity that is consummately active. Reading can exhaust us with its demands, not just to attend to the words as they give themselves to us, but to hold onto them, to crack them open and enter into the meanings they only reluctantly disclose. Poetry may be a gift, but it is a gift that requires the fullness of our conscious intellectual and emotional lives, if it is to be received. Another thing Arnold did not quite get: poetry may be in many ways a work of artifice and the imagination, but that does not mean it operates independent of principles in reality. To the contrary, the historical tradition shows us that it depends on and reveals to us many such principles. It is no idea set apart from "fact," but a receiving of and getting at truth and being by way of aesthetic form.

In the previous chapters, we have removed some of the clutter in which contemporary practice has buried the art of poetry; along the way, we also uncovered some of its essential components. Now, it is appropriate to offer a wholly positive, and systematic account. In the following pages, I would like to accomplish two tasks. I want, first, to enumerate seven principal notes toward a definition of poetry. I believe the future of poetry could be "immense," if more of us were conscious of what the art has been and what by its nature it can and should be. Reflection on the historical life of poetry reveals its permanent importance and essential nature, both of which finally transcend that history. We need not, and should not, settle for minimal definitions, but rather should come to as clear a vision as we can of poetry as a species of saturated phenomenon. Second, through these notes, I hope to suggest the way in which poetry's saturated quality derives in part from its being an art form that is, on the one hand, received passively from different directions—by way of inspiration, social function, and tradition, chiefly—and, on the other, one in which the active, fullness of the life of writer, auditor, and reader is always engaged. The future of poetry could be immense, did we but only know a bit more about it, what it is, and what it does. "To civilize is to spiritualize," and in the life of every spiritual thing, including the arts, there is no shortcut round the conscious intellect.

1/ POETRY IS THE PARADIGMATIC ART FORM.

Consider these words of the priestess Diotima, in Plato's *Symposium*:

> Well, you know for example, that "poetry" (*Poiesis*) has a very wide range. After all, everything that is responsible for creating something out of nothing is a kind of poetry, and so all the creations of every craft and profession are themselves a kind of poetry, and everyone who practices a craft is a poet . . . Nevertheless . . . As you also know, these craftsmen are not called poets. We have other words for them, and out of the whole of poetry we have marked off one part, the part the Muses give us with melody and rhythm, and we refer to this by the word that means the whole. For this alone is called "poetry," and those who practice this part of poetry are called poets. (205c-d)

Diotima here teaches Socrates that poetry is the paradigmatic art form. I use this term in a specific sense; as paradigm, poetry is, first, the prototypical instance of making as such and, second, is also the model to which all other instances of making refer by analogy. Her etymology, better founded than most Platonic etymologies, indicates that the art of poetry reveals something to us about the nature and significance of the human activity of creation, both in that aspect it shares with other kinds of making and in three ways it is set apart from them. Poetry instances most obviously what its name indicates, the human capacity for *making*, for bringing a new thing into being that transcends any parts from which it may derive. But, as Diotima suggests, if poetry clarifies what it means to create, it does so because it is a privileged kind of creation. Poetry is that kind of making which derives from something above us; as she puts it, the Muses give poetry to us with "melody and rhythm," which is her way of gesturing toward poetry's three other distinctive elements: it is a kind of making that involves a) *Memory*, b) *Metaphor*, and c) *Meter*.

I shall specify these three attributes in the subsequent notes, but under this one I want to highlight the significance of poetry as paradigmatic. It is the *first kind* of making, in the world, and so a certain mystery and also a certain prestige cling to it. The works of most artisans are always fashioned from materials already in some sense in our possession. The act of artifice—of making—gives form to what is already present for use. In comparison with this, poetry really is original. The poet introduces into the world materials that seem to come from elsewhere. Since the romantics, we tend to think of this in terms of creativity (and, of course, Diotima uses just that word in this translation) in distinction from making; that is, making involves working on what we already have, whereas creation is strictly *ex nihilo*: the poet brings the poem into being from nothing. But, as Maritain once wrote, in truth, "we have nothing we have not received." Diotima's account of creation is to be preferred then. In contrast from all other forms of making, poetry is "the part the Muses give us." The artist always receives his material from somewhere and something beyond himself; it is not simply there for the taking, but must rather be received.

The originality of poetry is therefore to be thought of in these terms: the poem is the place where something in some sense beyond this world first comes into the world. Homer, for instance, may retell the story of the Trojan war from out of the historical past, but the story itself is not simply lying in the past and waiting to be refashioned as a poem. The events have first to be

212

bundled up and given to him as a story, as something altogether new, by the muses:

Sing, goddess, of Peleus' son Achilleus' anger

This is poetry's mystery. What was not ours has been given to us. And it is also the source of its prestige. Even for those who do not read actual poems, poetry remains the point of comparison, the term of praise, for the well-made thing. This explains why those I have criticized earlier in this book seek still to call their arbitrarily lineated concoctions poetry, and why many a writer who might otherwise gain a wider readership and a more lucrative book contract as a novelist persists in calling his little paragraphs "prose poems." They sense, as do we all, that every act of making is an attempt to re-ascend to origins, to get back to the font at the edge of the world, where muse and poet touch.

2/ IN THE ANCIENT AND MEDIEVAL WORLDS, POETRY'S DIGNIFIED STATUS IS ATTRIBUTABLE TO THE THREE ELEMENTS OF MEMORY, METAPHOR, AND METER—AND THE SOCIAL FUNCTION THEY PERFORM: NARRATIVE.

What elements of poetry do the muses give? They are three. First, by *Memory*, I refer most directly to what the Greeks seem to have intended by an activity born of the muses. Of the nine muses, five govern different genres of poetry; but, more importantly, all nine are the children of *Mnemosyne*. Memory is the mother of the muses. This informs us that the Greeks understood the arts as an essentially story-telling activity; memory is the repository of those completed forms lifted from the past, ideal and organic wholes, that are stories, which are then wrought as a sequence of events, a plot, which may be taken in and contemplated in the

213

memory of its audience. Where, for instance, did Homer's muse, Calliope, get the materials she will "sing" as the story of Achilles? From memory, of course.

For Aristotle, in the *Poetics*, it was in the imitation of human action, that is to say, the making of plots, or story-telling, that the essence of poetry consisted, and which made it a distinctly philosophical activity. Important though they are, he denies that either meter or metaphor could account for what makes a poem a poem—only the plot-form can. By contemplating the total form of a story, all its plot, action, and characters together as a unity, the mind could rise from a knowledge of individual characters and events to the height of universals. Though it will be a familiar passage to most readers, it is worth quoting Aristotle's account of these points:

> The distinction between historian and poet is not in the one writing prose and the other verse—you might put the work of Herodotus into verse, and it would still be a species of history; it consists really in this, that the one describes the thing that has been, and the other a kind of thing that might be. Hence poetry is something more philosophic and of graver import than history, since its statements are of the nature rather of universals, whereas those of history are singulars. By a universal statement I mean one as to what such or such a kind of man will probably or necessarily say or do—which is the aim of poetry, though it affixes proper names to the characters. (*Poetics* 1451b)

Story-telling regarding human actions constitutes a mode of philosophical inquiry and so a means to *ethical* truth, which, for Aristotle, is a great, but not the

214

highest, kind. Later commentators on Aristotle group the *Poetics* alongside his logical treatises as part of the *Organon*, that is, that body of texts where Aristotle shows us the different routes we may take to arrive at knowledge. Exalted though *poiesis* may be, it was still related to a practical activity, human action per se, and so inferior to *theoria*, to the contemplation by the speculative intellect of the divine.

Everyone will recall that, in the *Republic*, Plato has Socrates speak of a supposed "ancient quarrel" between philosophy and poetry, one that provokes him to exile the poets from the city altogether. Having deprecated the poets for imputing salacious actions to the gods, in one place, and for being mere imitators of goodness who do not know the thing itself, in several others, Socrates will, in the *Phaedrus*, rank them as *literally* sixth-rate human beings. He does so for the very reason Aristotle praises poetry: it is a mere imitation, and so it is all too "earthly." But he says this in a very surprising context; Socrates is himself reciting a palinode, a poem where the poet repents of a previous statement. His poem, he says, will tell what no earthly poet's poem has ever told before; it will disclose to us that "place beyond heaven," the "plain where truth stands," where being truly is, and so the eternal reality of subsistent ideas that are "the subject of all true knowledge." He can disclose these things only because he is reciting a poem, a gift of divine madness, and poetry seems to consist of speaking by way of *Metaphor* in the broadest sense.

In its exemplary form, as Socrates conceives it, metaphor is a concrete image of a purely intelligible truth. Its elements of trope and analogy make it possible for the highest reality to be in some sense seen and known by the human soul. Socrates sings to us that the soul is a chariot drawn by two horses around the

215

circular horizon of the heavens; that the form of a material body figures forth and participates in the ideal form of Beauty itself. This is the second sense in which poetry is given by the muses. By the use of *Metaphor*, it reveals what the senses could not discover: the highest mysteries of reality, including the nature of being, goodness, truth, and beauty. Contrary to our expectations, Plato seems to hold a higher valuation of poetry than Aristotle. What Aristotle praises, Plato dismisses, but only on his way to resituating poetry as essentially metaphorical and therefore metaphysical. The true poetry is not an imitation of human action, but a disclosure of being itself.

Aristotle and Plato respectively honor poetry as divine in terms of the mnemonic and metaphorical muses, but Diotima's speech makes clear there is a third element to poetry that also sets it apart as the paradigm of making. She tells us that, whatever else the "Muses give us," they give it with "melody and rhythm." The meter, the measure, of the poem is what subtends and holds together its other elements. *Meter* is the ground of poetry, as being is the ground of reality. As such, meter holds memory together; it is time's plot. And meter enacts in itself an intersection of the individual and temporal with the universal and the eternal; it is intrinsically analogical and, so, metaphysical. We shall deepen our understanding of this below.

In the ancient and medieval worlds, Aristotle's understanding of poetry probably came closest to unanimous commonsense. That memory is the mother of the muses should tell us that the remembering of stories was thought to be both the source of the fine arts and their main social function. If memory is the font of the arts, then those genres whose forms are shaped around plot—above all, epic and drama—will be thought the highest, with all others following at a

216

distance proportionate either to how important is the narrative they can tell or how little narrative content they have. But, even here, it would be impossible simply to sort out the three elements from one another. Poetry's prestige began in meter, because it was meter that made possible the *public recitation* or performance of stories. Poetry could tell the "whole tale of the tribe," the stories shared in the communal memory and experienced together in the retelling. In brief, *meter* made poetry *memorable* (mnemonic) so that *remembered stories* could be *performed publically*. Poetry was an art of ancient tales and stately rhythms, and, as in Plato's account of metaphor, the public story revealed to a people the otherwise elusive truth about itself.

I argued, in Chapter 6, that poetry has retained and should retain its narrative modes in our day. But its social function has been reduced almost to nothing. The major media for the telling of stories, at present, are film, the novel, and to a much lesser extent the magazine short story and the prose stage play. All of these have proven flexible, but not necessarily superior, means of story-telling. We even read novelizations and watch film-adaptations of ancient epics. But, when I read the Mandelbaum blank-verse translation of the *Aeneid*, I see that meter can attain a dynamic power that prose seldom can. Consider the perfect pacing of action, emotion, and gravity in this scene from Virgil's second book. Aeneas is reciting to Dido and her court the sacking of Troy; in King Priam's palace, this decisive slaughter occurs, at the hands of the late Achilles' son Pyrrhus (also called Neoptolemus):

> But then Polites, one of Priam's sons,
> who had escaped from Pyrrhus' slaughter, down
> long porticos, past enemies and arrows,
> races, wounded, across the empty courts.

But after him, and hot to thrust, is Pyrrhus;
now, even now he clutches, closing in;
he presses with his shaft until at last
Polites falls before his parents' eyes,
within their presence; he pours out his life
in streams of blood. Though in the fist of death,
at this, Priam does not spare voice or wrath:
"If there is any goodness in the heavens
to oversee such acts, for this offense
and outrage may you find your fitting thanks
and proper payments from the gods, for you
have made me see the murder of my son,
defiled a father's face with death. Achilles—
you lie to call him father—never dealt
with Priam so—and I, his enemy;
for he had shame before the claims and trust
that are a suppliant's. He handed back
for burial the bloodless corpse of Hector
and sent me off in safety to my kingdom."
The old man spoke; his feeble spear flew off—
harmless; the hoarse bronze beat it back at once;
it dangled, useless now, from the shield's boss.
And Pyrrhus: "Carry off these tidings; go
and bring this message to my father, son
of Peleus; and remember, let him know
my sorry doings, how degenerate
is Neoptolemus. Now die." This said,
He dragged him to the very altar stone,
with Priam shuddering and slipping in
the blood that streamed from his own son. And
        Pyrrhus
with his left hand clutched tight the hair of Priam;
his right hand drew his glistening blade, and then
he buried it hilt-high in the king's side.

218

Virgil and his translator have given us a narrative of perfection. When I read Frost's narrative poems, I find also that verse facilitates a laconic voice for story-telling superior to that found in such prose minimalists as Ernest Hemingway and Raymond Carver. Mason may well be correct to assert, in the afterward to *Ludlow*, "verse is often more cinematic than prose." Reading or listening to poetry is not, however, anywhere near as passive an activity as film can be, and this alone will suffice to keep its social function for story-telling marginal. One just hopes its virtues might be more often appreciated and exploited, especially for those stories of either ethical import or cultural identity that a people most needs to hold in common if it is not to be a people in name only.

3/ POETRY'S PRESTIGE IN THE MODERN WORLD IS ALSO ROOTED IN MEMORY, METAPHOR, AND METER, BUT ITS MAIN SOCIAL FUNCTION IS LYRIC RATHER THAN NARRATIVE

With the invention of movable type, the lyric mode of poetry began its ascent from a minor to a primary rank in the hierarchy of poetic types. The "shorter poem," lyric or lyric-like, is now what most people think of as the paradigm of the art. Though this shift was already underway during the Renaissance, the lyric was still thought of as minor. As late as the twentieth century, poets such as John Crowe Ransom and Allen Tate viewed it as a tragedy, a sign of the impoverishment of the modern world, that the only kind of poetry they felt capable of writing was a "minor" sort, by which they meant the lyric. Where were the great themes, what was the acceptable form, they asked in frustration, that could help them fashion an epic for our time?

In the Renaissance, poetic drama and masques were of course widely performed—they define the age for us—and lyric poems were frequently intended for musical performance as madrigals or lutenist song. But, things were changing. Lyrics for music were collected in the various song books of the age, and, a century after the invention of moveable type, in the middle of the sixteenth century, an anthology of lyric poems usually called *Tottel's Miscellany*, or *Songs and Sonnettes* (1557), appeared in England. One could now purchase a book of short poems and read it silently, in private. As Paul Oppenhemier and other scholars of the period have argued, poetry was no longer conceived of primarily as public performance, but as an occasion for private reflection.

The lyric poem was one conceived on a "conceit," or subject matter, suitable for such reflection. It was composed in meter, and almost exclusively in rhyme, in part for mnemonic purposes, but primarily because meter, rhyme, and stanza were figurative. They served as signs of craftsmanship, constituting the poem as having a well-wrought, rhetorically intricate form. The use of scheme (the figures of speech of meter and syntax) was complemented by what we saw Hollander refer to as the language of the nonliteral, metaphors and similes, in a word, tropes. Scheme and trope were combined to make possible the representation of what would otherwise be unrepresentable—namely, interior states. In the modern period, lyrics attain to an almost complete inwardness and focus on subjective experience: they are increasingly read silently (internally), their conceit is on an interior subject, and, above all, the composite of scheme and trope excels at representing the interior life.

In the early days of what Yvor Winters calls the English native tradition, the lyric poem tended to represent what was unrepresentable only because it was abstract. Narrative poetry dramatized a theme or lesson, one might say, but the lyric could state outright its matter in a sententious, plain style, often beginning with what the Christian contemplative tradition calls a "simple proposal." Barnabe Googe, one of the most "brusque" poets of the plain style, begins "An Epitaph of the Death of Nicholas Grimald," with this simple summons to contemplate our mortality:

> Behold the fleeting world, how many things fade,
> How every thing doeth pass and wear away;
> Each state of life, by common course and trade,
> Abides no time, but hath a passing day.

Though everything he says here could be shown, his art is to tell in summary fashion. Googe's best-known poem enjoins a response to this mortal condition, but it is not that of Christian teaching. The author of *Everyman* would recoil in horror:

> Give money me, take friendship whoso list,
> For friends are gone come once adversity,
> when money yet remaineth safe in chest

George Turberville's "To One that had Little Wit" shows us how closely the plain style lyric can come to identity with the epigram, to a concentration with almost no room for the concrete image:

> I thee advise
> If thou be wise
> To keep thy wit
> Though it be small:
> 'Tis rare to get
> And far to fet,

'Twas ever yit
Dearest ware of all.

Many poems of the period are not only lyric and
undramatic because they are abstract, but because they
view human life as best attained when it retreats from
the world of action to the stasis of thought, as in
Edward Dyer:

My mind to me a kingdom is;
Such perfect joy therein I find
That it excels all other bliss
That world affords or grows by kind:
    Though much I want which most would have,
    Yet still my mind forbids to crave.

The lyric therefore summons us to a distinctly inward
way of life and does so by eschewing the allegorical
figures of a medieval play like *Everyman* or many
Renaissance narrative poems, such as Spenser's *Faery
Queen*.
Mention of Spenser leads us to observe that, during
the same period as this plain style lyric was being
mastered in English, the influence of Petrarch and the
Continental Renaissance was leading to an increasing
sophistication of how the interior life was to be
perceived and to be represented. The Petrarchan
movement made romantic love and its suffering a
major theme for the lyric, and thereby claimed the
interior states most worth representing were those of
complexity and conflict, in a word, ambivalence.
Winters and others have claimed this often led to
superficiality and silliness. They may have a point, but
the real contribution of the movement was its
innovations in finding poetic language adequate to the
representation of ambivalence. The plain style was

focused on the interior chiefly in the sense of giving us thoughts that are the final outcome of a previous, undramatized deliberation, and so have been distilled into abstract statements. In contrast, the Petrarchans developed the use of tropes to give a fullness of representation to the truly unrepresentable, concrete expressions not simply of thoughts but of conflicting thoughts and the resultant conflicted feelings. Thomas Wyatt's sonnet, "Description of the contrarious passions in a lover" is an English prototype of such poetry, if not itself a great poem:

I find no peace, and all my war is done;
I fear and hope; I burn, and freeze like ice;
I fly aloft, yet can I not arise;
And nought I have, and all the world I season.
That locks nor looseth holdeth me in prison,
And holds me not, yet can I 'scape no wise;
Nor lets me live, nor die, at my devise,
And yet of death it giveth me occasion.
Without eye, I see; without tongue, I plain;
I wish to perish, yet I ask for health;
I love another, and thus I hate myself;
I feed me in sorrow, and laugh in all my pain.
Lo, thus displeaseth me both death and life,
And my delight is causer of this strife.

Wyatt's poem represents ambivalence, passion with despair, in oxymoronic lines that are still abstract. But the Petrarchan emphasis on trope, already achieved here, made English lyrics increasingly sophisticated in their use of the figurative image. Poems rooted in the conceit of the "simple proposal" began to give way to another "conceit," what the Christian contemplative tradition calls the "composition of place." The poem begins in what the imagination *sees*: it is occasioned by a clear if implicit dramatic scenario, and leads us through a tripartite movement of the mental faculties. First, the imaginative composition giving us scene or scenario; second, rational reflection upon it; and third, a resolution of the will in response to it. All this converges in Michael Drayton's *Idea* 63, for instance, where the allegory remains interior and serves as a supple mode for representing love's sorrow, writing, "Now at the last gasp of love's latest breath, / When, his pulse failing, Passion speechless lies."

Though not usually regarded as a major poet, the Jesuit martyr, Robert Southwell provides us an especially important example of the potential of Petrarchanism, because so much of his work was devoted to advocating the migration of the lyric from the terrain of inward romantic emotions to the more purely spiritual themes of the contemplative life. Consider how much more imaginatively concrete and intellectually complex are these stanzas from the poem, "Look Home," than that from the Dyer poem we looked at above, though both are on the same theme:

> Retirèd thoughts enjoy their own delights,
> As beauty doth in self-beholding eye;
> Man's mind a mirror is of heavenly sights,
> A brief wherein all marvels summèd lie,
> Of fairest forms and sweetest shapes the store,
> Most graceful all, yet thought may grace them
>   more.

> The mind a creature is, yet can create,
> To nature's patterns adding higher skill;
> Of finest works wit better could the state
> If force of wit had equal power of will.
> Device of man in working hath no end,
> What thought can think, another thought can
>   mend.

I count eight concretely imagined tropes in twelve lines. So also, his meditation on a death's head, though little more concrete than a tersely imagined early effort by John Skelton, realizes the theme of mortality with a greater precision and vividness than did the Googe poem we read above:

Before my face the picture hangs
That daily should put me in mind
Of those cold names and bitter pangs
That shortly I am like to find;
But yet, alas, full little I
Do think hereon that I must die.

I often look upon a face
Most ugly, grisly, bare, and thin;
I often view the hollow place
Where eyes and nose had sometimes been;
I see the bones cross that lie,
Yet little think that I must die.

I read the label underneath,
That telleth me whereto I must;
I see the sentence eke that saith
Remember, man, that thou art dust!
But yet, alas, but seldom I
Do think indeed that I must die.

These are just a few of the poem's stanzas, but even in their short space, notice how they draw us from the picture as a whole, to the skull itself, and on to the motto beneath, tracing the interior or subjective movements of the speaker's mind. Southwell's example demonstrates the potential of the modern lyric to record the interior with perceptivity, precision, and concrete imaginative genius. It combines the moral and rational seriousness of the native style with the figural imagination of the Petrarchans to achieve a whole many times greater than either by itself.

All the elaborate developments the lyric would undergo in the romantic and modernist period, and even those farther flights we find in the contemporary variety, are already present *in nuce* in Southwell's poems. I mean this in terms of the radical development of the use of trope, but also in terms of the extension of the "conceits" of the lyric from profane to divine love, to the romantics' contemplation of the imagination as a faculty of the sublime and absolute, and on to the modernists' familiar focus on the "thingness" of things, the concrete nature of material reality, which finally serves as a pathway to the interior contemplation of being and Being Itself, whom we have come to know as God.

Some of the monuments of later stages of this development include: John Donne, "Good Friday, 1613. Riding Westward"; George Herbert, "Church Monuments"; Henry Vaughn, "The Lamp"; William Wordsworth, "Lines Composed a Few Miles above Tintern Abbey"; S.T. Coleridge, "This Lime-tree Bower, My Prison"; John Keats, "Ode to a Nightingale"; Alfred Tennyson, *In Memoriam*; Gerard Manley Hopkins, "Hurrahing the Harvest"; W.B. Yeats, "Among School Children"; Wallace Stevens, "The Idea of Order at Key West"; Allen Tate, "Ode to the Confederate Dead"; Yvor Winters, "A View of Pasadena from the Hills" and "To the Holy Spirit"; Richard Wilbur, "Love Calls Us to the Things of this World"; Helen Pinkerton, "Celebration"; and Kevin Hart, "The Room."

With the ascent of the lyric to primacy among the types of poetry, we come to think of the poem as a vehicle of the contemplative and imaginative life rather

226

than as a medium of public stories. And though, as we shall see, poetic meter was always thought of as intellectually and spiritually significant, its movements increasingly become identified with the movements of subjectivity, of the deliverances of the mind as a faculty of reason, emotion, and will. Blank verse, for example, with the achievements of Milton and Wordsworth behind it, will sometimes be called, "divinized prose," not only because of its spiritual subject matter and elevated style, but also because of its power to shape the interior man. Winters would define the poem as "a statement in language about a human experience . . . more or less rational . . . [using both] connotation and denotation," and "usually metrical." He elaborates on its function thus:

> The conception which I am trying to define is a conception of poetry as a technique of contemplation, of comprehension, a technique which does not eliminate the need of philosophy or of religion, but which, rather, completes and enriches them.

And, a few pages further on, he concludes, poetry

> should offer a means of enriching one's awareness of human experience and of so rendering greater the possibility of intelligence in the course of future action; and it should offer likewise a means of inducing certain more or less constant habits of feeling, which should render greater the possibility of one's acting, in a future situation, in accordance with the findings of one's improved intelligence . . . it is the richest and most perfect technique of contemplation.

These lines of definition could in principle apply to any poem, indeed almost to any work of literature. But what Winters captures with great power is how poetry comes to appear in the age of lyric. Story-telling has been reduced to "experience." The language may be literal ("denotation") but especial emphasis is given to the use of tropes to evoke the movements of feeling ("connotation"). The contemplation of the poem comes to correlate closely with the techniques of contemplative prayer developed in western monasticism and lay devotion, and in the Christian Platonist tradition more generally.

Despite the rise of the lyric to primacy in the modern imagination, however, let us keep in mind the ancient insight that narrative (gathered in memory) remains central to the arts as a whole, and that poets would err to surrender it completely, even if poetry will never again be our chief form for story-telling. Epic, drama, and the short story remain viable modes for poetry alongside the lyric, as do other short forms from satire to song, ballad, the epigram, and other sorts of didactic verse.

There is no denying the gain and insight the passage from Winters expresses, however. The rise of the lyric has helped poetry to realize itself in the mode Plato celebrates in the *Phaedrus*: poetry is ontology, giving us access to the abstract, unrepresentable, and ambivalent movements of subjectivity as it seeks to encounter and understand being and truth. Poetry never appears so powerfully as a gift or revelation as when it finds words for the invisible life of the spirit.

4/ Meter is central to the understanding of the art of poetry in the ancient and medieval and also in the modern views. Rhyme is a graceful complement to meter.

In the ancient period, *memory* appears as a primary element in poetry, whereas, in the modern lyric, *metaphor* comes to the head. But, in both periods, *meter* appears as equally important. Aristotle's comments on poetry as formed of plot more than of meter would become a source for later efforts to cut meter out of the heart of the poetic altogether. Sidney, for example, who defended the beauty of meter so finely, also bluntly denied its essential role for poetry when he spoke of most poets as having "appareled their poetical inventions in that numbrous kind of writing which is called verse." For, he proceeds to parse the word "apparel" to conclude that verse is "an ornament and no cause of poetry." In the context of Aristotle's work, we see this is misguided. In the *Rhetoric*, he tells us that prose should be rhythmical, while poetry is metrical. It is a "cause" indeed.

Meter is a further refinement of the inevitable rhythms of speech. Just as the growing child moves from halting words and phrases to sentences, and the orator formalizes our often ungrammatical speech into balanced periods, so the poet deepens the art of the well-framed sentence of formal speech by subjecting every syllable to measure. Why would the poet do this? Why would it seem so essential an element in poetry, ancient and modern?

The answer is fivefold, and I shall discuss them under the rubrics, *memorability, shaping, modality, ordering,* and *deepening*. I shall then offer a brief discussion of the late antique Christian development of rhyme as a distinctive complement to meter in Latin and the European vernacular languages.

229

As we saw in the second note, meter patterns speech in such a way as to make it *memorable*. It is mnemonic, not just in the metaphysical sense of coming from Mnemosyne, but in the more mundane sense of serving as an aid to memory. It inscribes a formal logic at the core of language so that those literate in meter can often discern what word comes next in a line because it *ought* to come, it fits. But also, the rhythm meter generates is generally resonant and haunting, so that even those unfamiliar with the technical details of prosody can nonetheless benefit from meter's presence. We all know this from our first encounter with nursery rhymes and songs, though we may sometimes mistakenly think it is melody rather than rhythm that causes these things to stick in our head. In the ages of oral, or primarily oral, culture, meter played an essential role in keeping the knowledge of a civilization in being, allowing it to be passed from person to person, generation to generation, through recitation and memorization.

Many will recall Socrates' story of the Egyptian god, Theuth, who has invented writing and promises it will help men remember things forever. King Thamus replies that it will in fact prove a recipe for forgetting. In the event, they were both correct. Writing would lead to the belated development of prose and the ability to record in lasting fashion ever greater quantities of information. But, it would also result in most persons having a diminished memory and an impoverishment of the arts of memory that sustained culture for millennia. That said, even in the age of Shakespeare, we know that the meter of the dramas continued to play a fundamentally mnemonic role for both the actors and those who attended the plays. This latter group included those who listened, memorized, and then reported what they had heard to publishers, so that pirated editions of the plays could be published.

We shall consider the classical quantitative and modern accentual-syllabic metrical systems in a bit more detail below, but here I would just note the *shaping* role of meter. I have repeatedly distinguished between the formal and material (or content), in these pages. Metrical feet give shape to the metrical line, and metrical lines to the total composition that is a poem. But, it is a strictly *formal* shaping. That is, it brings integrity and order to our words, unity to the poem, without in any way materially delimiting what those words can be or say. A rhetorical strategy like the classical periodic sentence constrains an author to establish certain mathematical proportions and parallel structures at the level of phrase and sentence. However mellifluous may be the result, it directly intervenes in the material content of the speaker. Such is also the case with, most obviously, the parallel structure found in the Psalms and many of the other material strategies free verse poets often embrace in order to give their poems the appearance of integrity (the use of anaphora, for instance). But meter is a purely analytical abstraction from sentence rhythm: "an abstraction from the live flexible movement of spoken language," as James McAuley put it. It establishes a subtle structure of feet that simultaneously gives every syllable a value and the line a perfectly regular order without determining the rhythm as a whole. Relative degrees of stress from syllable to syllable, the use of enjambment across lines, and the regular variations of the grammatical sentence (syntax and length), allows the perfectly regular metrical line to be generative of infinite variety. It is thus the most flexible formal property imaginable, but one which makes the order and integrity of a line of verse unmistakable to the eye and ear.

Another thing meter shapes is our expectations. John Hollander frequently wrote of the "metrical frame" and the modes of poetic form, both of which I comprehend under the rubric, *modality*. By the idea of metrical frame, Hollander intended that the use of certain meters or other poetic forms will create certain expectations in the mind of the reader, because that reader will already associate a particular meter with other, apparently similar, poems he has read, or with a set of familiar conventions. So, for instance, as soon as a reader recognizes a sonnet, the idea of sonnet will form a frame around the individual poem and this will, in turn, influence its interpretation. We might expect a logical structure built up over three quatrains and concluded with a final, epigrammatic couplet, and we might also expect the subject or "conceit" to be profane or sacred love. Even if those expectations are not met, they will still influence our interpretation of the poem. In the arts, disappointment is a technique.

In speaking of the "modes," Hollander refers back to the classical association of particular meters with specific poetic genres. This association was thought to be natural, according to Aristotle, but in our day we see them as more fluid, accumulating within the body of literary conventions, as additional possible sources of meaning. The ballad stanza, for instance, will be associated in most persons' minds with folk song and tale. That Emily Dickinson wrote on themes traditionally part of the lyric mode in this sort of stanza is one source of her work's eerie incongruity between the naïve and the profound.

The three attributes above are all practical in effect: they help the writer of verse to shape the work, and the auditor or performer to receive and retain it. But the next two attributes are of eminently speculative importance regarding the nature of poetry as an art. As we saw, Diotima refers to meter as something specifically given by the muses. What she seems to be referring to is the longstanding perception of the microcosmic order of the line of verse as a participation in, and revelation of, the *macro-cosmos*, the good *ordering* of being that constitutes the world as a whole. The *musica humana* of the poem is given by the divine music of the muse, and both harmonize with the *musica mundana*, the music of the cosmos.

From Pythagoras onward, the Greeks saw the discernment of number in contingent things as an apprehension of truth and being, of the eternal and the unconditioned. To recognize a particular circle—that of a wheel or a pancake for instance—as a circle is to put the mind in immediate contact with the eternal idea of circle that stands free from and above the existence of any actual circular thing. This is an insight found everywhere in Plato and Aristotle, where the perception of this good, true, or (especially) beautiful thing is a portal to the perception of Truth, Goodness, and Beauty writ-large. This Greek insight finds expression in Judaism in the book of Wisdom, where we hear that God "has ordered all things in measure, and number, and weight" (11:21). Divine wisdom is what gives number to the formless void, and our wisdom is the perception of those numbers. In the Christian Platonism of St. Augustine, we see him frequently advert to number as the primary instance in which we see the eternal *Logos* manifest itself in the created world to make that world intelligible to us. He offers a proof of the existence of God through reflection on the intellectual principle of number's presence in material nature. Matter is infinitely divisible, and so cannot be the source of the idea of one, of unity; the idea must come from a transcendent spiritual reality, and this is God. When Augustine wishes to understand how the eternal mind of God could produce the flux of historical events, he turns from mathematical numbers to metrical numbers. History unfolds like a line of verse, like a long poem with its metrical feet each distinct from one another (a dactyl, followed by two trochees, and so on, for instance), yet constituting an ordered whole. Just as the poem is one, though its parts rise and fade from existence on the voice, so is the whole span of our life one, though it stretches into the abyss of past and future and seems to exist only in the present moment. Just as the art of poetry is a simultaneous whole in the poet, but a sequential, temporal unfolding in the recited poem, so God is a simple, eternal presence, while his creation is "distended" across time and space.

This classical perception of the "numbers" of verse as indicative of the divine order was so far from being lost on early modern theorists of poetry that, in fact, it seems to have been their principal concern. Campion, even, in his desire to import quantitative meter from Latin into English, was inspired not merely because he found rhyme barbaric, but because he perceived the metaphysical significance of numbers. He tells us, like a good Pythagorean, "The world is made by symmetry and proportion, and is in that respect compared to music, and music to poetry." Sidney speaks of the "well-weighed syllables" of classical quantities, which make of poetry a "planet-like music," that is, a manifestation of the music of the spheres, of the *musica mundana*. Puttenham takes up the theme with enthusiasm. He compares the poet as maker to God, who "made all the world of nought." That they first perceive the order of things and then order it into speech makes them, as we mentioned above, the first in practically every enterprise of civilization:

> Poets therefore are of great antiquity. Then, forasmuch as they were the first that intended to the observation of nature and her works, and specially of the celestial courses, by reason of the continual motion of the heavens, searching after the first mover, and from thence by degree coming to know and consider of the substances separate and abstract, which we will call the divine intelligence or good angels (*daemones*), they were the first that instituted sacrifices of placation, with invocations and worship to them, as to gods, and invented and established all the rest of the observances and ceremonies of religion, and so were the first priests and ministers of the holy mysteries.

He is not done. They lived in chastity and "continual study and contemplation," so that they received divine visions; they were the "first prophets or seers," and all oracles given by the gods came in "metre or verse." Bringing this news of the divine order to the social order, poets also instituted culture and society, as "the first lawmakers of the people and the first politicians," who established commonwealths and brought order, virtue, and peace to the people. In the second book of the *Art*, Puttenham expressly states that proportion (measure or number) is the condition of beauty, and that meter is the proportion of verse. If the poet is the original priest, prophet, and politician—along with so much else—it is only because of meter's "poetical proportion."

This ordering principle, wherein the proportions of meter participate in or manifest by direct analogy the intelligent order of being as a whole, assigns to meter a consummate significance. And yet, it might also seem too simple, as if it were all just a one-to-one correspondence with the heavens. Thus, we should also remark meter's role in the *deepening* of poetry. Every work of art depends for its existence on being beautiful, as Puttenham claims, but beauty is classically understood as *form* and *splendor*. It realizes at once a concrete figure and the intelligible light of universal significance that radiates from it as an irreducible polarity. In contrast to the simple clarity of numbers as such, metrical numbers contribute simultaneously to the specificity and the universal significance of the poem. They particularize and deepen; they bring words to order but they also render them more complex, obscure, and layered with meanings.

John Crowe Ransom spoke of poetry as a rough composite of two parts. Its foundation is the logical or "prose" structure of meaning. But, to this, the poet adds in meter, rhyme, and figurative language, all of which he describes as logically "irrelevant," "local texture." This artificial cramming of what he sometimes calls the "scientific" structure into the intractable forms of texture ruffles and troubles the poem; it gives to the work those qualities that make it a concrete reality resistant to the rage for abstraction and use. Ransom's account is far too dualistic; as I have insisted, form and content are indeed distinct in reason, but they are one in being. Poets from Virgil to Ben Jonson, to yours truly, may sometimes draft a prose sketch prior to writing the poem itself in meter. But even here that does not mean that the meaning and texture, the content and the form, are distinct, or that the logical structure constitutes the skeleton and the rhyme or meter merely the "texture," the flesh tissue. Many poems begin as a line or two in the mind out of which the larger dimensions of the form emerge. Indeed, many begin as a sound of a metrical rhythm in the ear that only eventually takes on language; such was the origin of Turner's *Genesis*, for instance. The poem is a unified whole; any distinction along these lines is in the reason not the poem, and the sequence of composition has nothing to do with it.

These criticisms noted, Ransom has a point. All things are polysemantic; their meanings are deep, multiple, and at times in tension with one another. Poetry is the paradigmatic art form that exploits this depth found in reality as such in order to reveal and contemplate it. And so, myriad meanings blend within a poem, and meter in particular cross-hatches the "texture" of a poem so that new patterns emerge beyond those of syntax. The poem is a single being where a multitude of signs overlap with one another, and in which distinct orders—some logical, some alogical, some in concord, some in tension—coalesce into one.

Rhyme is something other than meter and is not as obviously essential for poetry. We saw that Campion associated it with the barbarians of the British Isles, who were only with difficulty civilized by the quantitative orderliness of Latin culture. He associates it also with the "Dark Ages," by which he means the Christian genius of the high Middle Ages. Puttenham and Samuel Daniel also remark the non-classical origins of rhyme, but perceive this as a sign not so much of rudeness as of an inheritance entirely venerable. It is a custom with all the force of common law, but also a new note, writes Daniel, "an excellency added to this work of measure, and a harmony far happier than any proportion antiquity could ever show us." Indeed, it "doth add more grace and hath more of delight than ever bare numbers . . . can possibly yield."

Rhyme first came into use in the Latin of late Christian antiquity, and this seems no coincidence. If the Greeks conceived the world as a Good-Order, and saw poetic rhythm as a participation in it, Christians joined them, but also conceived the world as a grace, a creation, a superabundance produced from nothing and for no other reason than out of God's eternal love. Rhyme itself suggests a superabundance upon meter, an order on top of an order, a grace added to grace. Meter constitutes a necessary order, while rhyme adds a note of gratuity. Like meter, it gives form to lines and stanzas; and, like meter, it cross-hatches a poem with an asyntactical logic; it attains a resonance not only across the lines of a poem, but between poems. In consequence, it adds to the deepening, ordering, modality, and shaping qualities of meter, while also making a poem much more memorable. My youngest son, who is two, is just learning his first poems. How do we proceed? I recite the opening of the line, and he provides the rhyme word. We shall build from there, no doubt as the first rhymers intended. But, someday, perhaps, he will read Wimsatt's essay, "One Relation of Rhyme to Reason," and conclude that the *mnemonic* function is only the beginning of rhyme's intellectual riches.

5/ IN ENGLISH, METER IS TYPICALLY ACCENTUAL-SYLLABIC, IN WHICH METRICAL FEET BRING TO ORDER THE TOTAL NUMBER OF SYLLABLES IN THE LINE AND CREATE A REGULAR PATTERN OF ACCENT OR STRESS.

We discussed, in Chapter 7, the difference between classical quantitative measures, which are always called "meter" in the tradition, and meter such as it is in modern English, which, because usually coupled with rhyme, the tradition often calls the two together either "rhyme" or "rhythm," both of which come from the same root. It should be clear that English meter ("rhyme") and classical quantity ("meter") operate on entirely different principles; one does not derive from the other and, indeed, they are not even mutually exclusive (Campion's poems in quantitative verse can also be scanned, he made sure, hedging his bet, according to English prosody).

The reader unfamiliar with the workings of English versification is referred to the appendix of this book. Here, I wish to make the general note that the main tradition operates according to the principle of accentual-syllabism. Of the Romance languages, French verse has end rhyme but, within the line, attends only to the number of syllables. The classical line of that language, the *Alexandrine*, consists simply of twelve syllables. In English, we attend to syllable count, but also to the number of accents or stresses in a line, and so also to how they are ordered within it. The unit for understanding this combination of syllable and stress counts is the metrical foot. From early on, English prosody has used the ancient Greek names for its feet, but an accentual-syllabic anapest or iamb is something categorically other than the quantitative feet that go by those names.

When Sidney distinguishes this prosody from the numbers of the ancients, he comments that modern verse observes "only number [of syllables], with some regard of the accent, the chief life of it standeth in that like sounding of the words which we call rhyme." Steele notes that "some regard" would be an understatement in reference to English, though it might not be for other modern vernaculars. Anglo-Saxon, much Middle English, and some modern English verse is purely accentual, attending *only* to stress-count. Though the practice varied over time, in brief, unstressed syllables may appear in any number and, sometimes, in any position. Overall, we can say that the earliest prosody in English *would* lead us to think accent was everything, that syllabic-count mattered only in the Romance languages, and that any strict concern with number, length, or weight, would be more appropriate to classical than to modern prosody.

Modern English verse, however, is a product of the slow intermingling of all three traditions. The distinctive development that made this possible as a new system was the introduction of metrical feet, so that both accent and syllable count provide a coordinated principle of order. Note well that the metrical foot is the unified, singular principle; one does not count syllables, then accents, or vice versa. Rather, one counts metrical feet. In consequence, there are many occasions where one might have one or two more or fewer unaccented syllables in a line and yet still have an appropriate number of feet. The syllabic line is sometimes used as an inaudible metrical experiment in our poetry, but, except in those cases where it is coupled with rhyme, it often seems little less arbitrary as a principle of order than does the typographic lineation I discussed in an earlier chapter. The historical development of English poetic rhythm must therefore be understood as the course of a Germanic language with a purely accentual meter coming into contact with the stricter mathematics of classical quantity and Romance language syllabism, so that it finally arrives as a synthesis of the two in the accentual-syllabic, foot-measured, metrical line. As we shall see, this was no arbitrary event, but one in deep and fruitful concord with the native properties of English. Indeed, Steele, Paul Fussell, and others have argued that it would take a dramatic transformation in the structure of our language to make possible the unseating of accentual-syllabism in favor of some other prosodic system. No such change has yet occurred.

6/ ENGLISH ADMITS A VARIETY OF ACCENTUAL AND ACCENTUAL-SYLLABIC METERS, BUT IAMBIC PENTAMETER IS THE MOST PERFECTLY SUITED TO THE NATIVE PROPERTIES OF THE LANGUAGE.

John Hollander once dismissed the efforts of such modern poetic theorists as Yvor Winters to discern a stress pattern in free verse analogous to that of accentual-syllabic meter, observing that,

> to try to scan free verse by counting the number of stresses and concluding that, in any event, the poem under discussion is roughly assembled of four—or five—stressed lines, may be merely to assert a trivial correlation built into the structure of English.

It is not uncommon, as we have seen, to hear poets complain of accentual-syllabic meter as if it were some arbitrary imposition upon meter. As I argued in my book on the poetry of Timothy Steele, even defenders of metrical practice, such as Ransom, often give us such a dualistic account of metrical-form as a shaping of otherwise free content, that they too seem to view it as a difficulty, a confinement, a challenge to be embraced, rather than as a principle internal to and in keeping with the nature of the English language. But this is to misunderstand meter and our language alike.

Structural linguistics provides us ample reason to conclude that accentual-syllabic meter is best conceived of as a consciously cultivated efflorescence of properties native to the English language, and that the iambic line is its paradigmatic realization. Casual speech and free verse will, therefore, typically seem like loose

241

examples of it—not because their author was consciously setting about something, but because he was speaking English. Steele's guide to prosody, *All the Fun's in How You Say a Thing* (1999), concisely describes those properties as follows:

1) English speech tends "to space stresses at roughly equal intervals"

2) The morphology of English words leans toward alternating stress

3) The "uninflected" character of our language: word order, rather than word ending, is determinant of meaning. This leads to the intermixing of "particles and pronomials" amid weightier words.

We see these three properties at work in lines such as "I like to play the saxophone, at night"; or, "The toilet's clogged again. Let's call the plumber"; or, "Whenever Mom gets here, kiss her for me"; or, "The paparazzi wrecked the conference"; or, "Matthew had Chicken Parmesan for lunch." Each of these lines is in iambic pentameter, though the second has an extra-metrical syllable at the end (a feminine ending) and the third has a trochee in the fourth of its five feet. It is also Steele's contention that this—the iambic pentameter—is the paradigmatic line for English verse, and so let us add a fourth item to our list:

4) Iambic Pentameter is subtle, flexible, and capacious. It is just long enough for its varieties to be "inexhaustibly exciting," while also perceptible, and irreducible to shorter parts.

English verse, at its origins, was not only accentual rather than accentual-syllabic, but also typically tetrametric, i.e. four-stressed. As Derek Attridge has observed, even in our day the verse of our popular music is organized according to lines of four stresses. A four-stress line is markedly audible: "Humpty Dumpty sat on a wall," after all, and everyone can thump out the beats of "Jack be nimble, Jack be quick." No one could miss it—even with the two unstressed syllables "on a" disrupting the heavy, regular stresses of that first line from Mother Goose. In modern verse, our several quatrain (four-line) stanzas tend to group lines of four, and sometimes three, stresses, and in every instance the result will seem to lend itself to song. I still recall some classmate of mine remarking, as if it were a real *coup*, that one could sing all of Emily Dickinson to the tune of "Mary Had a Little Lamb." Well, there is no shortage of melodies to which one could adapt her poems, because they are all in short-lined quatrains and most of our popular music is built around such lines.

If a four-stress line, accentual or accentual-syllabic, not only conforms to the nature of the language, but seems to provide our verse with its prototype, why would Steele suggest that the iambic pentameter line—with its five feet, or roughly ten syllables and five stresses—is the true paradigm? What earns it the adjectives we reeled off in the fourth point?

At least four attributes come to mind. First, being roughly two syllables longer than the iambic tetrameter, it can accommodate even the longest words in our language. "**An**ti**dis**establishmen**tar**ianism" is our longest word, my parish priest tells me, and though it would make for a very rough line, it would be a pentameter one nonetheless. But, second, being roughly two or four syllables shorter than a hexameter

243

or heptameter line, it will not tend to sound as if it wanted either to break in two even halves or into a tetrameter and a trimeter. If one inserts a pause (a *caesura*), as is very natural to do, at or near the midpoint of these longer lines, one winds up with what will sound like a half a ballad or short-metered quatrain rather than a single long line. The pentameter will therefore be the longest line in our verse that consistently sounds like one line. Every reader will know just where to break these lines so that it appears not as two, but four, as Dickinson wrote them:

> Because I could not stop for death, he kindly
>   stopped for me
> The Carriage held but just Ourselves and
>   Immortality

But who would attempt to chop these verses into smaller units, or extend them to longer?

> She sang beyond the genius of the sea.
> The water never formed to mind or voice,
> Like a body wholly body, fluttering
> Its empty sleeves; and yet its mimic motion
> Made constant cry, caused constantly a cry,
> That was not ours although we understood,
> Inhuman, of the veritable ocean.

We hear pauses, but, for a reason we shall consider, they are highly irregular ones and float free of the line-unit.

This leads us to our third, and most important, point. Though the iambic pentameter normally consists of an even number of syllables, each iamb comprises one unstressed, followed by one stressed, syllable, for a total of five metrical feet. This odd number tends to keep the line from feeling rigidly symmetrical, and therefore prevents it from seeming to break up into two audible units that might as well be separate lines. It also encourages a variability of syntax as words and phrases of different length run across the regular pattern of metrical feet in the line, and across lines, through the use of enjambment. In consequence, while the iambic pentameter may be the longest line we can normally hear as a line, it is also a line that can be rendered especially subtle, almost inaudible *as a line*, if the flow of enjambed iambs is drawn out long enough. The difference between the early and mature Shakespearean iambic pentameter is that between one in which each line stands out as a rigid whole and another in which the metrical line quietly gives minute order to the long cadences and complex sentence of extended periods. The blank verse of Milton raised this practice to a principle, where "the sense [is] variously drawn out from one verse into another." Overall, what one discovers in studying the use of the iambic pentameter line (as the poet Robert Shaw shows in his history of the line, *Blank Verse* (2007)), is an astonishing versatility from Marlowe to Wordsworth and Wallace Stevens, where the meter can become as assertive or subtle, as musical or prosaic, as the occasion demands.

A fourth quality presents itself. Granted, we say, the three mentioned attributes of the English language make an alternation of stressed and unstressed syllables inevitable in our speech. But, according to the third attribute, it would seem as if small, unstressed monosyllabic words would cluster around rarer, stressed syllables, in semantically weightier words. The regular alternation of unstressed and stressed syllables, in the iamb, would not seem to be our only option. First of all, meter could be trochaic, alternating stressed-unstressed, and, second, it could run with more than one unstressed syllable before each accented one—what is called anapestic meter. Trochaic and anapestic meters are, in fact, the only plausible alternatives to the iambic line, in English. They just lack the versatility of the iamb, and especially that of the iambic-pentameter. Why?

In any effort to write the trochaic line, we will quickly find that most sentences start with an unstressed syllable, that relatively few words end on a falling or feminine rhythm ("rhythm" is one such word), and, on those occasions when a sentence does start with a stress, it is easy, even routine, to follow with two unstressed syllables. If all three of these conditions obtain, one will find it more natural to write an iambic line with a trochee inserted in the first foot (an inverted first foot, as it is called in the appendix) than to attempt a completely trochaic measure. When a trochaic meter is used, one will find oneself stressing, at the beginning of the line, words that would otherwise feel, in the context of syntax, light or unstressed. "If I die before I wake" is trochaic tetrameter, but to hear it thus you must say, "IF," and the line still ends with a stress, as if it wanted to return to the iambic norm. This can be used to great effect. We have no shortage of trochaic poetry in English. But, it is simply not as versatile as the iambic norm.

The more interesting case is the anapestic line. While none of us speaks in all iambs or all anapests in our everyday chatter, it would seem that our speech *does* fall closer to a sequence of iambs with occasional anapests than to the opposite. When language is measured in iambs, it tends to sound more finely wrought, formal, and impressive:

When to the sessions of sweet silent thought
I summon up remembrance of things past,

When we order words into anapests, we find two things. First, it is almost impossible to use only anapests. Iambs keep slipping in here and there. Second, the result sounds more like a horse galloping than it does the speech of the classically educated army colonel riding on her back. Of course, sometimes a gallop is just what one wants, as in these stanzas from a classic poem by X.J. Kennedy:

In a prominent bar in Secaucus one day
Rose a lady in skunk with a topheavy sway,
Raised a knobby red finger–all turned from their
  beer–
While with eyes bright as snowcrust she sang high
  and clear:

'Now who of you'd think from an eyeload of me
That I once was a lady as proud as could be?
Oh I'd never sit down by a tumbledown drunk
If it wasn't, my dears, for the high cost of junk.

We all want to visit such a bar from time to time; we just would not want our poetry to abide there forever.

7/ METER, OR VERSE, IS THE CONSTITUTIVE FORMAL ELEMENT OF POETRY AND ALSO THE MEANS OF ITS PERFECTION, BUT POETRY IS A WHOLE TRANSCENDENT OF ANY ONE OF ITS PARTS.

A poem is a composite being, made from parts that the reason can distinguish even within the whole. But it is also a true unity, a whole greater than the sum of its parts. As I mentioned in the third chapter, the modernists had thought this entailed an absolute identity of form and content and their attempts to realize it were intended to be a distinguishing aspect of their work, a mark of its achieved consciousness. Winters, who was often considered a reactionary in his day and who certainly rejected many developments of the modernist period, nonetheless draws on the poetic theory of the proto-modernist Stéphane Mallarmé to express the character of the poem as a fusion, a simple unity. He tells us,

> The poem, to be perfect, should . . . be a new word . . . a word of which the line . . . is merely a syllable. Such a word is, of course, composed of much more than the sum of its words (as one normally uses the term) and its syntax. It is composed of an almost fluid complex . . . a relationship involving rational content, cadences, rhymes, juxtapositions, literary and other connotations, inversions, and so on, almost indefinitely. They partake of the fluidity and unpredictability of experience and so provide a means of treating experience with precision and freedom.

An absolute unity: a single new word. But also, a composite whole: a "fluid complex." Whose parts can nonetheless be distinguished: "a relationship."

If the modernists experimented with new ways of making that would realize that unity, they need not have done so. Those cultures informed by the Christian Platonist tradition have always granted to the being of the poem, to aesthetic form in general, an irreducible integrity, even as they have also accepted the rational distinctions between form and matter. This is why, as Remi Brague tells us in his *Eccentric Culture* (2002), the Romans did not just preserve the ideas of their Greek forebears, but their complete works, keeping them whole and commenting on them in part, rather than "digesting" them, and retaining only the parts they found useful. So also is it why the medieval Christians preserved the works of pagan antiquity whole, or tried to. They did not wish merely to harvest parcels of information they found true, but to hold onto works in their full aesthetic integrity, and for the sake of their inexhaustible depths. Our tradition has always assumed that things, including works of art, insofar as they are beings, are also indivisibly one. It has always retained this aspect of metaphysical realism, despite the atomizing and materializing tendencies so ubiquitous in modern western culture.

It is for this reason that we finally had to dissent from the otherwise attractive essentialism of Cunningham, discussed in Chapter 7. Cunningham wished to identify some base element, some minimal definition, that would unmistakably identify a poem as a poem, and the result was the phrase, "composition in meter." Poetry may do all kinds of things beyond meter, and these things will make a particular poem more or less good, but, though all of this is part of the tradition built upon the essential bedrock of "composition in meter," it is not to be taken as part of that essence. But this is inadequate. What makes a poem a poem is the actualized unity of the various elements that come together to make a composite whole. It would be strange to say that some of those elements belong to the essence while others do not. It would be, as we said, to attend to material causes but to reject final causality as a way of knowing; but all real knowledge is bound up with the principle of finality. We cannot know what poetry is only by turning to its beginnings; we see things through to their end.

So, then, how shall we define poetry? It is abundantly clear from the previous five chapters that most contemporary poets have failed to grasp its essence, and what they have produced in consequence is, on the whole, an embarrassment. Their work discredits the historical dignity assigned to poetry as does it make poetry seem an elusive, indeed an insubstantial, thing.

We have offered six notes toward a definition. It is the purpose of this seventh to clarify how they all not only fit together, but hold together as a transcendent whole. Let us say, then, that meter is the primary formal element of poetry. History is the basis of reflection in the Aristotelian tradition, and our history shows us that meter is what originally constitutes this thing called poetry. It comes first in time, if in nothing else.

Aristotle himself, we saw, tells us that meter is not sufficient to constitute the essence of poetry—you could versify Herodotus and would still have history—but I am not sure he is right. Those who read Lucretius's *On the Nature of Things*, read it first and foremost as a poem, and secondarily as a work of Roman epicurean philosophy; even those who do read it primarily *for* its philosophy still read it *as* a poem. If someone did set the stories from the *Histories* down in verse, they would be greeted as a poem, and probably a very good one. Furthermore, any reader of Herodotus will see that, in his representation of Solon, the historian is instructing us that the study of history is itself a means to rise from "singulars" to "universals," just as all thinking in the Aristotelian philosophical tradition presumes to do. Solon has traveled the world and learned the life stories of many men; therefore, we are told, he has the wisdom to define happiness and pronounce which men have best attained it (King Croesus has not). So, while I agree with Aristotle that poetry is indeed "philosophical," I think he errs in thinking meter insufficient to make a work a poem as does he err in thinking the historian, in principle, lacks a philosophical dimension, however much most historians may seem to.

250

One philosophical, if not historical, reason meter comes first in poetry is that it is, as Diotima tells us, "the part the Muses give us." As we have seen, if meter is in one sense a further refinement of language, it is also a manifestation of the primordial intelligible order of the *cosmos*. In consequence, it is *shaping*, in other words, it holds the poem together making it an ordered whole, a *microcosm*. And it is also *ordering* and *deepening*, giving to the poem a kind of final perfection, a splendor of and beyond the form that is constitutive of its existence and beauty. It opens onto the *macrocosm* at every pulse. I have argued elsewhere that beauty, in our experience and in reality, comes first and also last. My argument here is that we may say just that about meter. It comes first, from the depths of history, to order speech into poetry, but it is also the final perfection of the poem, a gift from an order beyond us, giving it a resonance with its origins in the true, good, and beautiful order of reality as a whole.

If meter comes first and last, it may be said to envelop all the other possible elements of the poetic essence: its memorability, its capacity for story-telling, for the representation of interior states, and for imitation (of human action or experience, *mimesis*), and metaphor (trope). None of these things would have come to be identified with poetry, had poetry not first been constituted by meter. But, it was, and they have. They are indeed elements that help poetic meter to attain its final cause, the perfection of the poem as a complete being. They do not stand outside the essence of the poem as poem, but help it to become more fully itself. The meter may provide a basis for them, but they also provide a basis for the meter. When we encounter any of these individual elements, they will appear to us as more or less poetic.

Let us phrase it this way. Meter constitutes the paradigm of poetry, as the muse-given art of poetry constitutes the paradigm of making. Just as non-poetic acts of making participate in the paradigm of poetry by degrees of analogy, so will non-metrical compositions potentially appear as poems to us, despite the absence of that paradigmatic element. Winters referred to *Moby Dick* as an epic, and others have referred to other novels and films in the same terms. An emotional speech is sometimes praised as "the song of one's heart." A work in free verse—lineated like Charles Wright's work, or in straight prose like some of Baudelaire's compositions—will appear to us as a poem because of its cadences and schemes, its use of tropes, or of moods and modes proper to the conventions of the lyric. We might be tempted, strictly speaking, to say these things are poems only by analogy, but in fact we will all experience them as poems, even if we soon become conscious of something vital missing. They will appear to us as poems *on the whole*, despite the absence of such a foundational and perfective element as meter. This has been a book about poetry, after all, and those radical limit cases I discussed I did as instances of degraded, vacuous, and pretentious poetry. I could only have been speaking analogically.

What is poetry in its fullness, then? Approaching it from the outside, we see that it is a hypostatic union of the made and the given, the gift passively received and the art actively undertaken, the human craft and the divine origin. This alone suffices to explain why a poem is always more than itself, a duality in unity, a perfectly intelligible mystery. Looked at from within, at its heart, we see that this union of art and gift result in something that has the character of a trinity. Memory, meter, and metaphor live together in a kind of

252

circumincession. Meter is already the first instance of memory, gathering and holding parts together as a whole. It is already the first metaphor, signifying what is beyond itself by its numbered nature. And so, memory and metaphor are at once other than meter and continuous with it. Meter may be present at the beginning, but, as first and last, it holds all together.

But this interior heart of poetry is always going out beyond itself. The three attributes enable poetry to reach out to, by their own essential and absolute natures, the most far flung and contingent of things— the remembered or imagined plots of story, the curious analogies of trope, the peculiar specificities of English or any language that give to their respective meters a strange necessity. Therefore, while, in one sense, it is beyond the tripartite essence of poetry, they are also, in another sense, proper to it that poetry can tell stories or represent interior states, can imitate and reveal, inquire and persuade, please and instruct—and do many other things besides. In each case, we have a potency, a possible function, diffused from the interior nature of poetry, that will lead a poem—the particular, individual poem—to become more fully itself.

The notes toward a definition of poetry I have offered here stake some big claims. Poems can tell us the stories we need to know, can help us remember them, and can put us in contact with the highest truths of reality. They can manifest those truths in meter and represent them by the power of metaphor. Poetry is a mode of contemplation and inquiry, what is normally called *dialectic*, even as it is also the furthest refinement of grammar and *rhetoric*. Its meter and rhyme are a natural ordering of language, and in conformity with the native properties of our tongue, but it is also a grace that transcends those things and reminds us of another Word. It is a craft of many parts, but also a real unity, a whole that is more than the sum of its parts.

All this we have seen traduced in our day, by the contemporary academy and by contemporary poets. I hope this book will seem a worthy response to their assaults, and that it will summon those with a love of well-made things, with a hunger for beauty and an interest in truth, not to wash their hands of a great art form just because its present predicament is so appalling. Were there no more good poems to be written, the art of poetry would command our attention simply because of those we already have. But good poems *are* being written. Richard Wilbur's "Blackberries for Amelia" and "For C."; Mary Jo Salter's "Welcome to Hiroshima" and "Goodbye, Train"; Helen Pinkerton's, "On Taddeo di Bartolo's 'Triptych of the Madonna and Child'"; Timothy Steele's "The Color Wheel" and "A Muse"; Ned Balbo's "Peacock"; Dana Gioia's "Haunted" and "The Angel with the Broken Wing"; these are just ten poems from recent decades that deserve the reader's attention now and to live in the memory henceforth. In an age that considers pure possibility the only true freedom, and the unmaking of every achievement an act of liberation, I cannot speculate what will be the fortune of poems such as these, much less the future fortunes of poetry as an art. That has not been my task. I have rather sought to explain what has gone wrong, to show us what we have had and what we have rejected, and to advocate its restoration. The rest is not up to me.

Appendix
Versification, a Brief
Introduction

1/ METER

English verse is traditionally written in **accentual-syllabic** meter. Indeed, the term "verse" originally refers to meter, and, by implication, in our language, to this mode of it. We can understand how this meter functions by explaining the two parts of the term. First, by syllabic, we mean that English verse is partially measured by the number of syllables that compose a given line of a poem. The traditional term **fourteener** (**iambic heptameter**) serves to denote that this meter typically allows fourteen syllables per line. One *can* just count syllables, and over the centuries many poets and theorists of verse have done just that, but this does not fully explain the way a line of verse works. To see why, consider two lines quoted by the Elizabethan scholar of prosody, George Puttenham:

> Not love but still be swerving

and,

> Love it is a marvelous thing.

Both these lines comprise seven syllables; as if to reinforce their similarity, they both contain the word "love" and end with the letters "-ing." But, on the ear, they are strikingly different; syllable counting of itself cannot explain why.

Verse is also accentual. By this, we mean that a given line should have a certain number of stressed syllables. When we say **iambic pentameter**, for example, we intend a line of (roughly) ten syllables, in which the even-numbered ones will be stressed. This is scanned, or marked, as follows:

```
  x   /  x   /   x /   x  / x /
```
Yea, hungry for the lips of my desire.

The "x" indicates an **unstressed** syllable, the "/" a **stress** (usually marked over the vowel, to indicate that the syllable itself is stressed, not some particular letter). I will use this notation whenever scanning complete lines of verse; otherwise I will use bold or capitals to highlight stresses in parts of lines. We do not typically talk of "stressing even syllables" in this or any case (even though that accurately describes what occurs in *this* line), because the best way to scan a line of verse is to account for the number of syllables and number of stresses in a line *at once*; the unit that results from this observation is referred to as a **foot**: every line of formal verse is normally defined in terms of the number of feet it possesses.

Hence, we say **iambic** (x /) to describe each of the five **metrical feet** in the example above, where the iambic foot consists of an unstressed and a stressed syllable. To say this line is iambic means that its individual feet conform to this pattern; to say a poem is written in iambics means not just one line but all, or nearly all, the lines conform to the pattern. The three other most prominent feet in English versification are: **trochees** (/ x), which are "inverted" iambs; **anapests** (x x /) and **dactyls** (/ x x). (There are many other terms for many other metrical feet, but, with one exception that we cannot go into here, only these four are strictly relevant for versification in English). Each of these terms may be used to describe a given foot in a given line.

By counting the number of feet in a line, or in the individual lines of a poem, we can arrive at a definition of the meter. First, one attempts to identify the types of feet present, and then one counts the number of stressed syllables in the line (in English, no metrical foot normally consists of more than one stressed syllable—with one exception we need not discuss). The line above is clearly iambic, and it consists of five feet and so five stressed syllables. We say, then, it is iambic *pentameter.*

Here is a list of the prefixes normally used to describe the number of syllables in a verse line:

Monometer	One foot (E.g. Iambic Monometer: x /)
Dimeter	Two feet
Tri-	Three (E.g. Trochaic Trimeter· / x / x / x)
Tetra-	Four
Pent-	Five
Hex- or *Alexandrine*	Six
Hept- or *Fourteener*	Seven
Oct-	Eight

Although poems can be written with different feet, or even a variety of feet, as their bases; and, although poems can be written in a significant number of different line lengths, the most common, because most natural, foot in English is the iambic, and the most flexible line length is pentameter. More than one scholar of prosody has calculated that seventy-five

261

percent of English poetry has been written in the iambic pentameter. No doubt that share has decreased on account of the nineteenth-century interest in balladry and metrical experimentation and on account of the swelling of production of poetry in the last century or so made possible, in part, by poets' abandonment of proper verse altogether.

When one scans a line, the general practice is to determine what the meter is through the poem (or stanza), and then to determine, foot by foot, line by line, where the author conforms, and where the author has perhaps used a **substitution**. A poem in iambic pentameter should have, as an abstract norm, five iambic feet for every line, and in the vast majority of poetry through the five centuries and counting of modern English verse, this is more or less the case. Occasionally, an author may insert one of the three other feet into a line to substitute for the iambic foot. Yvor Winters's "Slow Pacific Swell" strictly conforms to iambic pentameter in its first line, and in its second introduces the most frequent of substitutions, the trochaic or **inverted first foot**:

> x   / | x / | x / | x / | x /
> Far out of sight, forever stands the sea,
> / x | x / | x   /   x / x /
> Bounding the land with pale tranquility.

Notice the addition of a "|" which indicates the divisions of the line into feet. Notice also how "Bounding" must be stressed ("BOUND-ing") in the first syllable, and thus entails a trochee; if we tried to pronounce it as an iamb, we would get the awkward stress of "boun–DING." This trochee or inverted first foot is so common a practice that it might best be thought of as *not* a substitution of one foot for another at all, but as a **variation** in the meter that does not cause us to risk misidentifying the meter. Substitutions, as noted above, refer to the insertion of metrical feet other than the norm into a line in a particular meter.

Variations, of which there are many, refer to those alterations in a line that do not typically break from the metrical pattern. The two most common of these are the **trochee** in either the first, third, or fourth foot of an iambic pentameter and **feminine endings** (where an extra unstressed syllable appears at the end of the line). Less commonly, one finds trochees in the second or fifth foot of a pentameter. Historically, other variations crop up and fall out of favor: these include **headless** or clipped lines (where the first unstressed syllable of an iambic line is deleted); **broken-backed** lines (where an unstressed syllable in the middle of the line is deleted); and **feminine caesuras** (where an extra unstressed syllable is inserted in the middle of a line after a significant, punctuated pause; note that this *could* be defined as an anapestic substitution, but need not be, because it integrates so smoothly with an otherwise iambic line). We could list off several further variations, but the point here is to understand that variations in the line are not normally regarded as substitutions in violation of the metrical norm, but nuances within the norm.

The following short verse illustrates several possible variations:

Rain smeared the glass and we drove through a blur
[iambic pentameter]

Of haunted air half-lighted, and flooded road,
[feminine caesura or anapest]

Till silence and swift darkness of a tunnel
[feminine ending]

Broke upon us. As we steered ahead,
[headless; regular caesura]

We saw not light, but black clouds had raced
[broken backed on "black clouds"]

Before us, shutting us in a new dark.
[iambic pentameter]

Here are a few other variations from early in the modern English tradition; see if you can hear them, where marked in bold:

Broken-backed: The very **name signifie**th well (Thomas More)

Headless: **Like** affec**t**ions feeleth eke the breast (Thomas More)

Three Trochees: **Sid**ney is **dead, dead** is my **friend, dead** is the **world's** de**light** (Edward Dyer)

Here are three from a recent poem, David Mason's verse-novel, *Ludlow* (2007):

Headless: **That** was **how** John Lawson worked at first

Broken-backed: Take aim at the stuffed **elk head** that
        hung

Feminine Caesura: I don't fear anybod**y. I'm** going to
        tell

264

While variations like these are typical of earlier stages of English poetry, contemporary poets, as well as dramatic poets of the seventeenth century, tend to favor three-foot substitutions over the use of variations. Usually, this does not destroy the metrical norm, though it certainly can. The late Seamus Heaney pandered to modern tastes by using a very loose unrhymed iambic pentameter (unrhymed iambic pentameter in general is called **blank verse**). For example, in "St. Kevin and the Blackbird," he begins his poem with a line that conforms perfectly to the blank verse norm:

x   / | x   / | x / |x / | x   / |(x)
And then there was St. Kevin and the blackbird.

Perfectly? Well, yes, insofar as there are five iambs combined to compose the line. But this line has eleven syllables. That extra unaccented syllable at the very end is not a substitution, but, again, a variation, which means a change to the line that does not, strictly speaking, disrupt the poem's established norm of a given kind of metrical foot. As we noted, this exemplifies a feminine ending. The most famous line of Shakespeare's *Hamlet*, "To be or not to be, that is the question," also has a feminine ending.

Of headless lines, where the first unaccented syllable has been lopped off, leaving us an iambic line, but one with one fewer (usually nine) syllables, Heaney also gives us a fine example:

/ | x / | x   / | x / | x   /
As a crossbeam, when a blackbird lands

The first foot ends up being only one stressed syllable, rather than a pair or trio of syllables. Notice how the two disyllabic words, "crossbeam" and "blackbird" both take a stress in their first syllable; it just happens to be the case that most disyllabic words do this (and this is in fact our chief clue that "As," such a lightly stressed word, should be accented here). Similarly, trisyllabic words *tend* to take a stress in the middle syllable. "Tri**ump**hant," "an**noy**ance," "ag**ree**ment," "ap**point**ment," all are stressed in their second syllable. As such, polysyllabic words in general can often help you determine the meter of a line. But be careful, words like "**sax**ophone" or "**dang**erous" tend to scan as dactyls or (more likely) as trochees followed by another stress (/ x | /). When you are first studying meter, you should scan lines with polysyllabic words first, because they will aid you in abstracting the meter of the line from the sentence rhythm of the poem as a whole.

Metrical variations are extremely common; sometimes almost an entire poem will be composed in headless meter. Take, for instance, the first stanza of William Blake's "Tiger":

> Tiger, Tiger, burning bright,
> In the forest of the night,
> What immortal hand or eye
> Could frame thy fearful symmetry?

The first syllable of "Tiger," "In" and "What" are all stressed, and these stresses all begin the line, foregoing the first unstressed syllable normal to an iambic **tetrameter** (meaning four feet) line. "Could frame" (x /) however returns the poem to its actual meter, regular iambic tetrameter.

To return to Heaney's poem, we see that substitutions do sometimes occur:

```
/ x | /    x |  x    /  | x    x    /   | x
Kevin feels the warm eggs, the small breast, the
     /
   tucked
```

Despite only having one additional syllable, this line introduces two variations and an outright substitution. The first foot is inverted, common enough; but so is the second foot (i.e. it is also a trochee). Only in the third foot do we finally see an iamb, and this is immediately disrupted by an anapestic substitution in the fourth foot. The last foot is again in the iambic norm. Now, one could easily argue the second foot is just an iamb, rather than a trochee. Why? Because stress is determined based upon a) the natural stress of polysyllabic words, b) the speech-rhythm context of the line as a whole, but above all, c) the relative stress of syllables within a given foot. A monosyllabic word is not intrinsically stressed or unstressed, but only by context. I stress "feels," rather than "the," because I believe one must tend to stress the syllables that way naturally in reading the line aloud. Between b) and c) I here give more weight to b). We have no choice with "KE-vin," in contrast, although the difference in stress between the two syllables is relatively mild. Only when joking around do we say, "Ke-VVIINNN."

Similarly, we have no choice but to locate an anapest somewhere in the latter half of the line unless we want to convince ourselves that "breast" and "tucked" are unstressed (with "tucked" as a feminine ending), while "small" and "the" take the stresses. This is plausible but unlikely. Why? It is true that a monosyllabic word is not necessarily stressed or unstressed, and so we must refer to the line as a whole. In the present instance, it seems more likely that one would stress the weight-bearing words (nouns, e.g. "breast," and verbs, e.g.

"tucked") rather than an article like "the." However, it is quite possible that "small" should be stressed, in which case we get roughly the same metrical line, but the anapest appears in the final rather than the penultimate foot. Hence:

```
 / x|  /    x| x    /  | x   /  | x    x
Kevin feels the warm eggs, the small breast, the
     /
   tucked
```

But sometimes we *do* stress articles and other little words that might not normally receive stress either in poetry or everyday speech; we do so as a means of placing **emphasis** or creating **contrast**. For example:

> "James Wilson is *the* professor," announced Ronald.
> "You mean he is the professor for *this class*," corrected Judy.
> "No," said Ronald, "he is *the* professor. As in, the greatest professor of all time."

Or, another one more modest:

> "*I* see six white hens out in the yard," said Farmer Brown (in headless blank verse!).
> "And so, *what* is your point, my uninteresting spouse?" replied his argumentative wife (in anapestic tetrameter).
> "That there's six *white*! I thought they all were yellow," (he concludes, in regular blank verse).

To show one short poem that is full of substitutions, while still retaining an iambic tetrameter norm, let us turn, in conclusion, to W.B. Yeats's "The Nineteenth Century and After":

```
    /      x|  x    /  | x /  |  x   /
Though the great song return no more,
   x     /  |  x /  |x    /  | x  /
There's keen delight in what we have
   x / |x  x   /  | x   /  |  x   /
The rattle of pebbles on the shore
  / |  x   /  | x / |x      /
Under the receding wave.
```

Before reading below, see if you can identify any substitutions and variations in this poem.

Well, now, here's a poem of four lines: an iambic tetrameter, cross rhyming quatrain (incidentally called **long meter**). But only one of the lines is perfectly regular: only the second is all iambic feet—no variations, no substitutions. The first line has an inverted first foot. The third *may* have an extra syllable, which resolves into an anapest in the second foot (it is, however, **elided**: see below). The final line is headless, lacking one unstressed syllable in the first foot.

Non-iambic meters are fairly common—or used to be, particularly in the nineteenth century and especially in songs and popular rhymes. **Anapestic tetrameter** is the most common non-iambic meter in poetry ("Oh, what are you tapping upon your right knee? / The anapest meter of Thomas Har-DY"). That is, unless you reimagine headless iambic tetrameter as trochaic tetrameter with the final unstressed syllable sometimes lopped ("Ring around the rosey" is a good argument for trochaic trimeter)—but that just complicates a fairly simple system.

Some poets also use pure **accentual meter**. In this instance, a regular number of stresses occurs in a line, but a poet may use any kind of metrical foot for each stress; this means that the number of unstressed syllables may vary indifferently from line to line. In practical effect, what we usually see in accentual poetry is simply a line that moves back and forth between iambs and anapests (but other possibilities exist). **Anglo-Saxon alliterative** verse is accentual, with four stresses per line, and with at least three of the four stressed syllables alliterating with each other ("Buoyant and Burly the unbearable Burkhart" is a hideous but helpful example; then again, it is hard not to sound like a boisterous barbarian in such a verse form). Gerard Manley Hopkins' **sprung rhythm** is just accentual meter with a grand metaphysical scheme behind it.

We conclude with a concept twice mentioned above, and which may be the most overlooked but helpful element in the practice of metrical verse: **elision**. To elide a word or words means to slur, leave unpronounced, or to leave only slightly pronounced one or more syllables. We elide daily in our speech when we use what are called contractions: "I cannot see it" is frequently pronounced "ycan't see 't." Poets through the centuries have typically elided light or unstressed syllables in words in order to ensure that their lines conform to the metrical norm they establish in their poems. It is quite likely that Yeats, when writing, "The rattle of pebbles on the shore," intended not an anapestic substitution in the second foot but the form of elision called **synaloepha**, where vowel sounds in two adjacent words are slurred together so as to form one. If this is the case, "rattle of" should be pronounced "ratt-lof," so that the consonant in the final syllable of the first word phonetically adheres to the second word. This mode of elision is extremely common in casual speech and in the history of poetry, though it usually evades our easy detection. When Charles Algernon Swinburne writes the following, only with an ear conscious to meter do we sense that elision

270

must be intended: "I would earth had thy body as fruit to eat." One must elide (called a y-glide) "body as" to pronounce it "bod-yas." Whenever one encounters that once common phrase, "many a," as in "Many a night I stayed up late," one can be reasonably confident that the poet intends an elision so that we say "Man-ya night." Shakespeare does this several times in a single sonnet.

Elision takes several forms. Memorizing the names of the forms are unimportant in comparison with the ability to discern elision where it is intended by a poet. **Aphaeresis** and **apocope** refer to the dropping of, respectively, the first or last syllable of a word (not its slurring, but its dropping). "Better" becomes "bet", "against" "gainst." The more common forms of elision are categorized as **synaeresis** (elision involving the slurring together of two adjacent vowel sounds within a word. E.g. "interior" and "memorial" can be pronounced as three rather than four syllable words), **synaloepha** (elision involving the slurring together of two adjacent vowels in different words. E.g. "Th'expense"), and **syncope** (elision involving the suppression or omission of a sound from the middle of a word. E.g. "ta'en," "e'en," "mem'ry," or "clar'ty").

Thomas, Lord Vaux, gives us examples of two elisions in one line. In, "Do fly to thee by prayer to appease thy ire," "prayer" receives synaeresis with the "ay" and "e" in two syllables melding into one and reducing the disyllabic word to a monosyllable, then "to appease" is crushed by means of synaloepha.

What all forms of elision have in common is, first, their provision of a means of articulating the way in which human speech naturally tends, from time to time and by no means consistently, to alter—particularly contract—the pronunciation of individual words within the context of a sentence; and, second, poets

271

can and historically do intend us to pronounce words differently, as convenience requires, in order to fit language into their chosen meter. Poetry in previous centuries inconsistently but generally marked elisions where they were intended with apostrophes. Hence, John Milton might write, "th'eternal" when necessary to make his blank verse meter; elsewhere in his epic, *Paradise Lost*, he intended elision without marking it explicitly. It is up to the reader, having acquired a sense of iambic pentameter, to discern when elision is necessary and when it is not. This has become more difficult with more recent poetry (going back to the end of the eighteenth century), because poets generally do *not* mark elision with apostrophes. They rightly find the appearance of "ta'en" for "taken" or "heav'n" for "heaven" an unnecessary and archaic-looking mannerism. But it is important to recognize that elision is frequently present even when it is not marked explicitly.

Once one has had some practice at hearing the metrical patterns behind lines of verse, it becomes easier to detect it where it is intended. In the following verse paragraph from William Wordsworth's *The Prelude*, elision occurs multiple times. I have underlined the elided words to make them easier to detect:

> . . . all books which lay
> Their sure foundations in the heart of man,
> Whether by native prose, or <u>numerous</u> verse;
> That in the name of all inspired Souls,
> From Homer the great <u>Thunderer</u>, from the voice
> Which roars along the bed of Jewish Song:
>
> . . . from those <u>loftiest</u> notes
> Down to the low and wren-like <u>warblings</u>, made
> For Cottagers and Spinners at the wheel . . .

Strictly speaking "numerous" has three syllables; if we had no theory of elision, we would have to join its last two syllables to "verse" in the line and describe it as an anapest. But Wordsworth intends us to read it as "num'rous verse," eliding one syllable and thereby maintaining the iambic norm of the line. All the underlined words above function in their lines the same way. If this appears a small matter, it is not so. Proper understanding of the meter and the rhythm of these and other lines depends on identifying elision where it occurs. Many modern readers have assumed anapests or other substitutions where none were intended and have mistakenly believed that substitutions are more normal or necessary to poetic composition than in fact they are. In consequence, modern metrical poetry and modern poetic theory tend to stress unduly the importance of substitutions, whereas in past centuries substitutions were rare, elisions routine, and different metrical feet were used not primarily as substitutions but as the building blocks of different forms.

After elision came to be forgotten, ignored, or deprecated as a worthy technique for maintaining metrical integrity, older poetry came to appear less regular than it really was and metrical regularity became less obviously a virtue in verse. When the notion of "free verse"—of verse only occasionally conforming to a metrical pattern or not at all—was first floated in the late-nineteenth-century, it came into fashion almost unresisted—precisely because poets had either forgotten or come to look down upon elision, and so could no longer see in older poems the regularity their authors had intended. If Wordsworth vitiated blank verse with apparent substitutions, why should not modern poets break the loose chain of meter altogether? No answer was forthcoming, not because the advocates of free verse had transcended the bondage of versification, but because advocates of free verse and devotees of form alike had suffered a loss of metrical literacy. Without an understanding of elision, they could not see how regular the verse of the past had been.

As the contemporary poet Timothy Steele has frequently argued, all speech and writing has rhythm. A paragraph of prose can be as skillfully composed in terms of cadence as can a poem. What distinguishes poetry from prose is the presence of meter, which is nothing other than a regular pattern of relative stresses present in (but not exhaustive of) the rhythm of a poem and thus capable of being abstracted and discerned apart from that rhythm. Another way of expressing this would be to say that prose is language, and language is inherently rhythmic; verse is any language whose rhythm has been formed upon the regular pattern of meter; and poetry is any literary genre composed in verse.

Steele's published explanation of versification, which this guide closely follows (see notes), contends that the measure of verse gives order to speech without cramping or distorting it. Between the use of common variations, the various placement of **caesuras** in lines (any significant pause in speech, up to and including a period), the skillful use of **emjambment** (moments in a poem, where the grammatical sense forces us to read on through a line break without making any audible pause; there are varying degrees of this), of elision, and the modulation of *degrees of stress* within metrical feet, as well as the variation of word length and sentence structure, verse is an infinitely variable, infinitely flexible, medium. The iambic pentameter line is consummate in this regard, and does not require even the use of three-foot substitutions (anapests, normally) in order to accommodate the full rich expressive range of the English language—so long as we are willing to use all of these means of variation.

Let us return to the pair of lines quoted earlier from Puttenham. We will see that, though the syllable count is identical, the number of accented syllables, the types of variation, and the use of elision distinguish them from each other:

    x / | x   / | x   / | (x)
    Not love but still be swerving

    / | x / | x / | x   /
    Love it is a marvelous thing.

The first line is easy to scan: iambic trimeter with a feminine ending. Disyllabic words that end with the suffix "-ing" consistently receive stress on the first syllable, though, in a trisyllabic word, one would sometimes stress the first and third, as in "threatening" or "thickening," though not in "dispensing."

The second line poses an interpretative challenge. We might call it iambic tetrameter (as opposed to trimeter) and this is the most obvious difference between the two. It has four accents, and so four feet, rather than three, and so may seem a longer line to our ear. If it is an iambic, it is a headless one, with "Love" constituting a foot unto itself. Puttenham tells us it has seven syllables, and that is how I hear it, too, because I instinctively elide (syncope) "MAR-VEL-ous" to "MARVE-lous." We might be tempted to call it a trochaic tetrameter line to highlight how different it sounds from the feminine trimeter; Paul Fussell would tell us the first has a "rising," the other a "falling," meter. But, first, the "rising" meter ends with a fall, the falling one with a hard, high stop on a stress! And,

275

second, calling them both iambic emphasizes the normative character of iambic meter as the basis of spoken English, and so reminds us of what these lines have in common prior to our enumerating their significant differences.

Meter is essential to the recitation and hearing of poetry, as distinct from other forms of literature. Meter is not the "heart beat" of poetry—we require no figurative language to define it— it is its *raison d'être*. Just as the elements of grammar for prose composition are orthography, syntax, and punctuation, the elements of grammar for verse composition are orthography, syntax, punctuation, and meter. This guide seeks merely to make up for a dearth of instruction in the grammar necessary for those who would be literate. We will know it has succeeded, when readers and poets see that variation, elision, and rhythmic modulation rather than foot substitution constitute the normal, fruitful techniques of well-wrought verse.

2/ Rhyme, Form, and Stanza

Rhyme is a relatively modern invention. The Greeks did not use it. The Romans did not until the late-antique period. Only with the modern romance languages (Italian, French, Provencal, etc.) did rhyme come into regular, nearly universal, use. English is not a romance language, it is Germanic in origin, and the consequent structural differences result in proportionately fewer rhymes in English than in, say, French. Nonetheless, nearly two-thirds of English vocabulary derives from the romance languages, and it is an extremely large language (in terms of the total number of accepted words in its lexicon) compared with its romantic neighbors. Consequently, rhyme can be a greater challenge to the Anglophone poet even as the frequent saw of English as a "rhyme-poor language" seems a bit far-fetched. Indeed, there are abundant rhymes—but just few enough, perhaps, to make the logical importance of rhyme in English poetry more significant than in most other languages. In very sophisticated poetry, rhyme words often take on a great deal of meaning specifically in their capacity as rhymes.

Rhymes come in several possible forms. The most basic distinction is between **end rhyme**, meaning those words that rhyme at the end of lines in a stanza, and **internal rhyme**, meaning simply rhyme words that appear, sometimes by luck, sometimes systematically *within* a line or lines of verse. The second kind of distinction relevant to rhymes is between **masculine** and **feminine** rhymes. "The little boy / Played with the toy" exemplifies masculine rhyming, because the final, stressed syllable of both lines rhyme. A poem with the lines, "They killed the dark Rasputin / For his vile high falutin','" in turn demonstrates feminine rhyme. Note how, in feminine rhyme, both the final stressed and the **hypermetrical**, unstressed syllable rhyme. Effectively the last *two* syllables in each line must rhyme, with the last of them unstressed, for feminine rhyme. However, poets on rare occasions attempt **apocopated rhymes**, where one uses masculine rhyme, but one of the rhyming words has a feminine ending, as in, "I bought a gun / It wouldn't function," with "gun and "func-" rhyming, but the "-tion" hanging out as an unrhymed, hypermetrical syllable. A rare technique is **triple-rhyme**, where two hypermetrical syllables complete the lines and where they and the last stressed syllable all rhyme. Try this one on for size, a cheeky light verse lesson in sensitivity training:

> You said you liked me, but
> That it would sure be fabulous,
> If, on your cheeks and butt,
> I would both pinch and grab you less.

All the rhymes exemplified above are **full rhymes,** where the complete syllables of the rhyme words really do rhyme. But **slant** or **half rhyme** is quite common; these terms describe aural effects where the final syllables of two words are similar, but not quite true rhymes. Try rhyming "slant" with "mount" or "tall" with "cull," or "Flick" with "till," or even "bale" and "hate." Where only the final consonants match, we refer to this as **consonantal** slant rhyme, or simply **consonance**. (One may also speak of **double consonantal**, such as "dump" and "damp"). Where the vowel sounds only overlap—as in "tub" and "of"—we refer to **assonantal** half rhyme, or **assonance**.

We can denominate other, rarer, species of rhyme that poets use for different effects. **Eye rhyme** refers to words that appear to be rhymes when printed on the page, but which do not in fact sound alike. "Behind" and "find" rhyme. "Find" and "wind," as in to wind rope, rhyme. "Find" and "wind," as in, "the wind is blowing," are eye rhymes. *Rime riche* refers to the repetition of a word (or at least the spelling of a word), so that it rhymes with itself. Normally the words will be homonymic (same sound, different meaning), but not necessarily, as Yeats demonstrates in this early poem, in which the rhymes seem to express a passion simplified almost to silence by intensity:

> I would spread the cloths under your feet:
> But I, being poor, have only my dreams;
> I have spread my dreams under your feet;
> Tread softly because you tread on my dreams.

Rhymes arranged and coordinated with lines of fixed and repeating numbers of metrical feet normally constitute stanzas. However, we typically refer to **stanzas** as units of four or more lines. Fewer than that and we may refer to stichic verse (verse measured in lines, rather than stanzas); the line type then gives us a name for the **form**. In speaking of poems that have fixed number of allowed lines or stanzas we refer to **fixed forms**.

The minimal form in English poetry might be said to consist of one line and zero end rhymes. **Blank verse**, which normally describes any number of unrhymed lines of iambic pentameter is this minimal form (one could speak of blank dimeter or anapestic blank verse, as well; something counts as *blank* rather than *free* verse so long as there is a discernable meter; "free verse" is lineated prose and, lacking an internal metrical principle, cannot properly be called verse at all). **Heroic couplets** are iambic pentameter pairs of lines that rhyme; a couplet of any length is the minimal rhyme scheme that constitutes a form (as should be obvious, since one needs two lines to achieve an end rhyme).

In illustrating forms and stanzas, I shall use numbers (1-6) to signify the number of feet; capital letters to signify the foot type (I=Iambic; T=Trochaic; D=Dactylic; A=Anapestic—however there are almost no conventional stanzaic forms that require anything besides iambic); and lower case letters to signify the rhymes. Hence a heroic couple can be defined in the following code:

5I a
5I a

Shorter couplets are also possible, the most common of which is the tetrameter couplet (4I a / 4I a).

Three common poetic forms can be described as **tercets**. The standard tercet is simply a **triplet**, three lines in a unit that all rhyme with each other (a / a/ a). But **terza rima** involves tercets that interlock their rhymes in an unlimited train: aba in one stanza leads to bcb in the next and cdc in the following. *Terza rima* can be done with any line length, but iambic pentameter is most typical. Because *terza rima* can be hard in English, some poets try to imitate its effects with what might be called a **blank tercet**, where the first and last lines rhyme, but the middle one remains unrhymed: axa followed by cxc, and so forth (the "x" indicates a lack of rhyme, where one might be expected).

The most common stanza form is the **quatrain**, any unit comprising four lines. The major types of quatrains are **common meter** (4I a / 3I b / 4I a / 3I

280

b); **long meter**, where all lines are tetrameter and the rhymes either cross rhyme or couplet rhyme: abab or aabb; **short meter** (or **poulter's measure**), where the first two and fourth lines are in trimeter, but the third is in tetrameter, and where the rhyme scheme runs either abab or abxb (in this last instance, only the even lines of the stanza actually have rhymes). **Half meter** describes cross-rhyming iambic-trimeter (abab). And finally **ballad meter**, the prototype of all these stanzas, follows common meter in alternating tetrameter and trimeter, wherein only the trimeter, even lines rhyme (4I a/ 3I b / 4I x / 3I b). Another kind of quatrain, called the **Italian stanza** or the *In Memoriam Stanza*, involves envelope rhyming (abba); when called Italian, it generally is written in iambic pentameter, and when called after Lord Tennyson's famous poem, it is measured with iambic tetrameter. The final common form of quatrain is the **English Stanza** or the **Elegiac Stanza**, which means simply iambic pentameter that is cross rhymed (5I a / 5I b / 5I a / 5I b).

Longer stanzas that usually are written in tetrameter or pentameter include **cinq rhyme**: ababa; *sesta rima* or the **sixain**, (rhyming ababcc); the seven-line **rhyme royal** (ababbcc); and the eight-lined *ottava rima* or **huitain** (abab…abcc). All of these stanzas are used with great frequency in twentieth-century and earlier poetry. More complex stanza forms include the following:

The Burns Stanza: 4I a, 4I a, 4I a, 2I b, 4I a, 2I b.

Romance-Six Stanza: 4I a, 4I a, 3I b, 4I a/c, 4I a/c, 3I b.

Rubaiyat Stanza: 4I a, 4I a, 4I b, 4I a.

Spenserian Stanza: 5I a, 5I b, 5I a, 5I b, 5I b, 5I c, 5I b, 5I c, 6I c.

While fixed forms are generally longer than six, seven, or nine lines, the Spenserian stanza is the longest conventional stanza in English of which I am aware. However, it is important to recognize that the possible variety of stanzas is nearly limitless. Most poets routinely invent different stanzas for an individual poem, varying line lengths and rhyme schemes as one means of making each poem distinct and memorable. This is particularly evident in the ingenious stanzaic variety of the seventeenth-century metaphysical poets, John Donne and George Herbert. Nineteenth century, Victorian poets also invented a wide array of stanzas, but their experimentation tended to be more with the use of feet and line length rather than with rhyme schemes. Hence, Thomas Hardy's poems offer a veritable education in the use of anapestic tetrameter, and indeed the use of anapests systematically and regularly interspersed within predominately iambic poems.

Just as English "gets" its rhymes from the romance languages, it also gets all of its fixed forms from Italian, French, and Provençal practices. Aside from some amusing nonce forms, there are no fixed forms created out of whole cloth that were invented by English poets, although many stanzas have been so invented. In consequence, most fixed forms have evidently foreign names; the most common such forms are the **sestina**, the **pantoum**, and the **villanelle**. By far, however, the most fully adopted and adapted fixed form is the **sonnet**. Indeed, only this form has been truly naturalized. Poets write with some regularity in fixed forms, but in most instances, those forms are sort of "exercises," opportunities to show off one's technique. The sonnet, on the other hand, has proven to be an extremely docile, pliable form despite the fact that it consists of a mere fourteen lines.

An introduction to rhyme can get away with brief mention of the other fixed forms, but the sonnet is so central to poetry in English that we must give it considered attention. The first sonnets were written in Italian (as the word, which is Italian, should suggest). Hence, an **Italian** or **Petrarchan** sonnet is the prototype of all sonnets (Petrarch is the first poet to compose extensively in the sonnet form). It consists of fourteen lines in iambic pentameter. The rhyme scheme runs abbaabba in the first eight lines, called the **octave**. Usually the sonnet takes a **volta** or thematic turn after the eighth line. The final six lines, the **sestet**, can run in any of several combinations. The most typical rhyme schemes for sestets are cdcdcd, or cdecde. However, so long as the octave follows the pattern, the sestet can be altered in other ways without the sonnet losing its identity as Italian. English poets of the early renaissance were quick to adapt the sonnet to a native form that required slightly less constrained rhyming: having to find four "a" and "b" rhymes could be difficult. And so the **English** sonnet, usually called the **Shakespearean** after its most famous practitioner, runs with slightly more variety in its scheme. The meter remains iambic pentameter, but the fourteen lines are divided into three English quatrains followed by a final couplet: abab, cdcd, efef, gg. Early sonnets tend to use the major elements of the form as guides to the syntax and logic—at the least, in marking a turn in the poem between octave and sestet and, at the most, using the three quatrains of the English sonnet as a logical structure that is brought to sometimes clear, sometimes paradoxical, conclusion in the final couplet. John Crowe Ransom and Paul Fussell have both made strong arguments for the necessity of such close logical/stanza-pattern interrelation; for my part, I think it only a suitable option for some poems.

Edmund Spenser, whose Spenserian stanza outlined above attests to his taste for the ornate, composed sonnets in a slightly more difficult, interlocking rhyme scheme: abab, bcbc, cdcd, ee. Spenser's many stanzaic inventions have been imitated occasionally—during the nineteenth century, frequently—but with nowhere near the frequency as the two main forms of sonnets. It is worth noting that what distinguishes the sonnet from the other fixed forms listed above is adaptability. Sestinas require the repetition of six end words across multiple stanzas. Villanelles and pantoums require the repetition of entire lines. The sonnet imposes formal criteria only on the meter and the rhyme scheme, and so is a room that can be filled with nearly any thematic furniture. Stanza is derived from the Italian word for "room," in fact. In the English tradition, the adaptability of stanzas derives largely from the possibility of adjusting them and "filling" them in myriad ways.

While there are traditions that link form and content —sonnets are forever linked with love poetry for instance—these linkages are loose and provide occasion for violation as much as for conformity. The traditions that identify certain poetic forms with certain themes and content are referred to as **decorum**; in the English tradition, again, much meaning often lies for a particular poem in the ways in which it violates the conventions of decorum. Similarly, the manipulation of stanzas and fixed forms has often proven a source of inspiration for English language poets. When a fixed form, such as the sonnet, is modified in some way it is called a **nonce sonnet** or **form**.

Most recently, for instance, the poet Ernest Hilbert began publishing **Hilbertian** sonnets, a nonce form of the sonnet with the following rhyme scheme: abcabc, cdecde, ff (two sestets and a couplet). While only imperfectly metered, Hilbert's poems observe the boundaries of the little room of the sonnet marked by the rhyme scheme quite carefully:

Reality TV

Gossip often centers on TV shows
Viewers have in common. This is not strange.
What else can be so equal and shared?
Discussions of real estate, everyone knows,
Soon show that some can exist in a range
That surpasses what others ever cared
To know about. Talk of sex will reveal
That someone's not getting any. Talk of
New books won't fly, unless Oprah picked them.
Men have sports, but it serves most to conceal
How unalike they are otherwise. What love
Is squandered in this public fantasy, when
Families watch others choke on worms,
So familiar, now, no one even squirms?

With its lamentation of contemporary vulgarity and the loss of rich, shared conventions of decorum, artistic form, and intellectual tradition, Hilbert's sonnet occasions a few closing words about the status of meter, rhyme, and "form" at the present moment.

To those who would say the age of Oprah calls for a new prosody, one expressly lacking all measure and formal practice, we might offer Paul Fussell's judgment: "A 'new age' for metrics is a new philological age, not a new technological one: essential changes in the structure of the English language cannot be willed, and it is such essential changes that a new metrical system tends to reflect."

More generally, I would propose that the traditions, conventions, and crafts of ages past often appear baseless or primitive to us only because we have failed to understand their rational foundations, their actual nature. When we make the effort to discover them, we shall often find that such foundations were obscure to us only because the reasoning and intellectual faculties of our own age are less refined than were those that first established them. We flatter ourselves with having grown beyond beliefs and practices that, in truth, we lack the maturity and sophistication to perceive much less to transcend.

Meter, rhyme, and stanza must endure as the formal principles of our poetry, at least until that unpredictable dawn when English itself is no longer spoken. And, if poetry is to remain or become again a vital art, these things must be defended from those whose preening confidence leads them to dismiss what they barely perceive and have never understood.

3/ NOTES

The germinal elements of this guide were examples I provided to my students, when I was first teaching poetry writing classes at the University of Notre Dame as a beginning graduate student. Those examples slowly received surrounding paragraphs of explanation and, eventually, became a series of brief handouts I would offer in literature classes *in lieu* of proper instruction in prosody. Only a few years ago did I conclude that the bulk was sufficient and the format sufficiently convenient as to merit being fashioned into a small booklet for regular distribution to students and friends who were interested in learning the most basic elements of prosody. In that role, it gained in detail still further, consequent to my beginning to teach *The Poetry of Meditation* and *The Art of Verse* at Villanova University, wherein my little booklet served as a companion to the textbooks of the course. In keeping with this function, I have restrained, though certainly not excluded, historical detail and professional opinion from this outline of the subject. Nearly all of what is found here is *merely a teacher's reprise of original work done by others*, and it makes absolutely no claim to originality. I have chosen to reprint my little booklet as an appendix to *The Fortunes of Poetry* so that the reader new to the art of poetry and the arguments carried forth in the preceding pages may at least find introductory material necessary for its understanding in a convenient place. But it remains above all something written for my students, and is dedicated to them, especially to those students who have made the study of poetry such a joy for me; this growing number includes in particular, Charles Bates, Megan Malamood, Timothy Wadman, and Timothy Wilt.

Let me underscore how unoriginal I have tried to be in this guide. Nearly all its observations are drawn directly from Timothy Steele's *All the Fun's in How You Say a Thing* (Ohio University Press, 1999), which I consider the essential book on poetry for our time. I have also consulted James McAuley *Versification* (Michigan State University Press, 1966); Paul Fussell *The Theory of Prosody in 18th Century England* (Archon, 1954) and *Poetic Meter and Poetic Form* (1965 and still in print); Robert B. Shaw's *Blank Verse: A Guide to Its History and Use* (Ohio University Press, 2007); Brennan O'Donnell, *The Passion of Meter: A Study in Wordsworth's Metrical Art* (Kent State University Press, 1995); David Baker, Ed., *Meter in English* (University of Arkansas Press, 1996), and Joseph Bristow's *The Cambridge Companion to Victorian Poetry* (Cambridge University Press, 2000).

Other important studies of and guides to versification include: Timothy Steele's *Missing Measures* (1990); Coventry Patmore's *Essay on English Metrical Law: A Critical Edition with Commentary* (Sister Mary Augustine Roth, ed., 1961); George Saintsbury *A History of English Prosody, from the Twelfth Century to the Present* 3 Volumes (1923). David Caplan's critical study, *Questions of Possibility: Contemporary Poetry and Poetic Form* (2005) and his guide to prosody, *Poetic Form: An Introduction* (2007) are also recommended to the beginning student. The essays collected in Harvey Gross, ed., *The Structure of Verse* (Revised Edition, 1979) remain important, especially Otto Jesperson, "Notes on Meter."

Poems quoted are drawn from the following: Karl Beckson, *Aesthetes And Decadents Of The 1890s* (Academy Chicago, 2005); Yvor Winters, *Selected Poems* (Swallow, 1999); Seamus Heaney, *Opened Ground* (Farrar, Straus and Giroux, 1999); William Blake, *The Complete Poetry and Prose* (Anchor, 1997); W.B. Yeats, *The Poems*

(Scribner 1996); Charles Algernon Swinburne, *Poems and Ballads and Atalanta in Calydon* (Penguin, 2001); John Williams, *The Poetry of the English Renaissance* (University of Arkansas, 1994); David Mason, *Ludlow* (Red Hen, 2007); William Wordsworth, *Major Works* (Oxford, 2008); Ernest Hilbert, *Sixty Sonnets* (Red Hen, 2009).

James Matthew Wilson is the author of five previous books, including *Some Permanent Things*, a collection of poems, and *The Catholic Imagination in Modern American Poetry*, a monograph (both from Wiseblood books). A poet and critic of contemporary poetry, his poems, essays, and reviews have appeared in dozens of magazines, including *Measure*, *The Weekly Standard*, *The Raintown Review*, *The New Criterion*, *Modern Age*, *First Things*, *Dappled Things*, and *The American Conservative*. Wilson is an award-winning scholar of philosophical-theology and literature and teaches in the Department of Humanities and Augustinian Traditions at Villanova University.

Made in the USA
Charleston, SC
28 October 2016